RE-ENCHANTING ART THERAPY

ABOUT THE AUTHOR

Lynn Kapitan, Ph.D, ATR-BC is the former director and co-founder of the graduate art therapy program at Mount Mary College, Milwaukee, Wisconsin where she currently teaches art therapy students and is Chairperson of the art department. She has been exploring the interface between creative contemplation and social action as a form of peacemaking for many years, and is a frequent presenter at national and international conferences. She has served the American Art Therapy Association in numerous capacities including ten years on the editorial board of *Art Therapy* and currently as President-Elect. She has been honored the Distinguished Service Award from AATA and from the Wisconsin Art Therapy Association where she has worked to establish a vibrant professional community.

Dr. Kapitan holds a master's degree in creative arts therapy from Pratt Institute and a doctorate in Community Art Therapy and Leadership from the Union Institute. She enjoys painting in pastels, fabrics, and artist bookmaking with a particular interest in the practice of meditative art-making. Her twenty years as an art therapist began as one of the first school art therapists in her state and grew to include art therapy for youth in alternative education and other settings. Currently, she is a consultant to Capacitar, an international network of women's empowerment and solidarity, and is also working to establish internships and service opportunities in Central and South America.

RE-ENCHANTING ART THERAPY

Transformational Practices for Restoring Creative Vitality

By

LYNN KAPITAN, Ph.D, ATR-BC
Art Therapist and Supervisor
Associate Professor and Chair
Art and Graduate Art Therapy
Mount Mary College
Milwaukee, Wisconsin

CHARLES C THOMAS • PUBLISHER, LTD.
Springfield • Illinois • U.S.A.

Published and Distributed Throughout the World by

CHARLES C THOMAS • PUBLISHER, LTD.
2600 South First Street
Springfield, Illinois 62704

This book is protected by copyright. No part of
it may be reproduced in any manner without
written permission from the publisher.

©2003 by CHARLES C THOMAS • PUBLISHER, LTD.

ISBN 0-398-07371-6 (hard)
ISBN 0-398-07372-4 (paper)

Library of Congress Catalog Card Number: 2002032352

With THOMAS BOOKS *careful attention is given to all details of manufacturing and design. It is the Publisher's desire to present books that are satisfactory as to their physical qualities and artistic possibilities and appropriate for their particular use.* THOMAS BOOKS *will be true to those laws of quality that assure a good name and good will.*

Printed in the United States of America
SR-R-3

Library of Congress Cataloging-in-Publication Data

Kapitan, Lynn.
   Re-enchanting art therapy : transformational practices for restoring vitality / by Lynn Kapitan.
     p. cm.
Includes bibliographical references and index.
ISBN 0-398-07371-6 (hard) -- ISBN 0-398-07372-4 (paper)
1. Art therapy. I. Title.

RC489.A7 K357 2003
616.89′1656--dc21

2002032352

```
616.891656 K17r

Kapitan, Lynn.

Re-enchanting art therapy
```

PREFACE

Re-Enchanting Art Therapy is written in response to a growing anxiety coming out of recent, rapid changes in the field of mental health care. As contact with patients or clients decreases, case loads grow, and health care organizations downsize, upsize, and reorganize, therapists find themselves having to cope with often chaotic and sometimes toxic work environments that drain them of the vital creative energy they need to perform their work. In the field of art therapy, it is a crucial matter for therapists to be able to access their creativity, for without it they cannot offer the very knowledge and tools they have that are unique to their profession, critically needed in the world. Without free access to creative vitality, they become deskilled and disenchanted with their work lives. Many disenchanted art therapists leave the field, looking for better conditions in what is perceived as less risky, more prestigious professions; others look for ways to leave clinical practice while still maintaining their professional identity as art therapists. But the world suffers their leaving, for it is in these dispirited places and people where the gifts of art therapy are most needed to do their work of transformation.

This book is intended to be useful to art therapists, supervisors, students of art therapy, and colleagues in the related fields of mental health care who seek to approach their work with a degree of personal therapeutic artistry but find it a struggle to do so in the kinds of environments or populations with which they work. An understanding of toxic work environments, while a common experience among art therapists, has not been given much, if any, attention in the professional literature. As such, this text will be a useful companion to supervision texts or population-specific studies. But even more useful, I believe, would be as a different sort of companion: something pulled off the bookshelf when the time has come to reach beyond pragmatism and contemplate why the struggle, why so alone, why certain things have fallen apart or gotten stuck, or why that deadening feeling accompanying the casework or the work environment. For there is value in approaching these questions less directly than as problems to be solved. They are also invitations: openings or doorways into the deeper territories of our hearts, minds, and soul that are stirred by wounding. There is an angle in every supervisory or practice question that can't quite be pinned down and isn't satisfied with explanation or theory. A shift to contemplation of its deeper mystery, accessed through imagery and story, can awaken new and different insights, and put the questioner on a different path.

Beginning with the question, "What is killing the creativity of art therapists?" I formalized research to discover the roots of art therapist disenchantment in order to see and accurately know what we are dealing with as a phenomenon. Much has been written recently by art therapists about the need to pay more attention to their own art-making but the topic until now has been informed mostly by opinion and speculation. To further the research, I investigated the art, story, myth and dream imagery of art therapists who felt various degrees of disenchantment with their work. That art therapists do not value or have forgotten the importance of their own art-making was not found to be true. Instead, their art and stories revealed a larger concern for the pollution and sealing off of the creative function, disabling their ability to create or act in their work environments and making them toxic to others. They all sensed something was wrong, feeling cut off from the sources of creative vitality that their artistic and therapeutic practices depended upon, leaving them feeling dried up and gasping for creative energy. They were suffering various forms of "creative death" signally to them that what is not growing is slowly dying. If, as Eliade (1958) wrote, creative death is a call to initiation into greater life, then learning ways to welcome and embrace what most disturbs us, it would seem, is a valuable practice for restoring creative vitality and transforming our work as art therapists.

Re-Enchanting Art Therapy presents these findings and explores ways in which art therapists can develop a sustained relationship to the sources of their creativity. It re-examines what it means to "practice" art therapy and links practice to *vitality,* a word that imparts a sense of sustainable life or, in its absence, the ever possibility of dying. It situates art therapy as a living artistic practice, a socially responsive art form, broadening it beyond traditional categories of art and therapy in order to address a wider, more inclusive range of theories. It introduces the practice of "transformational rehabilitation" which links modern art therapists to the legacy of craftspersons living in partnership with a dynamic, reciprocating world that is alive with shapes, colors, textures, and expressive forms demanding artistic seeing and action, attention and response. The legacy we give to ourselves and others is this restored ability to create the vital connections needed in which to live and work, and thus claim our place among the world's *animadoras:* practitioners in the broadest sense of the word who "awaken and restore," breathing new life into and out of form.

Although I describe such practice, readers may find it objectionable to have to locate my methods of transformation in the slower-paced telling of stories, the witness of dreams, or the poetic offerings of unanalyzed artworks. We are used to measuring life according to the efficiency and pace of technology; we expect information to be presented in ways that are immediately functional, rational, and instrumental. But for the return of life's vital energies, it is imperative to slow down. As one of my companions told me, there is nothing wrong with efficiency but it will come to feel empty and sometimes corrupting if we don't also allow the contemplative pace of a walk of life. Slowing down, I am given room to attend more closely and care more completely for the world that is calling out for my response.

I am also aware that it will not be difficult to demonstrate the absurdity of this text and my belief in the vital life of images, stories, and dreams to re-enchant art therapists. It never is. We have a long habit of re-interpreting images as literalized history, psychology or science and, in the process, killing them. So I know that as others write practical, how-to texts on art therapy theory and methods, I may well be cast as a fuzzy-headed day-dreamer, not exactly current and not exactly an appropriate model. For the purposes of this text, I willingly threw out much practical knowledge I have of art therapy, but never was I self-deluded. I have attempted to write from the perspective of a pragmatic visionary, believing that "our daydreaming is what marks humanity in its depths" (Bachelard, 1969). To bring practice back to life, one has to reach beyond the literal and risk making a space for dreaming. What arrives in that open, prepared space will not necessarily be bliss. The antidote to disenchantment is not its enchanting, bliss-filled counterpart but a true awakening to the paradoxes and polarities that hold them both.

I am not the first to observe art therapy needs re-enchantment, and I owe the title of this book, in part, to Suzy Gablik who wrote *The Reenchantment of Art* (1991). I draw on aspects in her groundbreaking work that have inspired art therapists to re-envision the artistic traditions of their practices. Gablik, in turn, acknowledges the cultural historian Morris Berman, who wrote *The Reenchantment of the World* (1981), for the title of her text. Re-enchantment refers to a process of stepping beyond our modernist, enlightenment heritage of objectification in a way that allows a return of soul, and the integration of heart and mind in the ethic of care (Gablik, 1991). Because I was seeking a re-framing of art therapy my inquiry was intentionally interdisciplinary. To identify my contemplative practices, I turned to the fields of socially engaged Buddhism, organizational leadership, peace studies, depth psychology, improvisational music, and philosophical inquiry. I drew on the literature of world mythology, feminism, environmental activism, art criticism, and architecture to make some of the connections between the stories told to me and similar patterns found in other human experiences across time and space. I also am indebted to the poetry of Rainer Maria Rilke and Mary Oliver, and to the life works of Joseph Campbell and Clarissa Pinkola Estes for their acute observations of the human condition expressed in the realm of timeless myth. Where acknowledgment of these sources would disrupt the flow of the stories, I chose to footnote and locate them in chapter endnotes instead of the standard APA format.

I am also indebted to the acute observations and practices of living mentors who had the patience to teach me and inspire knowledge of my own. Dr. Arthur Robbins has had a hand in every question I have ever asked about art therapy, for there is no more exacting a teacher in learning the depths of the process and the practice of self-scrutiny. Dr. Shaun McNiff is a visionary who has known for a long time the same living truths I have only recently bumped into, and to him I owe my appreciation for the life of images. Dr. Fred Donaldson is the closest I have ever come to an apprenticeship with a shaman, which he disguises in the romping form of a "big white guy" who makes his living playing with children and wild animals. It is strange to me that this triumvirate of men has guided me in a field that is predominantly female and in great need of the feminine wisdom they have been instrumental in awakening in me.

For my research, I also acknowledge and thank the many art therapists who collaborated with me, shared their stories, and made a space with me for dreaming. I had only begun my inquiry when Lori Vance invited me to create the opening plenary for the profession's national conference on the theme of power and integrity. The art therapist's ambivalent relationship to creative power later became an essential finding in the study of art therapist disenchantment. I thank my collaborators Josie Abbenante, Valerie Appleton, Melody Todd Ashby, Robert Ault, Ellen Horowitz, Don Jones, and Cathy Moon who so willingly shared their insights on creative power and furthered my study. I had numerous conversations with art therapists interested in the same kinds of questions and thank Pat Allen, Janis Timms-Bottos, Suellen Semekowski, Deborah Linesch, Karen McCormick, Luanne Alberts, Stan Strickland, and Bruce Moon for their support and insights. Other art therapists, who showed me the depths and varieties of their disenchantment in the toxic work environment, were equally important contributors, although I have changed their names to protect confidentiality. I extend my thanks to "Danielle," "Leah," "Beth," "Sally," "Kari," "Val," and "Joy." When I put out an invitation to form a research group of art therapists who were interested in exploring the phenomenon of disenchantment in their lives and discover methods for restoring creative energy and transforming their art therapy practices, several art therapy colleagues willingly stepped forward though not all were able to participate. I am grateful to the "radical sewing circle" of my peers, Sonnie Albinson, Melody Todd Ashby, Michele Burnie, Min Kennedy, and Debbie Mickelsen for their wicked humor, wildish ways, and courage to encounter one another with a vulnerable fierceness of heart.

This research was begun in the early to mid nineties but found its focus beginning in 1998 with doctoral studies at the Union Institute in Cincinnati, Ohio. I remember walking into a seminar and discovering that everyone there—business leaders, human resource managers, educators, psychologists, religious practitioners, counselors, and one lone art therapist—were asking the same question: Why are so many workplaces killing us? I thank my fellow scholars for the tremendous support they gave me, especially Patricia Cane, Cherionna Menzam, Deborah Vogele, Cary LeBlanc, Julie Gatti, Marsha Tongel, Jim Stuart, and Jenifer Cash O'Donnell. I thank the seminar leader and my doctoral faculty, Barry Heerman, for his unending patience, humor, and affirmation of my scholarship. Finally, I thank my doctoral advisor Beth Hagens for her incredible support and trust in the creative process.

I owe a debt of tremendous gratitude to my husband Eddee Daniel who has traveled the artist's journey with me and who made a space for my dreaming throughout the months of doctoral studies. My daughters Erica and Chelsea are an inspiration to me in all their beautiful passion for living life fully on the rocky shores of adolescence. And finally, I wish to dedicate this work to my mother, Lee Kapitan, whose love and artistry so inspired my own life's passions and frustrations.

L.K.

CONTENTS

Page

Preface v

INTRODUCTION 3
    The Open Closing Door 3
    Review of the Literature: From Clinification to Therapeutic Artistry ... 8
    Methods of Artistic Discovery: Research Design and Questions 14
    Re-Enchanting Art Therapy 18

CHAPTER 1: ACCEPTING THE DEMANDS OF CREATIVE POWER 23
    Playing with Chaos 23
        Creative chaos and the clash of worldviews 25
        The suffering of taking things apart 27
    Stirring the Sleeping Dragon 30
        Shreading a life: Re-weaving its patterns 33
        The hungry dragon of longing 35
        The curse of the baby dragon 38
        It's alive! 40
        Up in smoke 41
        In the belly of the dragon 44
    Certification by Psychosis: A Final Dragon Story 48
    Dragon Fire of Creative Combustion: A Vital Life Sign 54

CHAPTER 2: OPENING TO ENCHANTMENT: THE ART THERAPIST AS *ANIMADORA* 60
    The Vessels of Our Transformation 60
    Therapeutic Artistry and the Craftsperson's Lessons of the
    Begging Bowl 66

    The Imaginal Space Opens 75
        Erica told me she had a hole in her heart .76
        Flota mi cuerpo sobre los equilibrios contrarios 78
        Waiting woman 80
    The Enchanted Landscape 85
    Art Therapy as a Socially Responsive Art Form 93

CHAPTER 3: A BOWL OF TEARS: WITNESSING ART THERAPIST DISENCHANTMENT IN THE TOXIC WORK ENVIRONMENT 103
    Introduction: Transforming Toxins Through Collaborative
    Witness 103
    Disenchantment in the Toxic Work Environment 108
        Turtle dreams in the cavern of jewels 110
        The journey to the other place 116
        The gardener 123
        The waters of St. Elm's 130
        The elixir of life 137
        The kingdom of the black river 144
        Jewels in the stream 150
    The Waters of Creative Vitality 157

CHAPTER 4: TRANSFORMING TOXINS IN THE CAULDRON OF COMMUNITY 165
    Introduction: Bringing Aliveness Back into Our Work 165
    The Reflective Circle of Peers: A Communal Practice for
    Restoring Creative Vitality 168
        The first circle: Walls and victims 173
        The second circle: Lovers in dangerous times 174
        The third circle: Feminine wisdom and the generational roots
        of violence 180
        The fourth circle: Bring back the peace we are all aching for 188
        The fifth circle: Searching for home 194
        The sixth circle: Necessary soul-work .199
        The last circle: Making a space for dreaming and
        returning home 203
    Making or Breaking: Art Therapy in a Violent World 207

CHAPTER 5: PLAYING ON THE THRESHOLD OF THE OPEN CLOSING DOOR 216
   Playing with Wolves 216
   Interlude 222
   In the Crossroads 225
   The Threshold 237
   Beyond Thresholds 245

CONCLUSION 251
   The Costs of Disenchantment and Lost Creativity 255
   Re-Enchantment as a Practice of Generosity 258

Bibliography 265
Index 271

FIGURES

Page

Figure 1. The open closing door, Lynn Kapitan .6
Figure 2. Falling into chaos, Lynn Kapitan 45
Figure 3. The eye of the dragon, Lynn Kapitan 47
Figure 4. The baby vessel dream, Lynn Kapitan 63
Figure 5. Waiting in the desert, Lynn Kapitan .64
Figure 6. Grandmother's bowl of tears, Lynn Kapitan 66
Figure 7. Portrait of Kathy's mother, Lynn Kapitan 79
Figure 8. The spiraling collective, Lynn Kapitan 81
Figure 9. Waiting woman, Lynn Kapitan 83
Figure 10. Gazing, terra woman, Lynn Kapitan 84
Figure 11. Danielle's disenchantment and response, "Danielle" 112
Figure 12. Lynn's response to Danielle's disenchantment,
          Lynn Kapitan 115
Figure 13. Sally's disenchantment and response, "Sally" 119
Figure 14. Lynn's response to Sally's disenchantment, Lynn Kapitan . . .121
Figure 15. Leah's disenchantment and response, "Leah" 126
Figure 16. Lynn's response to Leah's disenchantment, Lynn Kapitan . . .127
Figure 17. Lynn's response to Beth's disenchantment, Lynn Kapitan 134
Figure 18. Beth's disenchantment and response, "Beth" 135
Figure 19. Kari's disenchantment and response, "Kari" 142
Figure 20. Lynn's response to Kari's disenchantment, Lynn Kapitan 143
Figure 21. Val's disenchantment and response, "Val" 146
Figure 22. Lynn's response to Val's disenchantment, Lynn Kapitan 147
Figure 23. Joy's enchantment and response, "Joy" 153
Figure 24. Lynn's response to Joy's enchantment, Lynn Kapitan 156
Figure 25. Woman of authority, Melody Todd Ashby 176
Figure 26. The blanket of victim lies over her, Michele Burnie 177
Figure 27. Leaning away from life's push, Min Kennedy 177

Figure 28. Bear woman triptych, Melody Todd Ashby 182
Figure 29. Balancing on the head of a penis, Michele Burnie 184
Figure 30. Taking off the she-bear pelt, Sonnie Albinson 185
Figure 31. Winged sky-bear, Lynn Kapitan 186
Figure 32. Lost mother, Min Kennedy 186
Figure 33. You're here–the cycle's complete, Sonnie Albinson 189
Figure 34. No grail for me, Michele Burnie 191
Figure 35. The face of fire and ice, Michele Burnie 196
Figure 36. I made this place around you, Sonnie Albinson 198
Figure 37. Trapped in the cave, Melody Todd Ashby 199
Figure 38. Come out and play with me!, Lynn Kapitan 201
Figure 39. Playing with wolves, Lynn Kapitan 223
Figure 40. Nautilus, Lynn Kapitan 243
Figure 41. Open closing door revisited, Lynn Kapitan 253

RE-ENCHANTING ART THERAPY

INTRODUCTION

THE OPEN CLOSING DOOR

"Long ago and far away," I began, "there was a foolish young woman, caught in circumstances not of her own making." I couldn't explain it; I could only tell the story of how it came to be that I lost and found again the vital creativity that is the well-spring of my life as an art therapist. In the face of toxic, life-diminishing forces, I had been tracking an elusive question far into an unknown landscape.

"Was she a beautiful princess?"

"Not especially, and she wasn't a princess," I sighed. Who ever understood what art therapists did, or why the passionate intensity of their calling? "No," I said, "she was very ordinary. But she did have a talent for making things out of this and that, and telling stories to her children. On this particular day, though, she had a problem. She awoke from a disturbing dream and she was frightened."

"Was it a nightmare?"

"No, not really, the dream itself wasn't scary, but it stirred up scary feelings in her nonetheless," I said, shuddering from the memory of that image which came so suddenly in the night. At the time, I had been contemplating psychic deadness, seen in the faces of my colleagues and students. How could it be that they came to their work creative, joyful and life-affirming, only to become, a few years later, beaten down, cynical, drained of creativity and searching for a way out? I suspected that this pattern was a source of my community's lack of vitality and creative vision. It presented me with an ethical challenge that arose out of my work as a teacher who had witnessed a steady slide into disenchantment among new professionals: How could I inspire the many, creative, prospective students I talked to daily to commit to a calling that might kill them seven years after they've met me? And what of the lack of positive models they would encounter when they began their internships and formed supervisory relationships with deadened, non-creative art therapists looking to them to find their own healing? As I pondered these questions, the dream had appeared and awakened me.

"What disturbed her," I said, remembering the crushing weight of the dream image, "was this huge, black, metal door that was slammed shut and locked up tight. On the other side of the door was a most beautiful, enchanting place—she dreamed that she could step right through that doorway and into pure-blue sky! Only she wouldn't fall; she'd be floating through sky, and it gave her the most delicious feeling of freedom."

"I thought you said she was scared."

"Oh she was, believe you me! Because, how could that be? She didn't know how to fly! She was just an ordinary person. And the worst part was that she could only get to the beautiful place by opening that black metal door," I said, thinking of the obstacles to creative freedom art therapists describe as their suffering. "She sensed that there was some powerful force that was keeping it shut, and that made her scared, too."

"The next night, she had the dream again. Only this time, there was an old woman guarding the door, marching back and forth, this way and that, and all the while looking at her very, very fiercely as if to try to scare her away. The younger woman could hear her children crying and realized they were hungry and thirsty. She had to get the door opened! So she waited until the old woman marched away, and then ran up to the door and pulled it open just a crack. She could see a sliver of blue sky through it. But the old woman spied her and came storming back, pushing her out of the way and slamming the door shut!"

"That's how it went," I said, sadly shaking my head, having lived with this yearning myself. "Every time she managed to get the door open, that woman would come and slam it shut again. She woke up all in a sweat, wondering about that door and worried about what the dream meant and how it might come true. Why did the old woman frighten her so? Was a famine coming to her land? Was she or her children in danger of starving?"

"She got dressed and went about her business getting breakfast ready for her family, all the while thinking about her dream and its terrible dilemma. The blue sky had looked so inviting; there must be a way to go through the threshold behind the door. All that day she kept the dream in mind until finally, with her kids in bed and her husband asleep—"

"—She went to bed and had the dream again!"

"No, that is not how the story goes," I explained, describing an art therapist's method of artistic inquiry: "When all was quiet in her house, she decided she had to *paint* her dream and maybe that way she'd discover why it came and what it had to tell her. She went down to the cellar where she had a big sheet of dusty gray paper. With a piece of charcoal from the hearth she drew the black door and colored it in really solid, leaving just a tiny crack of blue peeking through. For no reason at all, she drew some lines across the bottom that looked like a bunch of twigs piled up in front of the door. When she was all done, she put the picture aside and washed the soot off her hands, staring at the painting—but not really seeing it because something else in her mind was trying to get her attention."

"So, even though it was very, very late, she got out another piece of paper—a white one this time. She just couldn't think of the door anymore because that crack of blue sky was calling to her, wanting lots more space. So this time she drew a wide, open space filled all in with a clear, clear blue, just like she had seen in her dream. She made it the shape of a doorway but left the paper white so the door was invisible."

Yes, I thought, this was the "open closing door," a painting I made to acknowledge the dream and to guide me into the paradoxical questions I was exploring (Figure 1). The door is open and closing at the same time; it is both a route to freedom and a means of containment. It promises a safe space that is protected yet constrained; it holds at the threshold the desires to act in the world and to withdraw in contemplation of it. I saw in the image both the desire for and the fear of creative power, calling me to set my inner and outer lives in motion, demanding renewal and reinvention in the course of my artistic, therapeutic practice. A key, perhaps, to the dilemma that is not really a dilemma at all. "When she was done," I continued, "she smiled with her heart's delight, and put the painting away. She crept upstairs to bed and fell into a deep sleep."

"Did she have the dream again?"

"Not right away, and that was fine since it had been scary, after all. But the next time the dream came she was standing perfectly still on the threshold of a blue-sky door. At her feet was the nest of twigs. She

Figure 1. The open closing door.

was wondering what to do when she heard a caw-cawing. She looked up. There high above her was a big, black crow. He swooped down and lifted her up, carrying her through the doorway and beyond. She was flying! She looked below her and saw the vast expanse of an abundant world with a deep, wild river running through it. She saw the shadow of the crow on the rushing waters of the river and realized it was she. She flew away, following the course of the river, and never came home again." Is that where the dream leads me? I wondered as I imagined stepping through the image of the open closing door. Who or what will carry me into the abundant world beyond to renew my creative spirit?

"She didn't come home? But what about her family? Did they starve without her? How did they get breakfast? Who would wash their clothes?"

"Oh, all right, fine then—she did come home," I sighed, slightly perturbed at this insistence on returning to the ordinary world and its responsibilities. "But I'll tell you a secret! She wasn't the same person as before," I added with a sly smile. "Oh no! She looked the same and she sounded just like the same mother they always had before. If you didn't look too closely, you'd never know she had had her dream-adventure. But let me tell you—every once in a while her children thought they saw a crow in the glint in her eye when she told them stories or in the flutter of soft feathers they felt when she kissed them on the cheek before bedtime. It was a mystery, you see. They never did figure it out until they were grown and started to remember dreams of their own."

* * *

It was a mystery, I thought, as I pondered the dream and the beginnings of my inquiry into what was killing the creativity of art therapists. Changes in health care had had a dramatic effect on the practice of art therapy in recent years. Born of the human potential movement of the late sixties and early seventies, art therapy began in traditional psychiatric hospitals, long-term care and geriatric facilities, and schools for children with special needs. But as diverse populations of people sought relief of mental suffering, art therapists expanded their practice to include drug and alcohol treatment, family therapy, physical and sexual abuse survivors, group homes, prisons, outpatient and community mental health agencies—any of the many places where counseling or clinical treatment is offered for adults, adolescents, and children. Gradually, art therapy has become recognized as an innovative but effective form of treatment where clients access their own healthy, creative functioning through art making and use the insights gained to make self-empowered changes in their lives. But since the early 1990s, when public funding for health care shifted to private insurers, art therapists have had to adapt quickly to major changes in the workplace. Today as a general rule, therapeutic relationships are brief, caseloads often are huge and made up of only the most severely disturbed or tortured people, treatment is overseen by insurers, practitioners must be licensed and regulated, and art therapy methods and outcomes are explained using the pragmatic, rational language of the clinic. Creative approaches to treatment frequently are undermined or devalued. As a result of these and other obstacles, many art therapists report being exhausted, discouraged, and disenchanted with the realities of their work lives, their creativity drained.

Yet art therapists must not lose their creative vitality, for if they do they can no longer offer the very knowledge and tools they have that are unique to their profession and critically needed in today's world. They need to be able to access their creativity as a primary, inner resource from which they draw their power and therapeutic skills.

Without it they become deskilled and disenchanted; like a heavy door slammed shut, all possible transformational energy becomes bound up in the painful toxicity of their life and work environment.

Throughout my pursuit of the sources of art therapist disenchantment I had been told many stories. Everyone seemed to have an idea of "why" ranging from the lack of fit for artists in the clinical world, professional envy, a lack of desire to engage in art making, a failure of proper training, a lack of support or invisibility in the institutions they served, and everyone's favorite scapegoat: managed care. All the stories pointed to the notion that the phenomenon itself is multifaceted with collective and individual, nuanced levels of truth. But over the course of my research I came to believe that the key for resolving what causes the most pain is to see it very clearly and use it as a source of creation. Poised on the threshold that opens to new sources of creativity, the challenge art therapists face may be to embrace the terrifying threat of resurrection to renew our practices, for how else will we be able to participate fundamentally in the creativity of our age?

REVIEW OF THE LITERATURE: FROM CLINIFICATION TO THERAPEUTIC ARTISTRY

My entry into the conversation on what is killing the creativity of art therapists began with heuristic research I conducted on the relationship between art and violence (Kapitan, 1996; 1997b). I explored the observation that less art and more violence seemed to go together, and its corollary, that by engaging in art-making experiences, violence would be lessened. The intensity with which I researched this premise produced the exact effect I was studying: Over time, the buildup of the imagery of violence surrounded me and its subsequent feeling states shifted me into an experience of pervasive numbness. Despite every intention to do so, I could not make art. I felt as though I were living in a void where all color, artistry, and life energy abandoned me. My exploration led me to look at the culture of fear and violence that is woven into the work lives of art therapists, its pervasive influence on current and future art therapy methodology, treatment models, and on professional identity.

The presentation of my paper at the national art therapy conference stirred interest among art therapists who had worked for a long time in violent settings and posed questions about a phenomenon called vicarious traumatization, in which the therapist who witnesses the stories and images from traumatized clients becomes traumatized and numbed in turn. Consequently, I was invited to participate on a panel called "Violence and Vulnerability: A Developmental Perspective" (Chapman et al., 1997). In a similar vein, a number of art therapists were addressing the "ravaged muse" or the impact of secondary effects of trauma on the art therapist (Wadeson, 1998; Malchiodi & Good, 1998; Sweig et al., 1998).

My initial inquiry was inspired by Allen's (1992) keen observation that art therapists were not making art any more, complaining they didn't have the time nor energy for it, not only with their clients but also for themselves. She described the difficulties of maintaining creative energies in the often dehumanizing and rigid institutions where many art therapists are employed. Allen's observation that art therapists were suffering from a lack of creative vitality in the workplace resonated with my own experience. At the time, art therapists were expending enormous energies toward becoming recognized and respected among an increasingly fragmented pool of competitors for health care dollars. We were adapting to the pressure by working for increased regulatory structures such as licensing and certification examinations, increasingly higher standards in education, ethics, and professional practice, and calling for more outcomes research to validate our work. But when a community throws itself into action without grounding in artistic contemplation of it, such action may become a frantic effort to survive against all odds. Violence may turn against the self as inferiority is internalized and artistic, expanded possibilities are blocked or lost. The antidote, according to Allen (1995b), is to recognize "a primary drive to know ourselves, others, and the world through our image-making" and remember our first responsibility: "to be aware of and tend to our own needs, our personal fire . . . [since] neglecting our own needs diminishes our capacity to be of service" (p. 165).

Allen (1992) named her observation the "clinification syndrome," a pervasive feeling of inferiority caused by art therapists needing to prove themselves to the clinical establishment in which they were working. Allen believed that art making ceases when clinical skills become the primary career focus. The artistic identity of the art therapist becomes secondary as it is forced to yield to an exclusive emphasis on the clinician's role. Allen saw the possibility of art therapists functioning in the role of "artist-in-residence" as a healthy alternative. Her experimentation led to the "open studio project" (Allen, 1995b) where art therapy is offered in the form of a non-clinical studio arts program, independent of any mental health service agency. In the "open studio," therapy concepts and practices are eschewed, no records are kept, dual relationships are often welcomed, and no emphasis is placed on roles (Allen, 1995b, p. 166). Usually few or no directives and more time are offered, and in-depth experiences with creating art are involved (Malchiodi, 1995).

Allen's insight resonated for me because I had observed the same phenomenon and had confirmed for myself that internalized violence leads to numbness and loss of creative vitality (Kapitan, 1996; 1997b). But I wondered whether those who suffered in this way necessarily had adopted a "clinified" identity that blocked artistic practice. Over many years the art-based education offered to my art therapy students integrated artistic practice and contemplation at all levels of their academic and clinical development, and it was one of the first graduate programs to require a studio component. Yet I had observed the same phenomenon among my "non-clinified" students and also among former students now serving as role models and mentors, as well as seasoned art therapy colleagues. The phenomenon seemed larger than something bounded by the clinic. Allen had identified the disenchantment, and our collective response suggested to me that it was something important yet still largely unknown, unnamed, and invisible. I chose to explore the roots of art therapist disenchantment so that the phenomenon could be named more accurately and brought into our awareness, rather than simply dismissed or allowed to influence us in unrecognized ways.

With "clinification" Allen provoked art therapists to rethink their relationship to their practice, but this term also creates problems, especially if the syndrome is actually something larger and not solely connected to performing a clinical role. In her own professional development and as the impetus for creating the studio art model, Allen (1992, 1995a, 1995b) acknowledged her struggle with the constraints of the clinic and her ambivalence in that role. She described how utterly defeated she felt by limited time with clients and the sterility of the setting, the boredom of listening to shallow discussions of superficial imagery by patients, and her cajoling to get them out of bed and away from the television set. Many art therapists would concur. But what of her belief that "the rules and regulations that [she] had painstakingly learned in order to practice art therapy paradoxically prevented art-making itself from being fully effective"? Or her comparison of the different, preverbal, nonverbal and even spiritual levels that art therapy accesses with the limiting, largely verbal level of psychotherapy whose rules "felt constricting, deadening, in fact harmful to the art therapy process" (1995b, p. 162)? Of her disenchantment, Allen wrote that she felt she was violating art therapy taboos or professional boundaries when she wanted to make art with clients, likely contributing to a breakdown of the tradition of professional distance. She said, "I began to feel the paradox that much of what makes psychotherapy effective and safe makes art therapy dead and lifeless" (p. 163).

At the time that Allen wrote of the death of creative vitality in the practice of much art therapy, psychotherapy itself was being revitalized by postmodern theories pushing the very boundaries Allen was chafing against. Their central premise is the larger relational system or field in which psychological phenomena constellate and where experience is continually and mutually shaped, known as the "intersubjective space" between client and therapist (Stolorow et al. 1994). The bounded, distant professionalism that Allen had learned was coming under criticism along with the "withering" of the therapist's authority as expert (Johnson, 1994; Spaniol, 2000) in a rapidly changing, postmodern era. Robbins (1973, 1987, 1996, 1998) articulated a theory of art therapy that places art within a field of oscillating rhythms of relatedness where both therapist and client experience and shape the energies occurring in the "therapeutic space" between them. Allen's work in the open studio project confirms this expanded concept of psychotherapy when she states that its primary attribute is energy: "The energy of those working in the space [is] the crucial, yet ineffable ingredient" (1995b, p. 164) where "viewing the struggles of one another through art causes shifts of perception on a deep level" (p. 166).

Clinification refers to a pressure to adopt the practices of others that do not value art, but it does not mean there is something wrong with clinical practice as some have interpreted Allen's work to mean. For example, my students sometimes have cited the horror of "clinification" to justify a distinctly anti-therapeutic stance, insisting that they don't really need clinical skills to practice art therapy if all they plan to do is set up open studios around the city and invite clients to them. At the same time, I know that the most effective, studio-based art therapists practice with considerable, well-formed and integrated clinical knowledge, although this is not always apparent to naive observers. Meanwhile, art therapists who work in clinical settings have complained that the "de-clinification movement" lacks scientific grounding and promotes fuzzy-headed rapture instead of clear and direct guidance for clients. Clearly, Allen's emphasis is on the centrality of artistic practice as a process of regaining and sustaining creative vitality regardless of where or how the art therapist works.

The studio movement arose from the tensions of an earlier era as well as the challenges of the present. From its very beginnings the profession has debated the place of art in art therapy. By 1973, art therapists had positioned themselves into two camps: "art as therapy" epitomized by Kramer's writings (1971) on the inherent value of art making as containing all the therapy needed, and the "art psychotherapy" approach epitomized by Naumburg (1973) where art making served as an adjunctive tool to engage the client in therapeutic change. This latter approach has also been identified as "clinical art therapy" (Landgarten 1987). Some art therapists today use the argument against clinification to promote a spiritual, blissful and inwardly contemplative side of art therapy over what they disparage as a grasping, worldly struggle for professional identity in the dog-eat-dog health care market. To paraphrase Palmer (1990), there continues to be a struggle between the inward search of the artist and the outward acts of the therapist, the silent communion with the art image and the engaged interactions of the therapeutic relationship, and a longing for the centered solitude of the art studio in the face of the dysfunctions of clinical practice settings. If one is called to contemplation in the art studio, this idea can be empowering. But as Palmer (1990) warns, "these same values can disenfranchise the soul [when] they devalue the energies of the active life rather than encourage us to move with those energies toward wholeness" (p. 2).

Whenever solutions to problems are conceived in terms of polarized ideologies there can be no reconciliation. But when we choose to learn from what disturbs or challenges us, we open ourselves to shifts in perception and response (Travis & Callendar 1990). Creative and productive means for meeting needs are freed up even if the conflict itself can never be resolved. For art therapists, this may well mean holding the creative tension *between* artist and therapist, the two poles that contribute to the primary identity of the art therapist, which is the core of the studio and of the clinic. McNiff, whose practice of art therapy has been based in studio settings over the past three decades, emphasizes art therapy's roots in the clinic or therapeutic community. He writes,

> Through participation in life enhancing environments with other people, we experience change. The studio spaces, the work of other people, the art-making process, and the images we make, all contain and transmit life-enhancing energies that effect change in individuals as well as communities. Art therapy animates and encourages us to go on living with increased vitality generated by the creative process. (1998, p. 130)

Clearly what McNiff describes is not necessarily open-ended, "more art oriented than clinically based," nor containing "undefined aspects of the facilitator's responsibilities and relationship to the participants who attend" the therapy session (Malchiodi, 1995, p. 155). McNiff's concept of the studio is "led by the space," embracing multiple possibilities. He emphasizes that "the vitality of the studio has more to do with the creative presence" in whatever space it is found; "we medicine the disquieted places, and this spatial transformation has a corresponding effect on us. The presence of the creative spirit can be felt everywhere a group is fully committed to its work" (1995, p. 182). Robbins (1998) identifies therapeutic presence as a key element in creating a healing space and describes it as a field of energy, a frame or container involving a holistic, intuitive, and receptive orientation, and a paradoxical state that is both focused, yet open.

Robbins has influenced my understanding of the dynamics of the creative relationship, capable of "a deep harmony not only with my patient, my artwork, the community, but also with myself" (1973, p. 184). As McNiff (1998) notes, the experiential aspects of the therapeutic relationship is perceived by Robbins as an object of aesthetic reflection that integrates the two primary aspects of the profession. Like Robbins, I believe that my job is "to be alive therapeutically for the other, whether that other is an individual, group, or community, which brings a profound spiritual connection, an essential aspect of healing" (Robbins, 1998, p. 23). Therapeutic artistry embodies a working towards meaning by shaping and forming the energy of the "studio" in the relational field. There we honor the symbols that emanate from a person's center and use them to create an engagement with the world

(Robbins, 1998). Disenchanted professionals who cannot acquire a genuinely felt sense of meaning through the culture in which they live and work cannot be centered in this way. Thus the "studio" in the largest sense is perhaps an archetype or deep structure wanting to be made visible and re-connecting art therapists to the places and communities they wish to belong in some fundamental way.

Therapeutic artistry is a practice that transcends the boundaries of populations, theories, and technique. Who we are as art therapists is the constancy we bring to the encounter. What changes, what shifts our process of naming this practice, is merely the container that also must be respected and understood. The container of the open studio form of practice is different from the container of clinical psychotherapy. But art therapy as a practice flows in and out of these spaces, adapting and transforming or co-creating relationships within the bounded fields of our work lives. After all, space is not empty but is filled with invisible fields; these are filled with interpenetrating influences and invisible structures that connect and subtly shape behavior (Wheatley & Kellner-Rogers, 1996). If we trust the inherent organizing forces of life, then new vitalities will emerge and authentic forms of practice will be made possible for all art therapists.

METHODS OF ARTISTIC DISCOVERY: RESEARCH DESIGN AND QUESTIONS

While much has been written by art therapists about the need to pay more attention to their own art making, the topic until now has been informed mostly by opinion and speculation. My research sought to address the underlying problem, that is, the need to regain and sustain creative vitality among disenchanted professionals, without which we cannot claim to be art therapists, the nurturers of creativity. I asked: By what transformative processes can disenchanted art therapists regain and sustain their creative vitalities? What outcomes are possible when we attend to the transformational energies of communal and creative healing practices? As I began to explore these questions I was challenged to find methods of inquiry suited to the unique worldview of art therapy and the core values of artists and art therapists. I was not interested in addressing these questions through a study of clinical methods or treatment techniques; neither did I believe I would find answers derived from the solutions-based focus found in "burn out" or trauma literature, educational theory, or psychological assessment. The strategies that I designed were directed at revealing the phenomenon aesthetically and transforming it in ways that would help art therapists claim what had been lost and sustain deep change. At base, my research method was that of an artist whose works serve as objects of intense, aesthetic reflection and subsequent action. Artistic practice is both a way of knowing and a means of discovery. With the unwavering attention of the researcher and an open, active, "listening" stance toward the phenomenon, layers of meaning are discovered. Art, story, and essay are products of this reflection as well as further means for reflection.

This methodology has a relationship to qualitative forms of research found in various fields. According to Braud and Anderson (1998, pp. 53–55), there are three major motivations for conducting research. One, in service of security and adaptation, is to learn as much as we can of the world, other people, and ourselves for the purpose of prediction and control. Research is approached as a series of problems to be solved. A second motivation is simply to understand the world in the service of curiosity and wonder; research questions are approached like a puzzle—the researcher wishes to know what the pieces are, how they fit together, and what sort of picture begins to be revealed when sufficient pieces have been assembled and put in place. For my purposes, I adopted the third motivation, which is also in service of wonder, but it is a wonder that accompanies discovery, surprise, delight, and awe. Research concerns are approached more like works of art to be appreciated rather than problems to be solved.

Art therapy research is often situated in the realm of in-depth understanding drawing from hermeneutic, heuristic, and phenomenological methods of qualitative inquiry. It can be described phenomenologically because art making is a contemplation of direct experience. However, as McNiff (1998) points out, artistic inquiry requires an active engagement with art images as a process through which an image reveals itself to us. While art therapy methods are closely attuned to the phenomenological approach to describing experience precisely as it presents itself, the experiences of phenomenologists are dependent upon language in order to exist as data. In contrast, the study of artistic images and the process of art making combine both material objects and experience. Where phenomenology relies on verbal description of experiences, art-based research also involves the study of objects that present themselves as data without dependence upon language (McNiff, 1998). Therefore, art-based research is something distinctly different from the methods described in phenomenological approaches.

Artistic inquiry is also primary in the practice art of therapy and in my research I drew on over ten years of prior experience with art-based research methods (Kapitan, 1998a). According to McNiff (1998), such inquiry is aesthetically-oriented and concerned with in-depth methods of artistic knowing as well as how creative activity influences people. Although methods that emphasize the researcher's relationship to the image often are the primary focus, I found it useful to broaden this with the practice of "therapeutic artistry" in which the worldview of the art therapist as an artist is brought to bear on the entire art therapy enterprise as a socially responsive art form (Kapitan & Newhouse, 2000). When artistic practice thus is placed in a context of social action, it builds on and extends feminist and transpersonal research, which emphasize the sacred, inclusive, subjective, experiential and contextual, transformational, individual and understandable features of the investigative endeavor (Clements et al., 1998; Valle & Mohs, 1998). It honors the plurality of voices—other ways of knowing and of other persons, particularly individuals and members of a previously unempowered group. The added benefit of artistic inquiry is that it not only embraces what has been unspoken, it provides a visual, tangible means for making visible what is unseen, for both the image and the person who creates the image. Becoming seen is a powerful means of verifying research findings and honoring existence.

My connection to the word "method," then, embraces an artist's practice of his or her artistic discipline. The method is the path into the unknown guided by an intense relationship to artworks and their surrounding fields of influence. Artistic discipline means attending to and being respectful of the art form's inherent nature. I hypothesized that when an art therapist engages in methods of artistic inquiry into the phenomenon of disenchantment, a deep connection with the essential nature of her art form will be kindled and a re-connection with the sources of her work will transform her relationship to herself and her world. If disenchantment is the result of being disconnected, then artistic practice would be an appropriate method of inquiry for both discovering the roots of disenchantment and transforming them with creative vitality.

I organized my inquiry according to several distinct modes of sustained artistic reflection and creative action, each a different path into the phenomenon of disenchantment and its transformation. Individually, I sustained heuristic inquiry through meditations recorded in art, journaling, and story writing that revealed visceral and aesthetic experiences with the phenomenon of my own disenchantment. Collectively, I designed and carried out a collaborative story telling project among several art therapists from different parts of the United States that revealed an ambivalence toward creative power, especially its destructive energies. A creation myth served as a vehicle for projecting their experiences of disenchantment, for processing them on a deep level and making them available for psychological transformation in the context of collective, organizational relationships. "Collaborative witness" was another follow-up project involving a confidential practice of witnessing several self-described disenchanted art therapists. It included an open-ended interview followed by silent, interactive art making and shared reflection, which in turn led to the revelation of a mythic narrative that amplified the essence of their disenchantment. Having studied the sources of disenchantment through all these methods, I designed an intervention for art therapists in my local professional community. This was a "healing circle" where a group of women art therapists came together in a weekly immersion-and-retreat format to explore re-enchantment, to release new stories and images for each other's inspiration, and to regain the energies of empowerment. Finally, I explored several unusual forms of "artist-in-residency" for revitalizing my own practice with adventurous play in a disenchanting work environment and for exploring the open, yet bounded space of the studio as an internalized structure that can be created and carried into disenchanted places or wherever the work is needed.

Consistent with Braud and Anderson's (1998) description of transpersonal research, simultaneous roles and functions began to occur throughout my inquiry in synergistic ways. All my interactions were research sessions that provided new information to contribute to the development of the profession. They also were clinical sessions in that my collaborators and I accepted the opportunity to bring to consciousness important issues and give them image and voice. Also common to transpersonal studies (Valle & Mohs 1998), my inquiry came to emphasize the container of the experience, intense emotional or passionate states in me and my co-researchers, a feeling of transcending time and space, an absence of fear and sense of surrender, sudden and insightful knowing, feelings of gratitude and grace, and self-transformation among all the participants.

In this text, my findings are presented in the forms of meditative art, dream, story, and essay in order to stay as close as possible to the original experience, and to give voice to images, to the experiences of my collaborators, and to my own voices within me. Story writing is a medium for preserving the archetypal integrity of the research and apprehending the many layers of meaning. In the subtle twists and turns of life being contemplated artistically, stories are an old and singular method for re-enchanting a listener's (or reader's) experience. The goal of a story is contemplation from which an individual will obtain meaning applicable to his or her life. Thus, the outcomes of my research cannot be reduced to a single set of interpretations but will be particular to each individual who contemplates them.

RE-ENCHANTING ART THERAPY

Overcoming the crisis of disenchantment is considered by some to be the greatest need of our culture at this time (Berman, 1981; Gablik, 1991). Disenchantment is described as the end result of a mechanistic world view, a modern vision of separateness that produced the objectifying consciousness of modernism, positivism, rationalism, materialism, secularism, and scientism (Gablik, 1991). In the art world, it is a product of the "disembodied eye" with which the viewer approaches a work from a distance, using objectified theory making to properly categorize and value what is seen. Art made to be approached aesthetically reinforces the rational over spiritual, intuitive or emotional reactions to art (Josephson, 1996). Pushed to the extremes of postmodernism, it takes the form of art that signifies the nihilistic, meaningless commodification or purposelessness of art and life. Art therapists, in serving their clients, attempt to create conditions conducive to art making in the face of the massive, disenchanting realities of their clients' toxic inner worlds, the work organization's dysfunctions, and our surrounding "culture of anesthesia" that shows tremendous contempt for the aesthetic dimension. Health care systems that are oriented toward the mechanistic worldview push the art therapist into an adaptive survival that further disenchants.

But if disenchantment is a state of being that dominates our culture, living in a state of enchantment is no better reality. Yalom, the existential psychotherapist who wrote *Love's Executioner* (1989), observed that the enchanted state of romantic love and psychotherapy are ultimately incompatible. Of his clients whose unattainable desires came to dominate their lives through illusions and obsessions, he wrote "I, too, crave enchantment . . . [but] I must assume that knowing is better than not knowing, venturing is better than not venturing, and that magic, however alluring, ultimately weakens the human spirit" (p. 13). It is infinitely more exciting to live life as it is happening than to wrap it in the illusory cocoon of merger that characterizes all states of bliss. Enchantment drains life of its edgy reality and obliterates new experience. One art therapist I talked to said that much as she loves that magical feeling of enchantment that sometimes accompanies her art therapy work, if she were to insist on maintaining that state, she'd be "bumping into walls all the time."

The rapture of enchantment appears in utopic depictions of art therapy that present an almost religious belief in its redemptive qualities of salvation from a dark, disenchanting world of environmental and human destruction. The future of art therapy has been envisioned as playing a major role in bringing art to heal entire communities, no longer practiced in mainly institutional settings with actual clients, and no longer using the terminology of therapy, therapist, or client/patient because "[these terms] will be unnecessary as the therapeutic uses of art will be assumed and understood by all" (Young, 1995, p. 195). In this text, I occasionally adopt a similar belief in the salvation of the world through art therapy and see it as a product of my heuristic falling into and out of love for art therapy again and again. I assert, in agreement with Gablik, that if our work is to succeed as part of a necessary process of cultural healing there must be willingness to abandon old programming, to make life alive again and discover that the world is enchanted and not dead. However, re-enchanting the world by seeing it exquisitely alive with all my senses is not the same as insisting that all my life spaces must be filled with bliss. Eventually I discovered for myself that re-enchanting art therapy takes place between the paradoxes, paradigms, and polarities of these states. There is a need to recognize our state of wanting and to live reflexively while holding that awareness rather than filling it with either bliss or a special victimhood. Re-enchantment is a cycling process that recognizes a unitary field where oneness and separateness, enchantment and disenchantment, intuition and rationality co-exist. Re-enchantment recognizes the states of both belonging and exile, seeing them simply as two necessary sides of one larger circle.

My discussions of re-enchantment begin, in Chapter One, with the story of a young art therapist whose life history is situated in the postmodern age with all its attendant fragmentation, speed, and incoherence. She is a challenge to my own worldview formed in a previous, modernist age with its beliefs grounded in universal truths and the ascendant, rational intellect that so often determines and fixes meaning. The story is a metaphor for the good intentions of the creativity killer in all of us, in dealing with disenchantment and the two sides of the paradox, either to control the flow and power of creative vitality or to play it into greater coherence. When we believe that the world needs us to keep it from falling apart, we are acting the part of Vritra, the mythic Hindu dragon of creation that has swallowed up all the space of the universe and has massed its hulk over the waters of creation. A lightening bolt is needed to pierce the illusions that tie up creative energy and get it flowing again. It is good to awaken the dragon, for it is a vital life sign. But what then? What will we do with all its unleashed creative power? We like the idea of art coming from chaos, but what of the reverse? To what extent do we realize that creative vitality also needs to flow back into chaos? The risk of awakening the dragon is to suffer creation's destructive energies, the taking apart of things that we have so carefully constructed for illusory safety and control.

Thus, I begin with the uneasy, ambivalent relationship art therapists have with creative power. When art therapists act as Indra, the hero in the myth who pierces illusions with the bolt of enlightenment, it is as if we wake up to renewed life, to get it flowing again. In Chapter Two, I explore the notion of the art therapist as an *animadora*—a word meaning "one who awakens the other to life." The Spanish word for giving birth, in fact, is *dar la luz:* to give light. I turn to the vessel where creative vitality is born, is shaped and is surrendered to. The birthing vessel, the bowl, the alchemical crucible—these are essential forms that can be used to describe a transformational conception of art therapy practice. I imagined holding out a bowl to the world and accepting with gratitude anything that is placed there as needing my attentive, transformative energies. As I opened my imagination, new images arrived in my "bowl"—some wanted, others unwanted. I come to see that the practice of making alive is an embodied practice of seeing the world ensouled. When we see the world as lover or as a loving partner we extend the human heart to the whole world. Thus, we make life in everything we touch and stand in readiness for any possibility that serves our deeper intent as art therapists. Such an attitude can transform our practices and re-enchant art therapy as a socially responsive, reciprocating art form.

I have heard art therapists talk of re-enchanting their practices by creating special places for their studios, like beautiful mountain or garden retreats where people can go to escape the pressures of living in a toxic, fast-paced world. I recall one art therapist who, tired of working with depressed people, was enchanted with the idea of hosting Caribbean cruises for art therapist colleagues to experience revitalization. I do not fault these strategies but they lead me to ask, what is driving art therapists away from the people and places that need them most? In Chapter Three, I explore the roots of disenchantment by seeking out the disquieted places, environments that are experienced as toxic to art therapists in both their work and deep within their own restless psyches. I practice bearing witness, which I believe the world needs much more than another quick-fix solution. As I listen to their stories and witness the images that appear, a larger, mythic story arrives that is common to each art therapist's experience: the great underground river that is the source of creative vitality has been blocked, drained, tampered with, or poisoned. The absence of the waters of creation creates the conditions of the wasteland and this is where disenchanted art therapists labor. For some, it is a state akin to soul death. For all of us, it is imperative that we detoxify and become clear channels of creativity again for ourselves and for those with whom we work.

In the landscape of disenchantment it seems we are craving aliveness and for this we suffer. Our workplaces have changed dramatically and they will never be the same. But as artists committed to a more just, compassionate world, we can choose the life-giving process of art making as an antidote to life breaking. Art transforms the violence and in this process we make peace. The inward quest for wholeness becomes, in peacemaking, a quest for outward relationship or community. In

Chapter Four, I present a community intervention called the Reflective Circle of Peers, which came to be known among the art therapist participants as their "radical sewing circle." Weekly, art therapists came together to explore their disenchantment and make magic from it. We kicked at the walls that bound us, claimed and surrendered victimhood, bore witness to suffering and challenged each other to live life between the paradoxes. Through these rituals we performed an ancient method of soul-retrieval and re-enchanted our practices by making a space for dreaming born into creative action.

Ultimately the question is not how to keep our creativity and ourselves from harm in the toxic, dispirited environments that need our compassionate attending but rather, how boldly will we live? In Chapter Five, I take up the challenge from my peers in the radical sewing circle and return to the spaces between the paradoxes. This is the threshold of "between" where I face that which keeps me from my own transformation: the encounter with the one who is me and not-me—whether that takes form in the medium of my art, the client, my inner selves or outer roles and personas, the externalized enemy or something alien I do not recognize, or other categories with which I define my experience. On the threshold, I let go of the rules to discover deeper rules; I enter the dream state that is nonetheless real and embodied, practiced in "adventurous play." I seek out thresholds in places of power and let go of intentional, purposeful action. I find "playgrounds" everywhere and eventually locate the *temenos* or sacred space of the studio as a capacity I carry within me wherever I seek to practice.

Someone once said, "When you love something so much, the only way to get out of trouble is to go deeper into it." We must enter into, not evade or fear, the natural entanglements of the dynamic, shape-shifting world in which art therapists live and create. Transformational practice holds both the desire to act in the world and to withdraw in contemplation of it. It calls us to set our inner and outer lives in motion, demanding constant renewal and reinvention. When we dare to move through what troubles us we trade some of our most precious, enchanting illusions for a reciprocating, living partnership with the world that has its own enchantment. This paradoxical relationship is the canvas upon which we re-enchant our practices.

Chapter 1

ACCEPTING THE DEMANDS OF CREATIVE POWER

*Things fall apart; the centre cannot hold,
mere anarchy is loosed upon the world.*
—Yeats

PLAYING WITH CHAOS

The myriad ways that the world conspires to keep art therapists from the creativity that feeds their practice are easily identifiable. Ask the question "What is killing the creativity of art therapists?" and innumerable answers will point to the constraints of time and place, the speed of daily life and the burden of ever larger expectations, the failure of employers to provide the conditions favorable to creative productivity, or the regulatory culture that has forced art therapy into a one-size-fits-all mold of the mental health care worker. More difficult is to recognize the obstacles we erect on our own when struggling with the demands of creative power to freely do its work of transformation. Our creative possibilities draw from the free movement of the psyche that may as easily wander into deep and formless, unknown terrains as bask comfortably in the light. Sensing the pull of fomenting chaos, no one is exempt from the temptation to block it since it stirs the excitement of new creation at the same time that it accompanies strange discomfort and fear.

I think of Mary, a graduate art therapy student who, for her thesis research, was investigating the hundred or so boxes, collages, and assemblages she'd made throughout her studies.[1] Her creative process exemplified the psyche's embrace of completely fluid, constant change and abrupt shifts of direction. She would carefully construct her pieces of creatively synthesized data but then suddenly would take them apart and reconstruct them, with exhilarating passion, as she discovered new arguments and insights in her inquiry.

I was her thesis advisor with an eye out for delivering her to graduation. I was a creativity killer, though I did not know it at the time. Maybe I was acting the part of the outside world's time-limited reality, like an employer looking at the bottom line or a disapproving head nurse armed with an efficient protocol for getting the work done. Mary's process drove me crazy. Reading drafts of her thesis was like rustling around in a paper scrap box: I saw lots of interesting pieces of things but nothing of a structure to hold and relate the pieces to one another. The incoherence surprised me: Mary had a background in fine arts, solid clinical experience, always wrote high quality graduate papers—what was going on? As a collage artist, I knew that she had to play around with pieces of data and imagery, rearrange them on the page, and use her artistic methods to discover hidden relationships. This in itself is not unusual among researchers yet Mary pushed far beyond comfortable limits. Tension arose as time drew short; I wanted to impose order on her process. I politely told her that I accepted how she had been guided by collage in her process, but the way she had paperclipped things together seemed random and I urged her to put some structure in the draft. Patronizingly, I explained to her what "chapters" were, saying "I am looking for the holding frame that says, in effect, 'these ideas group together as a chapter called 'x', here is an introduction to the ideas contained in this chapter, and this is a conclusion about why I think these things belong together.' This will go far in creating a sense of understanding in your reader's mind."

The chaotic rustling through the scrap box as Mary worked made it difficult to find and maintain a connection. I saw Mary's creative chaos as a problem where perhaps I should have seen it as a vital life sign, the proof of her courageous acceptance of the demands of creative power implicit in her inquiry. I kept wanting to give her advice that would "stick." One day I even told her in a near rage that she had to stop it and "glue things down" into a final form, after the fourth draft and two weeks before graduation when she had taken the entire thesis apart and reordered it into something completely new and unrecognizable to me. Only in hindsight did I see that Mary was teaching me something about her remarkable capacity to use her artistic process to sustain an open field of awareness. She was searching for some sort of internal logic and my imposing a structure on it, simply to manage my own anxiety, would have destroyed the integrity of her research findings.

Creative Chaos and the Clash of Worldviews

This fluid stance, which does not accept fixed or reductive causality, preferring "whole galaxies of meaning to emerge from a limited set of phenomena," characterizes postmodern thinking presently occupying our cultural habitat.[2] Mary's worldview, which rejects the idea of a single, universal reality, is part of a cultural "shift to incoherence" that is occurring, where there is no individual essence to which one remains true and committed.[3] Mary's process was tied to a postmodern belief that our present social and ecological disasters cannot be overcome until the worldview that created them is rejected.[4] Intent on deconstructivism, postmodern artists like Mary carry a profound disenchantment with the modern world. Their preference for freely appropriating, counterfeiting, mixing and re-mixing images violates the modernist view of creativity that is based in innovation, authenticity, and originality.[5]

Mary's highly relative, fluid process matched the flux of the fragmenting culture in which she lived. As an art therapist she was acutely aware that even though she and her clients didn't have identical or even very similar life experiences, "the larger, shared events of racism, sexism, terrorism, environmental disaster, mass murder, and war joined them together," she said, "as global residents and neighbors." The ideal of continual growth and progress, of reason triumphing over unreason, felt as unreal to her as a happy ending in a movie intent on repressing the reality of evil and despair. The postmodern view in art therapy takes issue with the presumed authority of our educational and clinical institutions while it also rejects simplistic or overdetermined treatment methods that favor a singular view of reality. In its concern for the multiplistic, overwhelming demands of today's therapeutic workplace, it insists that art therapists cannot responsibly treat the clinical issues of race, culture, gender, and socioeconomic status without including the impact of the outside world on how we construct reality.[6]

The key to the professional survival of creative art therapists in the face of toxic, unstable and overwhelming work environments may well be this creative capacity of Mary's, applied to shaping and reshaping a continuously adaptable therapeutic framework that is comfortable with chaos.

As Mary's thesis advisor, though, I was in trouble: my education and career were founded on modernist ideals rooted in a linear concept of selfhood that linked birth to death as a causal history of consequences.[7] Mary stood on the other side of the doorway: the postmodern heretic opposed to the notion of a rational intellect that determines and fixes meaning. She was skeptical of universalist ideas that downplay how distinct and different people really are and she was especially suspicious of positivist psychological outcomes linked to categorical diagnosis. She wrote of how insulting it was for her clients to be examined by a physician or psychologist only in the context of their disability, for the singular, narrow purpose of diagnosing a problem or dispensing medication with no attempt made to understand the person. As she put it, even the construct of "change for the better" in the eyes of a physician unfamiliar to the person might not be what the person or family would know as better. Mary saw in the shorthand taxonomy of clinical diagnosis a pessimistic "conclusion or grand narrative about an individual or meaning in his or her life."

As her advisor and supervisor I resisted this invasion of Mary's postmodernism into my authoritative, modernist domain and petulantly questioned whether there were any rules in this game Mary was playing. Negatively, I wondered if she and her clients also experienced each other as surfaces and fragments—as bits and pieces of whole people floating in amorphous, undifferentiated space with little to contain them. Her images and the meaning she assigned to them, I thought, all seemed to "slide past one another, dissociated and decontextualized, failing to link up into a coherent sequence."[8] So I reproved her, accusing her of having deliberately pulled everything out of the context and jumbled them all up just so the reader couldn't tell which came first, second, or third. "We need the unfolding chronology of time and space to help us find coherent order in our experience," I instructed her, alarmed, as she fluidly constructed and then deconstructed every draft. "We need the structure. *Put it back!*"

I heard my modernist plea for coherence and order in organizing and patterning Mary's lived experience. I had faith in the belief that people make sense of life by arranging their experiences in sequences across time. But in Mary's world people also arrange their lives as simultaneously presented pictures or compounded "scenes," not linear narratives. Their stories may be a re-assemblage of competing traditions, speaking in any voice that appeals. Their lives may be like the characters in soap operas, playing different parts in different stories, or enmeshed in simultaneous stories. No grand narrative is completed; life simply goes on with minor dramas postponed or abandoned and new stories emerging with each new scene.[9]

The Suffering of Taking Things Apart

In Mary's re-mixed collaging of preexisting images, like the rap music my generation loves to hate, a cyclic process was at work that could be discovered only by first suffering the formlessness of taking things apart. As I witnessed her art-based inquiry unfold, I learned that her worldview was not nearly as chaotic as it first appeared. Neither was it based in cynicism or negativity. Probably I would never have arrived at this subtler understanding of what she was doing had I insisted, as her mentor and advisor, that she bring closure to her inquiry sooner rather than later. Stretched along the continuum of the creative process unfolding are the two poles of deconstruction and reconstruction. Eventually disenchantment is transformed into its enchanted, reconstructed version. I would learn this over and over again as I conducted my own research. Both sides are part of a larger whole.

From her intimate relationship with the materials of artistic inquiry, Mary gradually was able to articulate her work as an art therapist in helping clients bring together the elements of their fragmented lives, lived in constant flux, into something newly whole. Her artistry found value in all the *bricolage* generated, discarded, found, traded, and created in a society awash in excess materialism, technology, and information. Her particular desire, she saw, was to bring the compassion of the art therapist and the focused attentions of the artist to what had been discarded and declared useless. She wrote that while she had been aware of this aspect of her creative process for a long time, she never thought she was making art or that she was an artist. "I was simply reconstructing what had been discarded, making something new from something old, or bringing something back to life," she wrote, since after all, "combining what appear to be unlike things often leads to a new perspective as the individual while unmatched fragments become transformed into a whole, new image."

Mary, and other postmodern artists coming of age as art therapists are creating a new art form of social and creative action since they do not view art as a separate enterprise that must be integrated into a therapeutic relationship. But to arrive at this new form, they need to deconstruct some of art therapy's most cherished ideas in order to see the world anew. Mary wrote:

> My responses, while consistent overall, are unique to each person with whom I work. It seems to me there is a continual cycle, or rhythm, of relationship. As an art therapist, skill in remaining fluid enough to allow for differences in relationship while maintaining my sense of self, is an ongoing concern. In this way, I work with the pieces of myself in new combinations or arrangements each time.

Mary was invited by the demands of the creative power that freely flowed within her to take part in her continuous formation, letting it operate and create what it wished of her. Working with Mary was like working with water, in the swirling combinations of essential stuff she was playing into existence and gradually finding coherence. Water has an impressive ability to adapt, to shift the configurations, to change the balance of power, and to create new structures.[10] Water is a unique "process structure" that can maintain its integrity over time without becoming rigid. What drives this organic adaptability seems to be a vital need to flow. It is as though we have within ourselves a river that constantly flows with vitality, whose energies are needed for a creative life lived in motion.

Unfortunately, such relational and process ideas can hardly be said to have penetrated very deeply into the consciousness of our culture.[11] A characteristic response to the fluid, chaotic reality of our age is to hammer organization and structure into place through the mechanisms of control, predictability and imposed order. We want to "glue things down" and "make things stick." Wheatley writes that the organizations and structures we create in this way are based on an underlying fear of things falling apart.[12] We resist the flow of creative power by building dams, locks, levies, and massive containment reservoirs. We manage it through parts, separations, subjects and categories, and complex planning for prediction and control. It doesn't work, though; the center cannot hold and chaos is loosed upon the world. One only needs to look at the Soviet Union in the late twentieth century to see what can happen when a centrally organized, controlling and rigid system is created to deal with the disparate fragments of a world in flux. Such a system will break up under the fossilized weight and stagnancy of its own bureaucracy, killing off the creative function in its need to stem the flow. What is required instead are multiple process structures that permit shifts and changes, rising up and disappearing only to rise again in different places and forms.

In the absence of externally imposed structures, the basic resource we have is ourselves, which we can use to engage the known and the unknown, and find ways to make contact and facilitate relationships, the basis of the postmodern world. Thus the function of both artist and therapist is as a connector or channel that gathers and passes on what comes to him or her from the depths, as the artist Paul Klee once said. The art therapist in touch with creation will seek connection in diverse places, creating multiple centers of connection and communities to hold it.[13] As an art therapist newly coming into her own power, Mary reflected on the chaos of the physical environment in which she lived and saw it symptomatically in the urban sprawl which blurs boundaries and lacks a center to hold our communal power and influence. Her intention as an art therapist was to create, in response, an environment for both her clients and herself that had a center or place of power for the imagination. At the same time she knew that she needed to learn to adapt functionally to the chaotic environments in which she lived and worked. "I find my own places of power, I recognize the alienation and fragmentation," she wrote, "but I continue to see alternatives to it deep in my imagination. It is there where I can form a protective environment for myself, a place that is my own. It is there that I can emerge from, and retreat to, and emerge from again in a continual rhythm, of oneness with the world."

I realized in my relationship with Mary that often I seek control when what I really want is order. Order born of harmony rather than control is a guiding principle of the postmodern age. The world wants organization but it does not need us to organize it. Whatever chaos may be present at the start of any enterprise, elements will begin to attract each other and combine,[14] and systems of organization will, in fact, appear if we pay close attention and allow them to do so. Mary's process was exquisitely beautiful on this point, as she wrote, "I lay my initial scrap on a sheet of paper without gluing it down. I add, rearrange, remove, and manipulate the materials until I am satisfied I have achieved an acceptable effect. My goal in making collage is in creating a unified design, whether I am arranging unlike images or images with commonalities." In parallel fashion, Mary viewed her art therapy practice as helping her clients use art to deconstruct their past, to reconstruct what was broken, or to construct a new version of themselves and the world.

The role and function of art therapists in the larger field of health care, I believe, is precisely to be in this business of tapping creative vitality to reinvent, reform and replace our outdated stories and images with better, more responsive and useful constructions. But to retain their life energy we must not get too attached—to our own stories, knowledge, authority, identity, and expertise—for this holding on to what we know stops the process of creation. We must suffer letting go for otherwise we will not be empty enough to receive what is newly playing itself into existence. Beyond the fixed versions we have created is the embrace of a deeper trust in ourselves continuously coming into form. Creative power thrives close to the chaos, for out of its flow the forms we create are born.

STIRRING THE SLEEPING DRAGON

But in choosing to embrace the demands of creative power, what will we do with its unleashed force? As I reflected on Mary's fluid access to the roiling sources of creation, my restless mind was halted by a whispered lullaby:

Sudden thunder
the crying child
becomes still.[15]

Something was rumbling deep within my consciousness, pressing for attention. "The way you answer the question 'Where do reality and power reside?'[16] reveals the foundation of your culture," I reminded myself. "Have art therapists forgotten that creation, the source of their work, is the most powerful force in the universe? It is the power by which the very universe came into being, is sustained, can be destroyed, and is transformed again and again."[17]

The Yoruba call it *Áshe*, the power-to-make-things-happen. To the Hebrew, it is *Yahweh;* *Wakan* to the Lakota; it is Buddha; Allah. The Hindu understand this dynamic universe where nothing is ever lost, nothing is static.[18] They see only the relentless flow of a powerful energy, with everything is originating, growing, decaying, and vanishing over vast eons of time beyond memory. The world is said to revolve around an invisible, symbolic center supported by the head of the cosmic serpent, the dragon, symbolic of the oceanic waters of chaos from which all life energy is created.[19]

The act of creation as the process of bringing order out of chaos is a powerful idea with art therapists committed to restorative acts of balance and the relief of suffering. As I have often observed, compared to other mental health professionals, art therapists seem to be uniquely comfortable with the messy, disordered chaos of the therapeutic studio in which their clients work. They intimately understand the disordered states of their clients' thoughts and emotions from which they help construct new consciousness. The connection between chaos and creation can be honored in the studio.

But against this idea there flows another current, one that reverses the pattern and views the act of creation as transforming order *into* chaos. As I knew from my struggles with Mary, this idea may be much more difficult to accept. Western tradition prefers the ascendant experience, of darkness into light. The poet Whyte says, when life is full and our moon is waxing, we feel powerful and successful. But when things are dying or falling away, even though this is simply the other side of the same circle, we may believe that something is terribly wrong.[20] Whyte observes that much of our distress comes from tying up energy in order to keep up a luminescent front when our interior surface is fading into darkness or descending back into the waters of chaos. Always moving in and out of clarity, focus and presence, so too, our creative vitality ebbs and wanes as we lose our connection to it and long to get it back again. Life is seldom at rest and requires an interplay between the polarities to prevent stagnation. The creative tension of the paradoxes generates a powerful energy of possibility, like holding together the two poles of a battery. Pull them apart and the current stops flowing; we become lifeless.[21] "This power, then," I read in the words of Whyte's poetry, "–you feel it wanting to pull your heart open. But there is no need to resist it–you will not fall apart but only fall into something larger than yourself."[22]

A great Hindu creation myth speaks to such times when things have fallen apart. Its image of stagnation is Vritra, a giant serpent dragon who is lying asleep, crouching on the mountains and filling up all the vast spaces of the cosmos with his coiled, limbless shape. The sphere of rebirth is symbolized world wide in this image of return to the womb, swallowed up by the cave, belly, or the oceanic sea where one finds monstrous guardians of indefinite form.[23] When the dragon has swallowed up everything, the vital waters of regeneration cannot flow forth. Then Indra, the hero, rides in on his powerful elephant to defeat the serpent. He flings his thunderbolt into the midst of Vritra's coiled mass, shattering the demon! The waters of creation burst forth from his encrusted belly and streams in ribbons across the land. Once again there is an opening space between heaven and earth where the serpent dragon had massed his ambitious, selfish hulk.[24] The creative process, in fact, needs this spaciousness and differentiation. That is why getting stuck always feels like some obstacle with no room to move. The problem is not with the chaos but with the fact that one is asleep to consciousness. One needs Indra's thunderbolt of truth to pierce the ignorance, deception, and illusion lying over the land. The dragon must be destroyed, not because it is evil but because it is holding back the life energy that growth and transformation depend upon.[25]

The awesome power and responsibility that comes with creation cuts close to the bone of the work of art therapists and may generate in us a fearful ambivalence. How can the hero live without his or her dragon? After all, a powerful hero needs a powerful opponent and once vanquished the struggle to awaken to life also ends. The bliss of the deep abode, Campbell writes, "is not lightly abandoned in favor of the self-scattering of the wakened state."[26] It seems a fearsome act, not simply for destroying the hulking dragon of the obstacles to creation that we have created. Perhaps we fear awakening its terrible powers and releasing the threat of renewed chaos flowing in our lives. Indeed, sometimes the Hindu story ends differently and Indra does not kill the dragon but merely shifts its coils so that a new space can be made. Other times he cuts up Vritra and places the pieces in the bellies of all living creatures so that whenever we crave power we pay tribute to Vritra as an aspect of the dark soul that resides within us.[27]

In my search for the sources of disenchantment among art therapists, I felt my heart and mind brush up against some large thing that was holding back fluid, dynamic forces of creativity. I glimpsed it lurking in

Accepting the Demands of Creative Power 33

the consciousness of art therapists who seem both attracted to and repulsed by often uninvited encounters with the dragon that held untapped, latent energies. In the collective voices of the profession, my own among them, I heard and saw powerlessness expressed symptomatically in a lack of vitality and in anger, apathy, and fear of "things falling apart." If the hero is especially unwilling, the disturber suffers an ugly shock.[28] Wanting to see it more clearly yet fearing its awakening force, I sought out other art therapists to tell me their stories of creative chaos. I questioned each one: "Had they seen the dragon holding back the power-to-make-things-happen?"

Shredding a Life, Reweaving its Patterns

Seven prominent art therapists agreed to read and reflect on the myth of the sleeping dragon that fills all the spaces of their creative possibilities, blocking the powers of regeneration. I was eager to interview them and co-create the stories based on their reflections.[29] In my first such encounter, I felt shy: I held Bob in high esteem, for he was one of the longest practicing art therapists in the country and a mentor to many.[30] I expected that I would be listening to a reminiscing mind stretching back over years and dipping into deep waters of memory. But instead he wanted to tell me about his most recent paintings, created in an explosion of pure experimentation and unlike anything he had ever done in over thirty years of painting. The genesis of this burst of productivity came from a single moment in a therapeutic relationship with a client going through great stress and difficulty. She was an elderly nun who was well known for her life's work in education. Depressed and in despair, she had just learned that her religious order had *shredded* all of her life work of thirty years. She felt destroyed. In therapy she drew a picture of herself being put through a shredder.

"The next session, I brought in my shredder from home and suggested we take finished paintings and shred them, and then reweave them back together into new art work," Bob said. "She quickly became caught up with the metaphor of weaving her life back together again. Out of her despair came new energy—for both of us. The acts of shredding and re-weaving opened up a new form of making art for me also. I could hardly keep up with the floodgate of energy that poured out—over thirty new art works made in a few months' time!" He reflected on how very much this process was a part of life, religion, therapy and art. For isn't it true, he asked, "that out of destruction and despair come spiritual reawakening or resurrection?"

He considered that for his client, the "dragon" was her community who now wanted her retired to a nursing home. Her whole life had been tied into that collective power; it had given her meaning, order, and joy. But he could see that the cycle had reversed itself and that now she was caught in a shredding of her very being. Yet killing this suffocating beast of her destruction, as Indra had done in the Hindu myth, was unthinkable—her community had been a valued part of her life's inspiration and her work. "She just had to figure out how to move it in some way," he considered, "to move the dragon just enough to free up all that energy bound up in her old patterns. Then her life could flow forward in new ways."

The dragon arrives at times when we are out of balance between the forces of tension and meaningful support. Bob offered the metaphor of a violin string, saying that one truly needs dynamic tension to make music. "If it is not tense enough it doesn't sound good and if it is too tightly strung it will snap or break," he said. "There's energy in both: the stress and the non-stress. The question is how to live in the space between them."

"You know," he said to me, "one of our real problems as art therapists is that we've always been ahead of our times and we have had to live with that stress in our agencies and institutions. I remember when I tried to start a graduate training program thirty years ago. They hired me but then sat on all the creative possibilities I brought to them, never allowing me to teach a single art therapy class on campus for three years. They claimed that the other departments would get too upset. It took a few years but I finally came to realize that they had hired me just to keep me tied up. Nothing was going to happen there or anywhere." He pushed this dragon: he resigned and moved the program to a place where they had the program up and running in a month. Twenty-five years later the program still thrives.

Bob smiled and remembered the hospital where he had worked for many years as an art therapist, where he was the first person outside the hierarchy of psychiatrists and social workers to be allowed to go through their psychotherapy training. Only after three years of asking them to let him actually use his training was he finally allowed to join the diagnostic teams. But they didn't know how to charge for his services. "So they didn't charge anything!" he said. "They called it 'research.' Then the patients started complaining about not being charged for what they said was the most meaningful part of their treatment. So they charged $3.50 an hour and then moved it to $10 an hour because social work was set at $30 an hour. Finally, it was set at $110, the same rate as the psychiatrists. But it took seven years!"

His point was that there was something in that adversity that made him a better therapist who knew more than ever the value of the art therapy process. But it also made him more sensitive to the oppression of working in a prejudicial system. "I was praised for my work at the same time that it was devalued," he said matter-of-factly. "One day I created a drawing of myself as a minority person in a prejudicial system. I started to become very conscious of the vulnerability that comes with powerlessness. Once I discovered that vulnerability I could expose the injustice and force the issue with my institution. I went through several major career changes there as a result."

"But that was also partly why I left. I couldn't stand the fact that my whole career was tied up in that dragon of injustice. I had to push and re-push the dragon over and over—never wanting to slay it, just to move it. As I did, I found a new source of creative power, namely my self-value and integrity. The bottom line is that a person's source of power is his or her integrity. It's the stuff that changes patients, the stuff of a 39-year-old marriage and what produced, for me, children who grew into wonderful adults. I think of the image of the volcanoes in Hawaii as they flow into the oceans that make new land. Or Puff: he's not a bad or hostile dragon, he's just asleep. Just like people who are asleep psychologically and need to have that shift happen for them," he said, thinking back to his patient. The relationship of destruction and resurrection is necessary in the creativity that moves all through our lives. As Bob put it, "life is a stream: that stream, it is you, it is them, it is me; the stream of life that we all move in and out of." This is a blessing we can take with us as we reweave and remake ourselves.

The Hungry Dragon of Longing

"Oh yes," my colleague Melody told me, as she lingered in the doorway of my office where we had been talking.[31] "I have met that dragon of chaos many, many times." It threaded itself all through her life as an art therapist and sometimes it got so close and blocked her vision so completely that that all she could see was the green of scales going by, just a couple of inches before her eyes. You couldn't know how big it was, she said, or where in all that mass was your own small self. With a playful glint in her eye, Melody told me about a very powerful dragon that once belonged to a small boy who'd been her client. His dragon was huge. It stood upright on two feet and towered over him, like a tyrannosaurus rex. But it was missing something, she recalled. The dragon could not see him and it couldn't see her. The dragon didn't have an eye. She asked the little boy to draw himself into the picture and to give himself something to tame his dragon.

"He drew himself standing next to that big dragon, holding the dragon's eye like a balloon on a string. This little boy, facing his own powerful dragon, knew the secret: that the way to tame it was to give it exactly what it needed. He named his dragon *EyeGone*." Melody marveled that children so easily toy with such power when so often all she could see was how much bigger the beast was than she and how powerless it made her feel.

Melody had encountered Eyegone many times before. Inside, she knew that dragon. Maybe, she mused, the dragon really has to do with longing—her longing to be seen, her longing for connection. There were myriad ways she disowned that longing and became disenchanted. She'd pretend it wasn't there or tell herself she didn't need anything or anyone. "How could I possibly go up to and touch that deep, deep longing?" she asked. "When the dragon of longing sleeps, I stumble toward it, struggling to free myself from all those needs that get tangled up like brambles, protecting the dragon and myself so I can't get too close. Oh, if I dare to stir the sleeping dragon. . . .", she paused and then considered it. "If it stirs, there will be an outpouring of longing. The dragon ROARS! Like in the story: 'It roars its terrible roar and gnashes its terrible teeth and shows its terrible claws. . .'."

And what if the dragon is hungry? she wondered. Isn't the creative process about a hunger for expression? Creating in art opens up our hunger, as though we've been sleeping or have been in hibernation and now need food. "How will I get fed?" she asked as she reflected on the dangers and necessity of using her latent creative power. "Is it at the expense of others? When I see little food available do I share? Or do I trick you out of yours? Out of that belief in the scarcity of things, my roar gets louder or my slumber gets deeper. My tail swishes others out of the way! I'm BIG NOW—there's no room for YOU!"

One day she glimpsed a dragon wrapped around a woman client who felt so afraid she couldn't see her own power. This dragon lived in a land where princes slay dragons and rescue princesses. She saw herself alone with the dragon, with no prince in sight. "Where is he? Where is he? I fear he'll never come," Melody exclaimed, giving voice to her client's need for rescue. As her art therapist, Melody recognized that feeling, "like being eaten up from inside until you feel so empty." The dragon's hot, needy breath warms and burns at the same time.

Melody thought of the enchanted, slumbering dragon inside that dreams of the perfect lover, the perfect job, a perfect self. When that illusion wraps around her it has to die to the realities of life she must accept so that she can see what is there. In any relationship something always has to be changed or compromised and the transformation that results does feel like a death. She described how her creative work begins with attunement, a centering. In that absorbed place she attracts what she needs rather than molds herself to what she thinks others want her to be. Making paintings or in therapy, she moves the paint and tunes into her clients in ways that create presence. But in so doing she encounters, inevitably, the dragon. "You can't stay in that oneness," she said. "What would it be like walking around attuned all the time? You might bump into walls. The whole world would start looking rather all one, the all-green of the dragon. You have to step back, get an edge, put it into a context, see the larger picture."

"And that is precisely when another dragon stirs," she added slyly. "His eye opens—a watchful, critical eye that judges me, observes and critiques. He clings to my insecurities and fears. I close my eyes in fear and cannot let anyone help me, for that would mean I am weak. My scales get thick; no one can touch me now. The dragon roars so loud I cannot hear. If I kill this dragon, I'll be nothing. What else can I do but feed him compassion? Then a new voice speaks inside me and I can open my eyes again and see. Then I can walk with the power of the dragon and it moves me out into the world."

Over and over again, when she asks people to draw their dragons and imagine taming them, what comes next is always a new possibility. "If you don't wake up your dragon, you'll end up carrying him around on your back!" Melody warned me, saying that the dragon will just get bigger and bigger. The power of her longing gives her the courage she needs to risk asking what is needed in each new situation. The gift in the battle is new understanding. "If this is true," she concluded, "then in the story's end the boy tames the powerful dragon EyeGone with his eye balloon and names him with a smile. He gives the dragon just what he needs—his dragon essence and his baleful eye. As for EyeGone, well, I think he'll go on to do something rather ordinary. He's probably out there today working as an eyeglass salesperson or an optometrist. Or maybe even as an art therapist who helps others see—and be seen."

The Curse of the Baby Dragon

In my encounters with art therapists battling dragons that blocked their creative energy and threatened them with creative, awakening chaos, I discovered a rhythm in their stories that moved in and out of focus. This business of dragons was a slippery matter gliding below my conscious mind only to reappear suddenly as another thread in the larger story of creative power being woven by my collaborators. Often this huge and powerful dragon force of creation would hide in the smallest child or in the simplest, most pragmatic gestures of art therapy practice. Ellen,[32] an art therapist who works in a traditional clinical setting, told me her encounter with the dragon in the form of a difficult case that was going nowhere and keeping her stuck. Knowing that this child client understood something important about power and powerlessness, Ellen playfully described the case in the imagery of a baby dragon who had put her art therapist under the spell of a curse.

"Once I knew a deaf baby dragon that had a terrible curse for all she touched," she began. "Her fury served to keep all at bay. She had no mother to teach her dragon lore. Rejected at birth, she had been stolen by a wicked man who rode her body daily and confused the vessel of love. Luckily she couldn't hear and this protected her from his assaults but it also left her unable to speak her truth. Living in dark, dank places, her deafened ears and broken eyes shielded herself from witnessing what had been so carelessly extinguished. She needed the protection of these and other walls that she kept between herself and her abuser. When I approached her, she would thrash out and ravage everything with her fiery flames."

"I hated working with this baby dragon," Ellen admitted. "She gave a new definition to the term 'Oppositional Defiant Disorder!' You can't expect a dragon to do anything in art therapy. She was too busy destroying everything in her path. She'd destroy everything I gave her. It didn't matter to her. She couldn't have cared less. She would grab anything that was nearby and use it all up, discard it, and then move on to the next kill. Use. Destroy. Discard. Use. Destroy. Discard... All the while, her dragon nature grew and grew."

"Months passed. Use. Destroy. Discard. Use. Destroy. Discard. It took a toll on me. It got so I just wanted to give up on her. I began to take her affronts personally. We both needed an awakening. After all, she wasn't the only dragon in the room. My own sleeping dragon wrapped me in a thick fog of countertransference and kept me stuck. A fiery dragon raged in her and a sleeping dragon grazed in me. I was blinded by her fire and drugged by my own indifference."

"Always unkempt and dirty, I couldn't get her to cleanse her fiery ways. Then one day, as she washed her hands at my sink, I saw her draw them to her flaming nostrils and delicately smell her hands. She liked the smell of the soap. It was really so simple but we had all missed it. Had anyone ever taken her shopping for her own soaps? No one had. So the next week, I took her to the mall. She bought shampoo, conditioner, and body soaps. She showered a lot after that and slowly the grime and dirt of those dank places that she'd had to live in washed away and her dragon scales began to fade."

"One day, as I laid newspaper on the table for her weekly course of destruction, an advertisement for a little girl's 'Bake-it-Shop' that was splattered with paint caught her eye. She began to cut it out with a nearby scissors. What was this? The horrible dragon was acting like other ten-year-olds and was interested in typical ten-year-old toys. We had all missed this! We had only seen the fire-breathing dragon in her, not this."

"Soon we started cooking together, like mother and daughter. While we were waiting for things to cook, I'd slip in a little art. We sewed pillows together, the old fashioned way, by hand. Then the little dragon made an entire meal by herself–flame-broiled, of course. I was amazed to see what happened when this fiery baby dragon used and controlled her own power. She was making order out of chaos. There was a connection now that gave her power but kept the space between us and that's a key difference. Alive and awake, we let our dragons out so they could co-mingle, create, and burst forth. The story goes like this now: Use. Construct. Create. Use. Construct. Create."

It's Alive!

I turned next to bigger dragons—dragons so powerful they dwarf the individual art therapist and shape the very landscape of our professional organization. Don, an art therapy pioneer, is the one who called my attention to it.[33] He called me one day to say he had "just a little story that popped into mind" when he thought about the image of the dragon in his life as an art therapist.

I remembered Don telling me how he became an art therapist in the days before it existed as a profession: he had served as a conscientious objector during World War II and was assigned to serve in a state mental hospital while all the doctors went to war. On his first day as an art therapist he walked into a bizarre scene, a single room the size of a gym, where a hundred disheveled people milled around with nothing to do. He was the only staff assigned to the ward and had no training beyond four years in art school. He was scared to death. Suddenly, a huge man from the very back of the room fixed on him and started striding toward him like a locomotive. He barreled up within inches of Don's face, abruptly stopped and made frantic, sweeping motions over Don's head. Apparently, the man had seen the dragon of fear that walked into the room with Don and was dispersing it to make everyone there safe.

But now my attention returned to the story Don called to tell me about. It happened one morning on a street in New York City, he said. He had been attending one of the first national conferences of the American Art Therapy Association at which, later that same day, he was going to be installed as its president. This was during a very chaotic time, in the early formation days when the idea of art therapy on a national scale was just coming into existence. He was quite naturally anxious just thinking about managing what he called "that rambunctious, non-parlimentarian bunch of artists."

As he was walking off the tension, casually sightseeing, something very odd happened. He became aware of a spontaneous memory, a suppressed image from his childhood. He was back in his little town in Pennsylvania and his mother was taking him to see a traveling circus that had come to town. He was standing with his chin directly up against a roped-off area, in complete awe of the great, performing elephants. He heard the ringmaster announce that the first ten kids who could reach the center ring could "Ride the Elephant!" Excitedly, he broke away from his mother's hand, ducking easily under the rope and dashing out to ride the elephant.

He remembers being lifted up. Amazingly, he was on its back—just a wee, peanut-sized, eight-year-old boy. But suddenly he was aware of his position on top of this gargantuan, undulating Jumbo. The mammoth creature reared up—and that was when he realized that this powerful beast was alive! He swallowed his rising fear in one brave gulp and from that deep space came the knowledge that he was on the heroic beast's back only by its grace and permission.

That insight, Don told me, has been a constant reminder for him ever since. It came to tell him something important as he was about to assume the power of leadership of the professional organization. "It is equally true for the immeasurable, transforming power of the sources beneath our creative efforts and in shaping organizational relationships. Like the mythic dragon power of the cosmos, that metaphor of riding the elephant has been a lesson and a guide," Don said. "It always has instructed me to think about where the power really is and who we are to think to wield it. We must remember and honor the larger-than-us, living being that carries us and gives us this grand ride. It is a matter of personal integrity, and no little humility as well, to realize that you are caught up in something that is so much greater than any of us."

"We are, after all, made of star stuff," he said, "connected to one another with the force of our survival." Art is what carries him especially and that is why he keeps it daily. He has felt duty-bound, as a sacred obligation and responsibility, to live daily in artful ways. "We all can celebrate the position we have with this magnificent, benevolent beast that is ever so much more than we alone, are and can become." Don paused and then added, "it may be that I have been called a 'founder,' but you know, it is really more about *being found* by this dynamic force. The arts have called, lifted up and carried me all through the exigencies of my private and professional life. In the beginning, you see, art was made to overcome chaos!"

Up in Smoke

There is one particular dragon in the work lives of art therapists that I know many would love to slay: that thing called "managed care," whose force in recent years has created abrupt change and much chaos. Often I heard references to managed care as the life-sucking thing responsible for the worst of our disenchanting powerlessness, completely coiled around our vitality. It is a familiar story to many. For Cathy,[34] an art therapist whose beginning career spanned the years before and after managed care, the story of its force in her life began: "Once upon a time, I belonged to a family of therapists and health care professionals who worked in a fine, old hospital. . . ."

Cathy had worked in the same place for many years. This reality gave her a "settled in" quality that wrapped her in an illusion of security. And, like many people who live in fine, old houses, she had collected things to fill up all the spaces—degrees, titles, those letters after her name—such things that other people could recognize as symbols of her worth. They were like talismans she used to ward off fear and insecurity. But of course, she realized, this state of affairs could not last. She was not yet aware of the undoing that soon would force her to become empty once again. The wind of change was blowing in her direction. She watched, stunned, as it swept wildly across the land. "Oh, it was the managed care thing coming, sure enough, big and awful! It took up residence in our hospital, beginning with the *downsizing*—getting rid of people is what it was," she said.

"Suddenly, we were no longer 'family'," she remembered. The sheltered world of the hospital had merged with and been consumed by a vast business enterprise with a whole different sense of power in the hands of different people. "It was like someone coming into your house and looking over all your things, telling you what to get rid of in order to make some room for who knew what. Yes, there was no doubt about it—change blew in and all our illusions caught fire and went up in smoke. That carefully built sense of security we had? Well, it was the first to go and things began to fall apart after that."

"What *was* this large and shapeless thing blowing through us like a forest fire, surrounding us, threatening to get on the inside of all of us and burn us to a crisp? It's hard to tell you what kind of creature it was," she said as she recalled the dragon's hot, smoky breath. "But one thing for certain happened: there was this 'evilizing' going on. Yes, you could say the creature coming in was the *Evilizer*. After all, we couldn't just stand by and get burned. We had to find someone to burn first. This force had to be personalized, you know; we had to evilize someone to carry everything that got stirred up. And the really strange thing was that this 'someone' kept shifting."

"The administration got evilized right away. But it didn't stay there. The evilizer would spark up somewhere else, like little fires burning first in one department and then in another. No one knew what to do or how to stop it from swallowing up everything. Then one day," she said, "*I* got evilized—accused of various things that were true enough but really just my way of surviving. Survival is a necessary thing but it does bring out the ugly in you. I didn't like it. When the evilizer got to me, I could feel it: that part of me that wanted to use the power in some sort of evil way, to step on people, because I was scared. We all were so scared. We wanted someone to lay the blame on. Evilizing became an obstacle in itself. It kept the power that we did have in someone else's hands. Because you see, with the evil ones there, we could be powerless victims. Giving up our power, we were reduced to a tiny scrap of who we really were and we believed in that image of ourselves when it seemed to be the only option."

"But one thing I am proud of," Cathy remembered, "is that I stayed with what got stirred up in me, to get closer to the dragon power that was pushing me. I was able to look at what I needed to do with it, be willing to change what needed to be changed, and to find the right place and time to let go and release it. While everything around me was all chaos and confusion, I held onto my center, my internal chant that was to remain true to why I was doing the work in the first place. And I finally did leave, but with my integrity intact. This was something I took with me and didn't lose."

The shifting and changing circumstances of the dragon finally forced her to let go and whooosh!—the energy it released propelled her forcefully through space to a whole different area of the country. When all that power shifted, Cathy had to decide what to do about the space that opened up once the dragon's coils had shifted. She discovered new seeds had germinated from the smoldering ashes of what had come before. She asked herself, what kind of new spaces did she want to occupy now? Where should she take her power, her energy? "Why, there were a million things I could do!" she realized. "The experience taught me that I could always create the space I need right in the middle of all sorts of chaos."

Like a forest fire, Cathy reflected, beautiful trees need to burn down in order to rejuvenate and restore life. She saw that the ability to settle in and get too comfortable gets killed off in the process of accepting the demands of creative power. "I wanted to build a new space then," she concluded, "and maybe a new family of therapists to give myself a sense of security. I suppose that as long as life goes along all hunky-dory, I think I don't need that and save it for only when something really bad happens. But it is a cycle that gets created all over again: I see myself watching out for and seeking that desire to get settled in again. I know that the dragon will come and take up space again. There is comfort in that but it can be stifling, too. It is dangerous. After all, you could get burned."

In the Belly of the Dragon

"I want no more hero myths!" cried Josie when I approached her to ask for her story of creative chaos.[35] "No more of this business of slaying dragons! What does it get us? We get swallowed up, stuck inside of the deep, dark belly of the dragon. The place reeks of shadow stuff! It is all around us, all the time, and it is constantly asking for our attention." I heard in Josie's words the lament of the art therapist's own shadow as he or she struggles to be freed from chaos and confusion. Josie was slumped next to me against the wall, taking a break on the floor of the carpeted room where we had been in a professional meeting for several hours and seemingly going nowhere. Much had happened in the intervening months between our meetings, and I could see that she was as tired as I was and wanting to cast off a heavy burden.

Valerie came over to join us by the wall, an art therapy colleague and friend who told of having suffered similar wounding and betrayals by her colleagues in her workplace, her frustrations and helplessness.[36] Our shared stories sat like a hulking dragon in my mind weeks later when I found myself unwittingly painting their images. So it was that I transformed its power to drain me by seeing through it clearly.

"I fell, screaming, into the abyss of the dragon place! I screamed and screamed and screamed into the wind, such that I couldn't hear my own voice as it rushed past!" Valerie began the story, revealing the fall into chaos I later painted (Figure 2). "I felt it becoming tiny as I flew into the void. I could feel the whirlwind move through me, dispersing all the atoms of my existence to the far corners of the universe, into darkness and chaos. My body fell through many levels of the world before settling like tiny seeds in the lower reaches between soil and

Figure 2. Falling into chaos.

bedrock. I fell through the layers of misunderstandings, miscommunications, outright lying and gossip. Their masks yielded to my passing as one after the other fell away and I saw the whirling forms of all who had supported me when I was building the space for the work and serving them with my art and labors. Who turned their backs to me and forfeited everything as I passed through the illusions of hierarchies and politics, the measurement of my truth against the cost of my services, betrayal after betrayal, on and on into the abyss. . . ."

"What set this terrible force in motion, you ask?" Valerie said. "It began with a tiny act: I challenged something that everyone knew enough to move stealthily around rather than disturb and endure it's awakening force. To challenge was to question my place and perhaps to face being cast out into who knew what possible chaos. Why me, why now? Why couldn't it have left me alone? But once in motion there was no stopping it. I was riding the howling winds!"

"Then, when the screaming died down, my soul in pieces settled though dispersed. The darkness turned inward and I felt my anger give way to a deep grieving sadness, and then a sense of disappointment and terrible loneliness. I was left with only myself; no one else could show me the way out of this terrible place." As Josie listened, she remembered what it was like inside the dragon of her own experience, its coils tightening. "How could I breathe? I needed oxygen. I needed space," Josie reflected. "I thought of how often art therapists complain of not getting enough space for our work out there in the world, but look! Look at our own tightness, a dragon of our own creation inside ourselves that's causing us to feel constricted! We cling to the certainty of our old, cramped past. When we get so narrowly focused in and against ourselves, we can't see. We can't breathe."

"And, oh, light up that passion! Bring it back! will you? But the first thing that we will do will be to bring up the old stuff, that 'No, no, you can't do that,' and 'No, *that's* not art therapy' and blah, blah, blah. The dragon shifts, stirring up all the old, stale arguments again and they've gotten really narrow, blocking any movement, as though life and passion are no longer allowed in the structure, this world we've created."

"And what do you do when the dragon is in your path, guarding all the treasure and keeping you from taking what you think is yours?" she asked (Figure 3). Do you think you can just go right up and slay it? Or maybe befriend the dragon, appeal to its sense of mercy by asking it to be nice? Sneak past it? Well, but for me, I just kept going up to it and giving it a poke. And it'd wake up and I'd back off! And then I'd go right back and poke it a little more and it'd stir again, and rise up and blow it's hot breathe over me, and yeah, I'd back off again! Finally, though, I just sat down right in the middle of it. Decided to lay down my battle axe and not have anything more to do with it."

"And oh, that dragon, it didn't like that it got dealt with that way and it started to flail its tail–saying no, no, that's not the way we want you to do this. You have to come over here and give us what we want so we can take it and then give you our judgment about you, you see. And this struggle just went on and on, anyway, no matter what I tried to do. I never know what to do with this dragon, how to keep from getting burned. I know it's a struggle with power. The system, the structure – it's such a killer. We could choose to play that game, I suppose... But I did it again, you know. Got seduced right back into it, thinking I could go off and establish art therapy in new lands, create something in the image I thought would be the best. Just ran right back into that same old dragon. So I bowed out, finally; I got out of there for sure this time. Told it 'Hey, I've been here before, I've met you before and I'm not doing this again! You can keep your lands, I will go back to where I came from.' So I left–walked away from it."

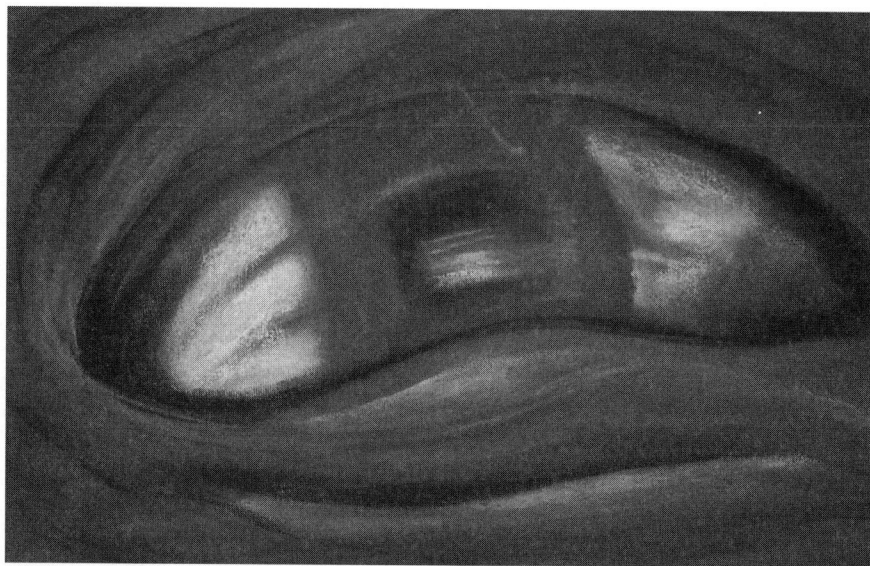

Figure 3. The eye of the dragon.

"What I'm struggling with now is that I really miss the lands I left behind; I'm still dreaming about them. I keep wondering how I can have that in my life again without getting stuck in the shadow stuff and I'm not sure where the answer is. Why take on another battle? Why not let somebody else do it this time? But then, you see, your integrity gets questioned: the little voice that says 'oh, you're being irresponsible'."

"I have been battling this dragon for years and years. Battling passionately for art therapy and trying to keep it alive and fighting all these people who want to kill it. I get exhausted. Exhaust: the remnant of engines firing, burning fuel. Yes," Josie reflected, "I am breathing my own exhaust. That's suicide, you know. We need some fresh air. It's hard to imagine how to create that open space, how to get to that needed breath of fresh air."

"Rest is what you need," Valerie told Josie, as she pondered the message of the dragon's story for all of us. "To rest and . . . maybe even, to go to sleep. To make a space for dreaming. From the dream place, deep inside the chaos of that dragon, you can rediscover images that will grow and burst forth into consciousness to become awake in you again. They offer a solution: you have to fully name the dragon of power and pierce the web of illusions that had brought you to this place and time of chaos. And oh, it is so liberating to name the dragon! It now lives out there—its presence becomes real."

Valerie continued, "I remember clearly that in the act of naming it, something surprising happened to me: my dragon turned over and shrank. It became tiny, like I was looking at it through the wrong end of a telescope. It was vulnerable and I felt for its suffering. We could co-exist. It wasn't so big and scary anymore. Once this happened, spaciousness took hold of me and I could begin to see a way over that great abyss where my fear was. As Rilke once said, 'Now take your practiced powers and stretch them out until they span the chasm between two contradictions, for the god wants to know himself, herself, in you.'[37] The riddle of the dragon is that you must wrestle with the mystery of the duality that is contained within you. That's how you become a dancer. You can't do otherwise. You have to do this work."

Josie considered these words and said, "Ah yes, the dragon has a life of its own! It's stirring again, shifting; I can feel it. I wanted to slay it to restore the world to order again. But it doesn't really work that way. It is just as important for things to go *back into* chaos from time to time. We're so afraid of that. So afraid, we block that dynamic possibility at every turn. We forget that's where the power comes from, where the creativity comes from. The more we move away from the art, the more we move away from the chaos. And the farther away from the chaos we get, the more we move away from the creation that is coming out of chaos. Why do we hold on so tight? Life–death–life. It's a cycle where some things must die for something else to be born."

"Breathing lessons. That's what the dragon gives us."

CERTIFICATION BY PSYCHOSIS: A FINAL DRAGON STORY

Breathing in and breathing out: two sides of a larger truth the dragon teaches that invisibly connects us, makes us alive and whole. They seem separate and they do have distinctly different functions but there is unity found in their harmonious rhythm. The other side of oneness, I believe, is not separateness but diversity. When we are at our best as a community, Palmer writes,[38] we invite diversity because diverse viewpoints are demanded by the manifold mysteries of things; we embrace ambiguity not because we are confused or indecisive but because we understand the inadequacy of our concepts; we welcome creative conflict not because we are angry or hostile but because conflict is required to correct our biases and prejudices about the nature of great things. We experience the power-to-make-things-happen only when we respect its life force.

I turned, now, to my own dragon pressing for recognition and Indra's thunderbolt of insight. What could be more banal, I had often thought, than to stand in the midst of this astonishing universe and allow the dragon to squeeze all its wonders through a reductionistic screen, debunking enchantment with data and logic, downsizing mystery to the small scale of our own minds?[39] My dragon lived in a flat, desacralized landscape created from the banality of reductionism, regulation, and the categorizing of creative flow. I remember the day it caught up with me, with a simple mandate on a piece of paper that arrived in the mail at the college. Tucked into the newly revised standards for the training of art therapists was a small item that stated: "To uphold the highest credential of the profession, program directors must be board certified." Ah, it arrives, I thought. Like a piece of torn-off fabric carried on the wind, it snapped and fluttered, and finally settled in my corner to demand attention.

For years I had held off and refused. I simply could not accept the toxins introduced when this import began to take up space in my professional culture. In a blink of an eye, it seemed, we had a shiny new certification examination like everyone else. All the creative, expressive, and diverse practices of artist therapists were funneled into a paper-and-pencil exam of 179 multiple-choice questions. Many honest people with integrity argued that it would deliver us as well as create needed standards. What was wrong with that? It's just a hoop. Get over it, they told me. Forget about it, write the check, and start studying.

In reality, I was afraid of it. Below my reasoning, rational mind some repellent thing caught me up. Something in me was tangled up with the mandate, going unanswered and denied. I would make art out of it, I decided, and transform the dragon to release my creative power. I wrote a letter that asked for help and guidance to all the art therapists who'd taught, supervised, mentored, and befriended me. I asked them to send me pieces of fabric from something they no longer needed, which I would use to create a protective, ritual garment to wear when I took the certification exam. I would sew art therapists into my robe just as I had sewn their teachings into my professional life. In this way

I would honor those to whom I was indebted and grateful; their energies would protect me in the toxic belly of the certification exam.

For several weeks, packages came in the mail with swatches of fabric accompanied by handwritten notes from people I loved, telling me why they had chosen what they did and affirming my decision. Soon I had a pile of wildly diverse fabrics of all colors and textures. How much like my profession it was. I quilted the fabric together, creating relationships among the colors that I imagined were people coming together in conversation and community. Two pieces joined to two others; four pieces joined a group of seven, a dash of satin against the rough linen. Whatever anxiety I had about the exam went into the artwork, where I could recover what I had rejected and disowned in anger. As I sewed, I remembered my community and the essential love I have held for my profession all these years. The process of making art to transform the toxins sustained me. In the end, the robe was a rich tapestry, a riot of color unified by its common purpose and function.

I felt blessed and filled with borrowed grace as I donned the ritual robe and entered the sterile examination room. I am sure I was an odd sight to the room monitors. But no matter. I had made my peace and was ready to engage the dragon. The test began; I stared at the test booklet and read: "What art media is best for hyperactive children?" Markers, I think automatically, not watercolors—too hard to control. Easy one. Next. In a glance, I take in a line drawing of a house, obviously from the House-Tree-Person test.[40] The house has a roof that looks like a birthday cake. Easy: this person suffers from an excess of fantasy. Next.

I read a case vignette, two lines long. A woman is irritable, refusing to comply with the group therapy task assigned, and leaves abruptly only to return in anger and distress. What is my diagnosis? *Borderline.*[41] I went on to the next item, but my mind lingered, distracted by the image of the woman with the borderline personality disorder. Why is she irritable and refusing to comply? Why so quick to make her behavior pathological? Who knows her story? What else is going on? Unbidden, my mind conjured the image of a woman I once knew who seemed a little slow but had good clinical skills despite an impoverished ability to write. After two years in supervision, one day she told me her story. She was from a farm family, the loving embrace of many brothers and sisters, parents and grandparents. In the crucible of adolescence, she came to believe that God was calling her to vocation. She left home and entered the convent. I imagined her culture shock as she tried to adapt to the new rules: Silence. No touching. Keep your eyes lowered, your head down. Contain your exuberance.

She finally confessed to her superior her confusion for this new life. The next day, she abruptly was sent away, without her personal items or saying goodbye. She was taken to a psychiatric hospital and confined against her will for an entire year. She was given over twenty electroshock treatments, after which she was suddenly discharged and sent home on a train with no explanation. With clenched teeth, she told me that vast stretches of memories were gone forever. Many years later, she returned to the hospital to see her case file. She was desperate to learn who had labeled her eighteen-year-old self with a diagnosis that justified electroshock treatment and involuntary psychiatric confinement. She read: *The patient is confused about her sexual identity.* They thought that electroshock would cure her of homosexuality and the normal sexual strivings of a young teenager away from home for the first time.

Let me out of here, I thought, in a wave of anger; I can't take this exam anymore. I know too much. I've heard too many stories and seen too many pictures. I look at a sketch of a family, drawn by a seven-year-old girl. They are five people, lined up in a row with smiles on their faces and identical, stick figure bodies.[42] What does the picture mean? I am asked. I am offered four, one-word choices: A. Cheerfulness. B. Isolation. C. Confusion. D. Conflict.

Oh, hell, I think. I don't know. How could I know? I can't do this—I can't reduce the complex, multilayered richness of the art of children to one word, one label, one pathological condition. One right answer. My mind doesn't function this way. To do my work, I invite divergent thinking; the multiple, many voices and stories are allowed to enter, mix, and take new, unexpected paths toward meaning.[43] It has always served me better than compressing everything to a single point. I don't believe in one right answer. I don't even believe in one right God. God may be the One, the Whole, but s/he doesn't wear one face. S/he lives in many cultures, tells many stories, and has many ways of being in the world. Why do we discredit that?

What was the little girl's story? What if the stick figure family she drew is really a manifestation of the Divine? What if this stereotyped image expressed a longing for oneness, for the safe harbor of a family where everyone wears the same smile in recognition of her divine state of being? *Stop it, you're hallucinating,* I told myself. *You know the answer; choose. God will forgive you.*

Safe harbor . . . I remembered Jeremy, a slight young boy with a colossal temper. Every time he arrived in my art room disheveled, enraged, I would hand him a piece of paper and markers and he would draw silently and intensely for ten minutes or so. Then he'd brighten, ask me what we were doing that day, and join the rest of the children in an art task. He was *emotionally disturbed*. But to get to my room, he had to navigate the imposing terrain of an emotionally disturbed facility designed to have every room open out into a large common area. From the safety of his self-contained classroom to the safe harbor of my own, he had four minutes to cross the territory of rival gang members. Of course he arrived with a bloody nose and torn clothing.

I shifted in my seat and heard the soft jangle of beads. I considered my emotional disturbance at taking this exam and the robe I was wearing, enveloping me in a warm embrace. The wisdom of many people was holding me and reminding me of who I am and what is important; their presence was palpable. I created the robe to transform my experience; at first it did, as I chose to believe in the intelligence of creative test writers challenging me to reason. I dove in confidently and calmly answered every item with no more concern than I'd have solving a crossword puzzle. But the calm was not long lasting. With each question, unknown lives, untold stories, and invisible pictures layered with meaning accumulated in my awareness and, in my distraction, pressed for justice. Fighting the dragon now, I could feel my mood change from alert curiosity, to irritation and frustration, followed by existential angst and despair, and finally smoldering anger and defiance.

I read an item, "What was the rationale behind Kwiatkowska's recommendation to use hard-edged colored pastels in the family art evaluation?"[44] A. Economy. B. Hardness. C. Durability. D. Brightness.

I don't know and I don't care. At the start of this four-hour, multiple-choice marathon I would have answered this one easily, but no longer. I am transformed into a rebellious teenager, randomly filling in choices just to get the damn test over with and be released. I looked up at the examiners sitting passively in the front of the room, and oh yes, it was a transference reaction all right: I hate them. They are my sophomore history teacher, eighth grade math teacher, and that old biddy Mrs. Schmitz all rolled up into one. Their bright, rat-like eyes shine confidence, superiority, authority. *Stop it. For god's sake, concentrate on the exam.*

Let's see, what's the answer to this one? I ask myself. Well, I stubbornly think, hard-edged pastels *are* economical, and maybe ol' Kwiatkowska had to do a couple hundred of these things every week. Then again, she was a doctor's wife and probably bank-rolled her whole pioneering art therapy program back in the fifties or whenever it was, before she got immortalized in a textbook[45] . . . Did I read that book for the test? I pictured it on my bookshelf at home, last read twenty years ago for a final exam in family art therapy. I smiled, fantasizing that if I ever got out of this place and wrote the book I wanted to write, someday there will be an item on the test: "Why did Lynn Kapitan recommend . . . ?" *Stop it, Lynn. Just answer the question. It is simple. Pick "brightness." You are thinking too much, distracting yourself.*

Maybe I am in the wrong profession, I muse. Made the wrong choice twenty years ago. The killing voice of the dragon whispers: *Maybe I am just too stupid.* I turned to look at the hundred or so people in the room bent in concentration and wondered: Was a similar process going on inside all of us? If we listened in on the testing minds, what kind of negative, destructive chatter would we hear? For my own part, I considered the fact that I always had been a successful student, and, aside from math anxiety, mixed dominant handedness and a little dyslexia *(stop it, you are diagnosing yourself)*, I never needed to really fear taking a test. Unlike my father, whose inner city junior high school was called the Penitentiary, or my mother, whose valedictorian scholarship to the university was denied simply because she was female and poor, no one ever told me I wasn't good enough. I had not been judged by the color of my skin or the parentage of my ancestors, and my midwestern accent had only occasionally inspired ridicule. What must it be like, I wondered, for those who did not have my confidence and privilege, to endure this test? What are we doing to people and why must this be necessary in the course of getting a credential?

I was getting angrier, the dragon power smoldering inside me. I knew the robe was worthless if it was only a creative rationalization to endure an oppressive monoculture built from righteousness, smug superiority, and a psychology for preserving the status quo. So easily we adapt to the violent draining away of life and not see it operating in these simple hoops we believe we must jump through. As my thoughts caught on the rough dragon scales of the exam's reality, I recalled

Krishnamurti, the philosopher who saw the connection between the world's vast misery and our many, local actions against things, people and ideas. To understand violence, he said, "there must be clear awareness of violence in its various expressions: nationalism, class antagonism, acquisitiveness, the lust for power, and the innumerable beliefs from which our minds suffer—all bring about violence. The real causes are hidden in our unwillingness to keep inwardly, psychologically free. As long as we are not ready to abandon our beliefs, dogmas, ideologies and the various compulsions which are merely the chains provided by society, the problem of violence will continue."[46]

In order to uphold the highest credential, program directors must be . . . Seventy odd years ago, in Vienna, the sentence ended with the word *German*. In the south, it was *White*. In the Catholic Church, the one correct answer is *Male*. In the military culture, the unspoken ending is *Heterosexual*. Of course I knew that a profession's board certification is quite small compared to these larger, heartless, and insidious dragons. Perhaps, I thought, I really was just making a big deal out of nothing. But as I focused in and out, and played with the dragon's shifting scale, I felt deeply uneasy. There must be a better way, one less destructive and less antithetical to the deep values of helping people and the diverse ways in which we go about that enterprise. As I left the examination room, the beautiful robe I wore felt heavy and burdened.

DRAGON FIRE OF CREATIVE COMBUSTION: A VITAL LIFE SIGN

Joseph Campbell said that if we do not awaken to the deeper mythic resonances that make up our lives, they will rise up and take us over. If we fail to live out our place in the myth consciously, the myth will simply live us against our will.[47] The encounter with the dragon of creative power is none other than art therapy's natural entanglement in the unfathomable, shape-shifting world in which we live and create. In seeking control rather than order, or naming this power as a problem in need of reductive solutions, we fail to live in and experience the messy foment of creative chaos that is the source of so much life vitality. The art therapists in this chapter's stories all were challenged by the demands of creative power and often relinquished personal power rather than endure its alchemical ability to shatter illusions of stability, safety and immunity. The poet Whyte affirms that ironically, the place of refuge that we seek is the same place where the devouring animal of our own disowned desire lies, and that our refusal to go there is the refusal to be eaten by life.[48] "The delusion is that there might be a possibility of immunity from the natural failures that accompany the soul's exploration in the world. But you are going to be swallowed by something greater one way or another. The question is whether you will give yourself to that greater life consciously."[49]

The awakening of the dragon is a vital life sign. Accepting the full presence of creative power helps us begin to deal with the hidden forces that are a source of continual disruption welling up from the very grounds of existence. The organizations and structures we create, however, often place enormous energy into the unconscious attempt to hold back the shifting, oceanic qualities of existence.[50] We glue things down to make them stick or funnel the flow of diversely textured, multiple life stories into streamlined, multiple exam questions. Slowly, the spaces and silences congeal into an unmoving, sterile landscape and a desperate longing to free the trapped waters of regeneration. With the longing comes disenchantment, needing someone like Mary at the start of this chapter to transform it into its enchanted, reconstructed version. Whatever chaos may be present at the start, we know that organizing elements will appear, will begin to attract each other and combine into new organization—if only we pay conscious attention and allow them to do so.

Creativity has always been a form of combustion.[51] As each of these art therapists described, we need the fiery possibilities associated with artistic life and imagination "not only to see our way through the present whirligig of change," Whyte writes, "but also because artistry asks for accountability to a human community, for rootedness and responsibility even as it changes."[52] The dragon's breath burns hot with passion and intensity; we are warmed by it at the same that we fear getting burned. Dragon fire carries "not only the heat of primordial creation but the dance of energy that devours and sublimates the outworn."[53] When it enters the fine houses art therapists have built in their practices, it not only can warm their identities but just as likely can burn the house down to the ground and force them out into the outer darkness of frustration. It teaches how to breathe, with new but unknown life, into the silent void. Whyte writes reassuringly, "Out of the silence the soul startles us by telling us that we are safe already, safe in our own experience even if that may be the path of failure. The textures and undulations of the path it has made through the landscape by hazard and design are nourishing in themselves."[54] The thunderbolt of consciousness shatters illusion and awakens us to find our place in this alive landscape where we apply the breathing lessons of the dragon's creative power to freely do the work of transformation.

NOTES

1. The chapter's opening story has been reprinted (with revisions) with permission from the American Art Therapy Association, Inc. Originally published in *Art Therapy: Journal of the American Art Therapy Association,17* (2). Quoted material is from Mary's thesis, entitled "Personal, professional, and creative holding environments: An existential and postmodern approach to art therapy" (Milwaukee, WI: Mount Mary College, 1999).
2. Byrne, P. (1995). From the depths to the surface: Art therapy as a discursive practice in the postmodern era. *The Arts in Psychotherapy, 22,* pp. 235–239.
3. Gergen, K. J. (1991). *The saturated self.* New York: Basic Books. p. 228.
4. Grentz, S. (1996). *A primer on postmodernism.* Grand Rapids, MI: William B. Eerdmans.
5. Gablik, S. (1991). *The reenchantment of art.* New York: Thames and Hudson. p. 30.
6. Riley, S. (1997). Conflicts in treatment issues of liberation, connection, and culture: Art therapy for women and their families. *Art Therapy: Journal of the American Art Therapy Association, 14,* 2, pp. 102–108.
7. Byrne, p. 237.
8. Gablik, p. 30.
9. Gergen, p. 132.
10. Wheatley, M. J. (1992). *Leadership and the new science.* San Francisco: Barrett-Koehler. pp. 15–16.
11. Gablik, p. 55.
12. Wheatley, p. 17.
13. Robbins, A. (1999). Chaos and form. *Art Therapy: Journal of the American Art Therapy Association, 16,* 3, pp. 121–125.
14. Wheatley, M. J. & Kellner, M. (1996). *A simpler way.* San Francisco: Barrett-Koehler. p. 6.
15. Rossiter, C. (1985). Sudden thunder. In *Modern Haiku, 16,* 1, p. 55.
16. Palmer, P. (1998). *The courage to teach.* San Francisco: Jossey-Bass. p. 19.
17. Miller, A.L. (1992, Winter). Living with sacred power: Promise and threat. *Parabola, 17,* 4, p. 4–9.
18. Zimmer, H. (1946). *Myths and symbols in Indian art and civilization.* Princeton, NJ: Princeton University Press.

19. Campbell, J. (1949). *The hero with a thousand faces*. Princeton, NJ: Princeton University Press, p. 40–41.
20. Whyte, D. (1994). *The heart aroused*. New York: Doubleday. p. 285.
21. Palmer, p. 65.
22. Ibid., p. 84.
23. Campbell, p. 90.
24. Zimmer, p. 3.
25. Smithers, S. (1992). The sleeping dragon and the waters. *Parabola, 17*, 4, p. 29.
26. Campbell, p. 207.
27. Smithers, p. 27.
28. Campbell, p. 207.
29. This series of stories is adapted from Kapitan, L. (Coordinator). (1998b). Gathering the village, stirring the sleeping dragon. Opening plenary of the 29th Annual Conference of the American Art Therapy Association, Portland, OR. Denver: National Audio Video. [Audio tape 121-1].
30. Robert Ault, MFA, ATR, HLM co-created this story with me. The founder of the graduate art therapy program at Emporia State University, Emporia, Kansas, and the Ault Academy of Art in Topeka, Kansas, he has conducted studio art therapy for more than twenty-five years. An exhibiting artist, he retired as an art therapist on staff of the Menninger's Clinic after thirty years of practice.
31. Melody Todd Ashby, MA, ATR co-created this story with me. She has practiced art therapy with children and adults in a variety of inpatient and outpatient clinics, and is currently the director of the undergraduate art therapy program at Mount Mary College in Milwaukee, WI, where she also supervises graduate art therapy students.
32. Ellen Horowitz, Ph.D., ATR-BC co-created this story with me, which also has been published in her book *Leap of faith: The call to art* (1999, Springfield, IL: Charles C Thomas). Ellen is the graduate art therapy program director at Nazareth College in Rochester, New York, and a practicing art therapist at Hillside Children's Center.
33. Don Jones, ATR, HLM co-created this story with me. A founder of the American Art Therapy Association and one of its first presidents, Don worked at the state hospital in Columbus, Ohio, and was hired as the first art therapist at Menniger's Clinic in Topeka. He founded the creative art therapy program at Harding Hospital, Worthington, Ohio, and practiced there until his retirement. He continues to volunteer practice with the prison population and is an exhibiting artist.
34. Catherine Moon, MA, ATR-BC co-created this story with me from her many years of practice as an art therapist at Harding Hospital in Worthington, Ohio, after which she moved to Scranton, Pennsylvania, where she had a studio art therapy practice with children and adults.
35. Josie Abbenante, MA, ATR-BC co-created with me a part of this story. At the time, Josie was an art therapist at the New Mexico School for the Deaf in Santa Fe, New Mexico after many years of work as an art therapist educator in two places of higher education.

36. Valerie Appleton, Ed.D., ATR co-created with me a part of this story. Valerie is an assistant dean and former director of a professional counseling degree program at the Eastern Washington University in Spokane, Washington, where she teaches, supervises, and conducts research in the fields of art therapy and professional counseling. I created the paintings that accompany this story over a period of several months prior to the first telling of this story. Their relationship to events in the story is synchronistic.
37. Rilke, R. (1995). As once the wing'd energy of delight. *The selected poetry of Rainer Maria Rilke* (Stephen Mitchell, trans.).
38. Palmer, pp. 107–108.
39. Ibid., p. 111.
40. The House-Tree-Person is a well-known projective drawing test administered by psychologists. The patient draws a picture of a house, followed by a tree, and a person of each gender on each of four sheets of white, 8 1/2" x 11" pieces of paper in pencil.
41. *The diagnostic and statistical manual of mental disorders, 4th edition* (1994, American Psychiatric Association, Washington, D.C.) states that the diagnosis of borderline personality disorder is made when there is a pervasive pattern of instability of interpersonal relationships, self-image and affects, and marked impulsivity beginning by early adulthood and present in a variety of contexts, as indicated by five or more of the following symptoms: frantic efforts to avoid real or imagined abandonment, unstable relationships with extremes of idealization and devaluation, unstable self-image, self-damaging impulsivity, recurrent suicidal gestures or behavior, affective instability due to a marked reactivity of mood or anxiety lasting a few hours, chronic feelings of emptiness, intense or inappropriate anger, and transient, stress-related paranoid ideation or dissociative symptoms.
42. This type of drawing would be familiar to a reader of the text *Actions, styles and symbols in kinetic family drawings: An interpretive manual* by Robert C. Burns (1972, New York: Brunner/Mazel), a manual of graphic indicators found in projective drawings used to assess a child's psychological view of his or her family life.
43. McNiff, S. (1989). *Depth psychology of art*. Springfield, IL: Charles C Thomas. McNiff attributes the word "abuse" to the fundamental problem of an individual expert who authoritatively tells us what an image or artwork "means." It does not take long within the art therapy studio to discover that the image has the ability to generate multiple interpretations. "The objects and events of our lives can be known in different ways, at different times and in response to different needs. This multiplicity of certainties contrasts to the way in which people try to convince the world that there is one truth. . . . *Polyveritas* [many truths] affirms our ability to know and understand our experience," pp. 56–57.
44. Hanna Kwiatkowska was one of the founders of the art therapy profession, practicing in Washington, D.C. in the 1940s and 1950s. The "family art therapy evaluation" is a protocol she designed which asks a family to complete a series of six drawings in a specific sequence, as follows: 1) free picture (no subject is assigned), 2) a picture of your family, 3) an abstract family portrait, 4) a picture started with the help of a scribble, 5) a joint family scribble, and 6) a free picture.

45. Kwiatkowska, H. (1978). *Family therapy and evaluation through art.* Springfield, IL: Charles C Thomas.
46. Krishnamurti, J. (1993). The way of peace. *The Sun, 206.* (Original work published in 1948), pp. 12–13.
47. Campbell, J. (1988). *The power of myth.* New York: Doubleday.
48. Whyte, p. 70.
49. Ibid., p. 71.
50. Ibid., p. 10.
51. Ibid., p. 96.
52. Ibid., p. 10
54. Ibid., p. 82.

Chapter 2

OPENING TO ENCHANTMENT: THE ART THERAPIST AS *ANIMADORA*

THE VESSELS OF OUR TRANSFORMATION

I watch my husband sitting on the back porch step, silently forming a small pinched bowl in his hands. I never see him so calm, relaxed, and centered as when he is shaping an elegant pot out of a rough lump of moist earth. He attends first to compression and the rounding. When sufficiently reconciled to the form, he presses his thumb into the center and, with visceral delight, gives into that moment of opening. Rhythmically, he turns the clay in his practiced hands, pressing and hollowing out the expanding interior void held by gradually thinning walls.

I eye my artist husband closely; yes, it is undeniable: he is enrapt. The clay bowl is his lover; they are forming each other's inner and outer spaces in communion. Longing stirs within me for that vibrant touch he freely gives to this other. But how could I be jealous? I have known and loved him for over twenty-five years. He has favored me with many pots and bowls, the vessels of his artistic love affairs. I come home from work and there on the kitchen table is a bowl, still warm from the kiln and giving off occasional tinkling sounds of cooling glaze. Often, he leaves the exterior walls of these pots unglazed, roughly cracked and textured with broken impressions, like so much brokenness in life. But there is tender wisdom inside his bowls for as I peer inside them, I see that he has glazed the inner spaces an impossible clear blue–the color of our child's eyes, the deep lake waters of the north, or the open sky above the canyon.

Anything can be placed in the bowl we have created, as an offering or a place to rest. But sometimes I am ungrateful. I fill the bowl with the acrid smoke of hate, sadness, bleak despair, or disenchantment. I feel the compressing and rounding, the relentless pressure with which we wear down each other's unsightly bumps, the frustrated knowing that I or the other—whether lover, employer, client, child, or simply "the one who is not-me"—will not change, will never be molded and shaped into the forms I long to love. Exhausted by that passionate desire, it is hard to imagine how an open and protected space can be created where needed rest is possible. "To make a space for dreaming," as one art therapist said in her story of the dragon. It was in the enchanted dream place deep inside the chaotic forces of creative power where she rediscovered images to awaken her and bring her back to creative life. So it seems the materials of renewal are always at hand, deep within the artist's imagination and the longing of the heart. To stay vibrant and alive, we need to make a clear and open space from which to awaken and see the world differently. There our artistry becomes a life-enchanting experience infused with the sense of being a loving partner with the world.

But this mystery has divergent pathways of insight that can be obscured with too quick a facile and ready explanation. Transformational images often come in dreams, like the bowl I once dreamed of—it was sticky red, alive and flesh-like. A pulsating orb of energy. Human at times, organ at other times, pure energy sometimes. The bowl had a warm powerful body with a cool spring inside it. Like a resting place for my soul, it seemed an oasis in the desert. In my dream, I placed a fiery, red blossom on the water inside it; it became the warm, human clay body of him, my lover. I felt enveloped by his gentle yet powerful strength and knew that had I never been held in that power, I would not know how to let go and surrender to the mystery of the inner spaces that shape us. Inner spaciousness opens when I am held in the embrace of life's vital energies, transformed by its fire and cool waters. When I am thus filled with love, I am able to give love generously to others. Then my bowl is open and receptive. I place my two hands together and magically they hold water and reflected sky.

I read about the begging bowl that Buddhist monks carry daily to sustain their lives. Theirs is the pragmatically spiritual practice of accepting with complete gratitude whatever is placed in their outstretched bowl, whether good or bad, lovely or horrible to behold. It may be that day's food; it may be brutal insults. *Any* material placed in the begging bowl is understood as a gift that sustains and transforms the monk's life. This metaphoric image offers the possibility of how art therapists, drained of creative vitality by the toxins of their work lives, can renew and transform their practices. With this insight, as though working its way up through layers of old habits to be discarded, I had another dream: I am walking home from somewhere and step into a pottery studio. As I talk to the potter, I casually pick up a colorful, jug-like vessel and neatly slice off its spout with a carving tool. It leaves a more rounded, feminine form that I am pleased with. The potter recoils from my destructive act of phallic power, saying "You have made this your bowl now, it is your responsibility."

As I hold the bowl in my hands, it begins to throb. It seems to have its own plan; I can do nothing but hold it while it takes its shape. It moves and throbs, growing bigger and bigger. Soon I must sit down under the weight of it, still holding it tenderly. The bowl transforms into a baby. Then I see that she, too, is changing with dynamic, throbbing growth as she transforms from baby, to child, to young woman. A mound is growing in her belly and I know that she is pregnant. Soon her birth pains begin and I see her infant emerge. Later, I paint this baby vessel (Figure 4), thinking that she is like the monk's begging bowl which I simply and attentively must hold as it forms itself from life's own energies. My memory flits down another path while I paint, recalling the early morning of my daughter's birth when I dreamed I was standing on a beach before the ocean, looking across the waters toward the horizon. Far off in the distance a large wave steadily approached. I watched it come nearer and nearer. When it reached the shore and broke on the beach, I awoke with my first contraction. My daughter was born in the afternoon; the very next morning I was packed up and sent home, closing the unprofitable birthing unit. Too fast for my mother to see her newborn granddaughter before I was whisked home, my day-old infant strapped into her car seat.

How different it is in southern Mexico when she who has given birth is attended by women who take her to the sweat lodge, remove her clothes, wrap her in soft towels, and offer her prayers for her healing. In the transition between her lives before and after the birth, she needs a physical, emotional, and spiritual cleansing. The sweat lodge deliberately evokes the womb of the feminine and a process of regression. It reminds her that she, too, came from the womb of her mother. As

Figure 4. The baby vessel dream.

she waits steadily in the belly of the darkness, sweet herbs infuse the steam bath; she breathes in cleansing breaths, breathes out the accumulated pain and toxic stresses of her body that had given birth. When she stoops to leave the sweat lodge and emerges through its narrowed passage, she receives clean cloth wraps like a newborn baby herself. She is cradled on the knees of a healing woman, who kneads and massages her body, the bowl, the vessel, restoring it to natural health. The women in her community give her this healing gift, and she is affirmed in her own creative power to *dar la luz*.[1]

Contemplating these dream memories, I know that many art therapists long for such an embrace from their community, in recognition of their work to restore the wounded spirits of their clients. Where do they go to be cleansed? I wondered. I put this thought aside and paint once again, now with the intention of acceptance for what has been placed in my bowl. Like the waiting, about-to-give-birth woman, this time I face not the fertile sea, but a vast expanse of desert wasteland (Figure 5). It is empty of all life; the baked earth is bone-dry, hardened clay. The bowl-like horizon forms against the deep blue sky. There is nothing to do but wait. My head is covered in a blue scarf against the harsh wind and sun; my white shirt sticks to my back with sweat. Near

Figure 5. Waiting in the desert.

the horizon, I see a figure walking slowly toward me. She is my grandmother. Otherworldly, she walks toward me over the parched, hardened earth where no rains ever fall. She carries, in her outstretched hands, a bowl. I know that she is bringing me her sacrificial offering as I contemplate the barren desert of my disenchantment. I see the bowl's clear interior and I smile, anticipating with deep longing my acceptance of her cool, blue gift of water in this hot, dry place. I think that I am open and patient, believing that I will be rewarded for my passive waiting–I have been good; I am the dutiful granddaughter, entitled to drink from this bowl. But as she comes closer, I see it is not the pure, clear water I had envisioned drinking. The bowl is filled with her salty tears. What am I to do with these tears?

My dreams open me to sources of enchantment but the path traverses narrow, constricted places, like thresholds between birth, life, and death. One evening, I sit with a group of angry women who are hard at work transforming their pain of living. Our circle forms a bowl; we hold the rim, explore the roughened edges between us, and the silent presence of the generative center.[2] On this night, the bowl of our longing was terribly harsh. Some of us placed ugly thoughts and feelings there—anger, fear, hurt, and shame—while others placed sweet and tender things, or the spice of fiery passions. Where once we longed for perfection, on this night our tears softened the hardness. We blended all—the ugliness and our most tender passions—holding the polarities and transforming these materials and ourselves into a proper offering.

The next week, our circle transformed again as the insights born of our imagery slowly worked their way into consciousness. We made magic; we made it rain. We considered that with a gentle rain our desert will bloom again and what was dormant will burst into sudden bloom where there was just dried earth before. Seeds sown long, long ago await the rains, however long they are in coming. Evoking the grandmother of my dream, I was reminded that this process started long before my time and is not mine alone to complete. In my painting from that night (Figure 6) I called out to her, from a childhood memory, saying:

> Grandmother spirit, you hold the bowl of the world and your tears nourish the planet. I saw you once, that day as a wild child when I ran and ran and ran, deep into the woods. Little did I know that I was running in a circle. In the opening ahead, I glimpsed the glittering lake. I came to the edge of the cliff, eyeing the promising blue waters—running so fast I ran right into air! I dove, then, into the deep lake waters, coming up to the surface still reeling from the shock of the cold water.

Art therapists can revitalize their work by claiming their place among the world's *animadoras*. Practitioner in the broadest sense of this Spanish word, the *animadora* is one who "awakens and restores." As artist, he or she breathes new life into and out of form. Spiritual traditions all over the world refer to the mysterious juice we draw upon in that act—the *chi* in China, *kundalini* in India, *mana* in Polynesia, *manitu* among the Iroquois, *élan vital* in France—believing that a person is a vessel or conduit through which the force of life flows.[3] Its manifestation in the psyche is termed *libido;* in the cosmos it appears as the structure and flux of the universe itself.[4] Art therapists, kin to midwives, know the power to *dar the luz* (to birth; in Spanish, "to give light"). Held by that larger, procreative force, they hold the vessel in turn and see, in the still, generative space where rest is promised, that any things placed there are the materials for transformation. Restoration begins when art therapists practice active partnership in a world experienced as alive and pulsing with shapes, colors, textures, and expressive forms, demanding artistic seeing and creative action, attention and response.

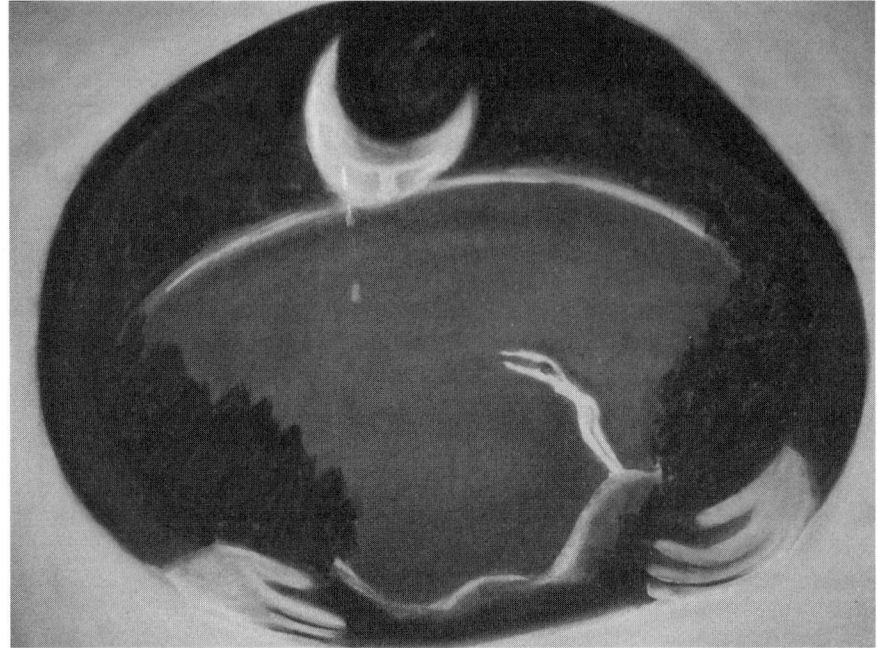

Figure 6. Grandmother's bowl of tears.

THERAPEUTIC ARTISTRY AND THE CRAFTSPERSON'S LESSONS OF THE BEGGING BOWL

The legacy that art therapists give to themselves and others is a restored ability to create vital connections needed in which to live and work, especially within a society that, in the main, practices dream suppression on a large scale. Transformational rehabilitation is a practice that links art therapists to the legacy of craftspersons living in partnership with a dynamic, reciprocating sense of their creativity. I re-learned this value recently in my return to the artistry of making books by hand, a medium I had worked in long ago when I was young and impatient and in love. As with clients in art therapy, making books requires great caring. Nothing can be rushed; the mind and heart has to still themselves in order to pay attention to what the materials and steps in the process are saying. This paying attention and stilling myself to be in the moment is like listening with great care and great love. When I listen, both to my own essential nature and to the nature of the material in my hands, I begin to sense something opening between us.

I discover something being formed, not by me but through me. It is then that I awaken and feel life's enchantment; a new love stirs for the work and life.[5] When I began as an art therapist, I couldn't draw upon such knowledge. It was hard to be patient with what I was doing in order to understand what was required. I see now that this was my "monkey mind"—always thinking ahead about what the work was going to look like, and how I would feel when finished and had an end product to verify my efforts. I was so focused on the dream that I did not listen to the journey, what would happen along the way. In sewing and binding a book, I think about how a thread knots up if you don't wax it first. A book artist I know says that you should heavily wax the thread to prepare it for sewing a book together. But I don't like the feel of waxed thread and find it less workable. I realize there is another choice: not wax the thread but *slow down* so it doesn't bunch up and knot as you pull the thread through the text block. It is a matter of presence and listening—really listening—to the unseen thread silently slipping through the pages.

My return to making books is like falling in love again. I am giddy with the feel of textures and colors, of rice paper, handmade paper, creamy buttery Rives, flecked and speckled banana paper, flower paper, thin fibers spun into a matte surface, translucent paper, ribbons and boards, needles and thread, stick-flat-glue spreading over paper, the balanced weight of the folding bone, or precious photos framed in time and space. I see their enchanting possibilities everywhere. Alive as images, they accompany me on my walks, glimpsed in the tangled clumps of shredded bark along the riverbank I discovered after a flood last summer, or in the smoky, thin slab of wood I pick up from a tree that has been charred by a lightning strike, and I think, "what kind of book can I make with this hallowed energy?"

I remember going to the paper shop and my irritation in watching the salesclerk's clumsy thumbs as she flipped up the corners of my carefully selected papers in order to count them. She handled that paper so roughly, completely without care. I could see that her mind was on something else. As in any therapeutic practice, even the most mundane, the touch that is required must be present, nonaggressive. It is a kind of touch that transmits loving attention; it absorbs the contact and allows energies to meet each other. More than just a gentle touch, the book artist is intimately aware of the paper, yet does not leave a mark or dent by handling it roughly or by grasping the paper to control or dominate it. The touch required gives with the paper, slides along the surface, yet is still equal and firm in its contact.

I thought of that touch, of both art therapist and craftsperson, when I turned the pages of the text block, aligned the edges, opened the signatures to sew. In sewing multiple signatures on tapes you need to handle the pages a lot. The beauty of it is that in the end there is no evidence they've been handled at all. At least, not on the surface of the page. No dents, no dings. But below the surface, yes, the paper has been handled with loving care and attention. So all the pages go together; they coexist well. They have been bound with loving, careful, and gentle contact, allowed to settle in with each other in a way that is true to their nature. As an art therapist, these insights please me and accurately describe my skill. In my reverie as I sew, my mind flits onto a thought about someone I am having a conflict with, creating a problem needing resolution. Just as I have this thought, the thread I am sewing tangled up. I realize that if I get angry and irritated, the book I am creating will be bound in anger and irritation. So I put the thought away and returned to the task at hand, becoming present again.

Images store deeper levels of meaning and insight than words do alone. Working from book image to text word accesses and opens me to insight. Then, when I shift this insight back into making the book, the detailed physicality of it feels like an evenly hovering, suspended process of working through, transforming my perceptions into new consciousness. I am pulled into a focused and sustained reverie as my hands attend with loving attention to concrete, sequential, and focused tasks. The process feels like I am being re-wired, synthesizing information and allowing the reverberations of insights just learned to be contained and held in the process of making a book. I am invited to take part in my own formation,[6] to be the sculptor of myself or at least to allow the forces that shape me.

When my mind is thus focused, small sequential tasks don't seem tedious at all, though they most certainly would be if I could not be open to staying present in the moment. The firm attitude of "sticking with"[7] reveals its power to open me to a depth experience. My attention is held by how straight the ruler lines up with the paper, for example, making a pin-prick to mark the line to be scored or cut, since a mark as fat as a pencil dot would throw off the measurement. Such detailed care—it amazes me that I have cultivated this patience at all, and how enjoyable it is to me now. I remember an autistic child I worked with in my school art therapy program who, after weeks and weeks together, one day gave me eye contact—an electrifying moment that ran all through me. A friend looked at me with pity when I told him, saying "How terrible, how boring it must have been to wait so long for that one moment of clarity!"

His words resonate the frustration we have when we are attached to a certain result, expectation, or desire to achieve a certain goal. Most of the time we pick and choose from what gets placed in our bowls. It is an attitude that constantly shapes our therapeutic practices. Some things are wanted; they're *good*. Some things are obstacles, or ugly, tedious or unexpected, or do not give eye contact; they're *bad*. Push them away and start over with the search for what is desirable, ignore what is placed in the bowl as not right, not good enough, not worthy of attention. But it is a circle, you see, with no inside and no outside, just the pulsating of life everywhere. It excludes nothing. Yes, I choose according to what is appropriate for my medium or therapeutic practice, alert to the possibilities of certain moments along the way. But I am not passionately attached to what I choose, for everything offers me some new possibility to work with. Bernie Glassman says, "If we could live in the world as if everything mattered, we would take care of each situation that arises in a natural and spontaneous way."[8] But almost all of us exclude something or someone.

Last winter, I had only one day to frame and mat my paintings for a show. I did not have the resources to have someone do it for me. And after all, they were my paintings, so matting and framing them were part of the process of taking care and continuing my relationship with them. I decided to make a ritual of the day's work. Every step of the way, from selecting the color of the mat board to measuring and drawing down the knife through the board, I attended with complete mindfulness and a relaxed attitude. I discovered how much my anxiety about slipping up, making a mistake, and ruining the board contributes to such things actually happening, because my mind is engaged not with what is happening right before me but is attending instead to a sort of phantom experience or hypothetical or future/past expectation.

How similar this is to sticking with what I see happening in a session with clients, accepting the process as being placed in my bowl to work with in gratitude rather than the competing image that materializes in my mind of what should happen (an ideal) or what might happen (fear or joy) or what must have happened (bias, pre-condition). How hard it is to *be with* the person and the process unfolding, instead of shifting my experience to some preferred other thing that is not really there at all.

When I made that day a ritual, all the little tasks that contribute to a well-matted, well-framed work added up and the pieces were finished with loving attention. The tasks themselves were not "creative" but they opened me to a creative process nonetheless. Each was like an element in a Japanese tea ceremony–creating a whole that is attentive, beautiful, thought-filled. The tea masters, I have read, make divine wonder out of an experience; out of the teahouse that influence is carried into the home, and out of the home into the nation.[9] My husband remarked that he was surprised I had not thought to use the Dexter, an expensive mat cutter that makes the task faster, easier and foolproof, but that instead, I had cut such precise lines with a simple utility knife. I knew that my practice–the ability to have this control–did not come from technique or a plan, the way much therapy is conducted. Rather, control came from attentiveness formed in the actual, unfolding relationship–from listening to whatever is there and responding accordingly, with slower, more mindful movement, a centered heart and a clear, unwavering contact between hand and material, self and other.

The craftsperson's lessons of the begging bowl have guided and deepened my understanding of art therapy. The bowl teaches me about opening toward and being solicited by the world within my hands and beyond. It is a practice of intentionality, as Maitland writes, of occupying and creating spaces with spacializing intentions, purposes, energies and desires.[10] The bowl holds an opening, sanctified space inside the limiting structure of its walls. Anything placed in my bowl–whether problems, tedium, obstacles, fears, or joys–demands some kind of creative response from me. The passage into this inner immediacy of knowing occurs by way of transformation.

Lately, I have been thinking about art therapy from the lessons of a craftsperson rather than artist. When I reflect on creative experiences that have given me peace and joy, what I remember is sewing clothing or making these artist books. I bring a hovering, peaceful attentiveness to these works without the noise of the ego striving to "express myself!" as I so often feel with painting. I am grateful not to bring that artist's insistence into every therapy session. In such encounters with my craft, I feel connected to those traditional societies where there is no abstract concept of "art" so everyone may be an artist in how they go about creating their arts for life's sake. Our peculiar heritage of specialization in the arts so often makes art a problem to be dismissed, ignored, made irrelevant or exclusive.[11] But research has found that art's function in the human species is not as an object but as a behavior or propensity to "make special," particularly the things one cares deeply about or activities whose outcome has strong personal significance.[12]

"What is *this*?" of the craftsperson includes and is a bigger question than "Who am I?"[13] The paper of my books, the clay of the bowls, the people with whom I work—they are responsive but cannot be forced against their nature. Violence and toxins are introduced whenever and however one attempts to do so. I dream of beautiful shapes and colors. I need to dream, but in the actual making I learn that both "the clay and the creator are subject to the laws of the Creator."[14] I may not be able to define these laws but I encounter them all the time in trying to make my visions real. In meeting the demands of my craft, I develop an inner strength that can meet the demands of my life. At the same time, as a craftsperson I always sense my place in relation to forces greater than myself.

There is something more materialistic, less intellectual or individualistic, which comes to me when I think "what is *this*?"—alchemical processes surely are taking place when I create my books or practice art therapy. Eliade said that "the alchemist must be healthy, humble, patient, chaste; his mind must be free and in harmony with his work; he must be intelligent and scholarly; he must work, meditate, pray...."[15] I wonder how many artists or therapists would characterize themselves in this way. I do know this is true of many excellent craftspersons, for how else could the beautiful object by their hands come into being? Alchemy is about becoming; as in the traditional processes of initiation, there is suffering and purification, death and resurrection of the god or the neophyte, represented by the substances in the crucible or by the material of the craftsperson[16]—the symbol, like the begging bowl, of transformation.

The patience that is the quality most vital to the craftsperson is, in the final analysis, a kind of suffering applied to the process of creation, operating in and upon me. The Latin root of the word *patiens* is from "pati" which means "to suffer."[17] I have learned that the substance, whether material or human, must change its character, must surrender to some larger process or be torn into separate elements in order to be reformed into something new. It must die in order to be reborn. Ah yes, I think, affirmed in my practice as I suffer the scoring and cutting through of the beautiful sheet of creamy paper, or the scissors making its first cut across the richly woven wool fabric. I must slice off the spout of the vessel in order to create the opening for the child to be born.

In the practice of my craft, I share a strange belief with the alchemist that matter is alive and I carry this attitude into my art therapy practice. The society in which I live teaches me this cannot be the case, that alchemy is an ancient practice of quackery among superstitious peoples. I must be a hopelessly confused, animistic heathen for I know the aliveness of matter to be true! I shift the handmade paper around to avoid the spot of thinned fibers or to capture and make use of a cluster of petals embedded in the sheet, reminded that *this* paper—as with *this* client—like no other has a history, a character, and certain needs or possibilities. I must feel and understand this life so that a relationship can appear between it and my own life. A craftsperson will say that she accepts that the pattern for her work is not hers—it comes to her from somewhere else—but neither is her work (whether therapeutic or artistic practice) merely to obey and to imitate.[18] We bring to it our own peculiarities or personality something from us that joins with the other, the living material in our hands. Otherwise the relationship doesn't exist and is indeed dead. Or perhaps the material isn't dead but is merely breathing too subtly to be perceived, and it is my attitude is that needs to be restored to life's enchantment.

The photographer Paul Capronigro also links the practice of his craft to alchemy, saying that what is most important is to gather and use materials lovingly, from what Maitland would call the allowing-will.[19] When you embrace limitation with an attitude of allowing, you take the most important step toward creative revitalization and transformation. Limitations begin to suggest new possibilities, as life is always lived suspended between limitation and possibility.[20] Capronigro writes, "Along with inner attitudes, the art of waiting needs to be cultivated . . . Standing in readiness for any possibility allows recognition of other conditions that might serve one's deeper intent. Recognition is the ambassador of seeing."[21]

As an art therapist, I have long understood my work as suspended between limitation and possibility. In my case, the ideal trajectory of a clinical practice was interrupted with unexpected career changes, financial challenges, and the demands of raising children. At times I wondered whether I was still an art therapist, when circumstances reconfigured the most familiar patterns of my practice. Being forced to accept and accommodate to my life's limitations, I discovered that my authenticity as an art therapist remains intact whenever I am connected to serving my deeper intent. I have learned not to confuse the outer forms of art therapy with its substance, nor to pin my identity and worth on fixed categories that may have little relationship to my life's journey. Most assuredly, *this* is a constant within me even though the container of my art therapy practice keeps changing and demanding different things of me.

Capronigro tells me it is a fine thing to surrender to the limiting or bounded subject according to the artist's or therapist's ability to contact his or her own source. He speaks of the centered heart that guides deeper intent when he says,

> True art is produced by means of an intelligence of love, a love that makes the gymnastics of the ego pale by comparison. This exists apart from emotional agreements between individuals, immature bargaining, or mere chemical affinities. This higher love permeates and feeds all dimensions of being; it does not meander through sentimentality or extol cleverness as does the intellect, but exudes a quiet, radiant, and elevating substance. This intelligence of love . . . it is not a jealous lover, but a sustainer of something higher. Works of art that have been created from this source have unfailingly nourished, for such art embodies a profound mystery.[22]

I take up a lovingly crafted book and open it: there are blank pages at the beginning called endsheets, which are special papers, usually too fine or expensive for text. Turning them serves the function of clearing the mind before reading. The twin pillars of the portal to the inner sanctum are the front and back covers, which guard the opening to new awareness and hold the polarities of life and death, good and evil, hope and fear. The approach through the handheld experience of an unopened book leads from opening, to journeying, and finally to arrival, the fulfillment of a resonating experience as one closes the book. The book sanctifies the experience of the encounter, invites a journey through time, space, and consciousness. Like the therapy session, there is within the pages of a handmade book a little interior world of safe, protected intimacy. I do not know until I behold it what will arise in my experience when I take up a book and start to read. Inside the covers of my books is an imaginary field, a place of "as if" where the reader is invited inside to participate in some ritual of self-transformation while living briefly suspended between the worlds of illusion and reality. I close the book and return to ordinary experience, knowing that what has just transpired was both not real and real. So, too, do the therapist and clients who enter the studio, a *temenos* or sacred space, to re-enact an ancient practice of hospitality. The therapist or keeper of the studio is a host, who is stationary. The guest or client arrives, halting life's movement long enough for a relationship to be formed between them, each one changed and nourished by the encounter.[23] Close the book and clear the space and mind; now you can empty, let go, and wait for the next encounter.

The guest or client comes seeking sanctuary, a safe place of protection where wounds can be carefully cleansed and healed. But where is the sanctuary, if not fundamentally in the hospitable heart of the host or therapist who is willing to face this living encounter and courageously open to it? When we suffer, feel isolated, and disconnected, we look for healing and wholeness everywhere but right where we always and already are. We attempt to create sanctuary through bounded categories of professionalism, expertise, or specialization. Or we search for some transcendent other place where life is free of painful limitation. An extraordinary magical place *out there* while rejecting or passing over what is right under our feet.

McNiff states that the spatial variable may be one of the most important influences on the quality of the therapeutic experience.[24] Indeed, we need to attend with care to creating artistic sanctuaries in the world where people can generate the creative energy needed for transformation. But ultimately this space of sanctuary—and the spaciousness there we so long for—can and must be found in the art therapist's ability to contact a larger, creative source that flows through him or her. After all, as Capronigro said, all life is one great cathedral where anyone, regardless of time or place, is free to worship.[25] Sanctuary is created out of one's own relationship to a subject: a loving attention that imbues the encounter with a nourishing substance. Whatever image or soul arises in that encounter is alive and seeking its own transformation. It is the open bowl, the alchemical vessel of the heart that awakens to life and to life's response and witness.

THE IMAGINAL SPACE OPENS

*The smell and taste of things remain poised for a long time,
like souls, ready to remind us, waiting and hoping for their moment . . .
and bear unfaltering, in the tiny and almost impalpable drop of their essence,
the vast structure of recollection.*

—Marcel Proust[26]

I draw a spontaneous picture in my notebook to record the feelings I have of opening and witness. The image invites me in, to be enlarged by "witnessing the unfamiliar and strengthened by witnessing the resonant," as Allen writes.[27] Images follow images; they come in dreams, in sessions and classes, in staff meetings, in the studio. I feel a familiar rhythm of call and response in all these spaces of shared encounters; the particulars of their origin are somewhat inconsequential. These images are my soul's familiars that come to me as collaborators in the creative process.[28] Creation is a sentient and instinctual flow, McNiff says, and the deep movements of the psyche made visible through the paint welcome spontaneous visitations of expression, unending in their depth, surprises, and challenges.[29]

From my sketchbook, images enchant and haunt me, and call me to story them. In doing so, I animate and awaken them, and in turn they restore me to awakened life. When I explore the inner surfaces or inscape of my therapeutic knowledge, I recognize that my worldview forever has been shaped and influenced by my creating with living, artistic materials. As Hillman says, the practice of "making alive" or personifying simply offers another avenue of loving, "of imagining things in personal form so that we can find access to them with our hearts."[30] Caring with loving attention is a practice of knowing, especially knowing from the place of the centered heart. This method is generally dismissed by therapeutic practices based in a scientific worldview, which tends to regard such expression as too emotional to be useful. The poetry of myth that underlies human striving is interpreted as biography, history or science; living images are reduced to remote facts. A missing element in scientific practice toward the world is the heart, since the mind and its rational processes are the valued means for knowing. If we want to return to caring for the world, seeing it personified through the human heart is an intelligent method that integrates heart with mind, and "returns abstract thoughts and dead matter to their human shapes."[31]

Hillman says that naming with images and metaphors has an advantage over naming with concepts, for personified namings are never dead tools but living psychic subjects we are obliged to be in relation with.[32] To embrace art therapy as an *animadora* would, we must trust that the material we come in contact with in our practice is seeking this relationship. On the pages of my sketchbook, images arrive from somewhere in my inner landscape. In my mind's eye, I look into the inscape of the bowl and see that they had been placed there asking for my attention and response. In caring for them, I shape them into stories infused with their energy that give form to the hidden patterns and inner surfaces, in this case, of my own disenchantment. I personify them and they become familiar spirits here to listen to a heart that had been broken. They come to re-enchant me, and help me regain what has been lost.

1. Erica Told Me That She Had a Hole In Her Heart

That was her matter-of-fact, seven-year-old way of explaining to me what had happened, and how she was feeling about it now, several weeks later. How was she going to go on living, she wondered, with a hole in her heart?

A spontaneous sketch drawn in my notebook invites me to revisit the memory of driving along the highway, retracing our route taken earlier on the first day of our family vacation, helplessly unable to undo a small tragedy. I could feel the edges of icy blackness creeping in as the light cast long shadows across the road. Darkness could get inside her, now; scary things could slither into the wound in my child's heart. My journey back to the day's beginning seemed a crazy undertaking, a vain attempt to push back time and space to the innocent days of my newborn daughter's soft breath upon my neck when I held her in the warmth of wholeness.

I told her I would be right back, but that had been hours ago. I drove slowly along the crumbling shoulder of the asphalt as cars rushed past in a blur. I was oblivious to them, focused on the edge between the road and the nearby fields. Everything for me slowed to that single, still point, searching for something I was convinced would be there. Something I would soon seize triumphantly to put things right.

Darkness was encroaching upon the pink and orange light of the dying sun deepening into blues and purples. Caught on the edge between continuing on and turning back, I feel suspended in mid-air, and groping for the thin line of the amorphous, middle space. Like an abyss opening below my feet on either side that is glimpsed in the cracks between teetering wooden planks, in my mind's eye I see an image: the tourist's footbridge suspended over a fake chasm at Fort Dells, a delightfully decadent place in Wisconsin where I vacationed as a child. But the terror is real enough. I believe that if I move ever so slightly to one side or the other I will fall forever into nothingness. In the hot summer sun, a cold sweat trickles down my back, the only motion in my frozen state. I look up, across the gulf between this side and the other. The taunting voice calls out, "What are you, chicken? Aw, come on, you stupid girl! What a scaredy shit you are!" Riveted to one spot, I cannot will my feet to action and step into what I am deadly certain is thin air. The illusion of the suspension bridge convinces me and I cannot trust my experience to tell me otherwise.

Thinking I'd heard a baby's cry, I jerked my attention back, in a sudden panic, to the busy lanes of traffic. A wailing siren from a police car streaked past me and disappeared into the darkness. Some new accident had occurred up ahead, but my thoughts only returned dully to the vision of my crying child when I arrive empty-handed. It had been a futile journey; I had always known that. She had a hole in her heart. My daughter would learn this over and over again.

Such folly, I thought, to have driven more than 200 miles along the shoulder of the road, looking for a baby's blanket that had somehow slipped out of the open car window earlier that day and left abandoned on the side of the road. Why did I do that? Did I really believe, as perhaps she had, that I would find the tattered, beloved thing? It was too dark now and if I had missed seeing it before, surely I would never see it now. It slipped into the darkness and was gone.

Is it true that when one thing is taken from us, something else has been given? Often my impulse is to turn away from the shunned, discarded image and refuse the gift that enters in these moments of wounding. Erica has a hole in her heart, I think to myself. In my mind's eye, I can see the precious thing lying on the road, abandoned to the crush of wheels and the roar of the traffic. Or blown into the side of a wintry cornfield and left dangling from a barbed wire fence. I went in search of a baby's blanket but it was my own heart left trampled and exposed that came to haunt me now. I had yet to learn that the soul prepares to enter where an empty, lost space has been opened. There was nothing else to do, but go on.

2. . . . flota mi cuerpo sobre los equilibrios contrarios

(My body floats between contrary equilibriums)
—Federico García Lorca[33]

I see now that I had forgotten how to pay attention and so my mind was vulnerable and open to the distractions of my fears. In the crush of combining full-time work and family, I had made myself accessible to the swirling energies that pummeled me, as though I were lying in the middle of the road. Carlos Casteneda's mentor Don Juan told him that when you cling to anything out of desperation, you are bound to get exhausted or to exhaust whatever or whomever you are clinging to. He said, "You must take yourself away. You must retrieve yourself from the middle of the trafficked way."[34]

I have made a drawing (Figure 7), as Kathy (a pseudonym) tells her story of unraveling her father's secret life. She seeks the truth with a brutal zealousness. I can feel her retracing the steps taken, perhaps to undo fate or to atone for his guilt. She directs her single-pointed focus in the search to recover the father who was lost. But my sketchbook drawing reveals the murky, floating body of a woman suspended in a fog that is neither here nor there. I think it is a portrait of the other lost one, her mother. Is she, I wonder, the shunned one, an image that was exiled from Kathy's soul?

What is the truth of this mother, who is unknown to me except as portrayed in Kathy's words and my imagination? The image that emerges from the motions of my hand across the page is terribly vulnerable. Her aging, rounded woman's body is nude, her stance awkward. She doesn't seem to know what to do with her hands and she places them in her lap, not quite covering her nakedness. She slumps in an almost hidden gesture of resignation and her twisting head, looking away and almost over her shoulder, seems pained and needing protection from the cold stare of her witness. She looks into empty space toward some unknown future or in reverie for something lost to her. Her body floats in suspended space; an inky gloom surrounds her. It mutes and softens her rejected, woman's sensuality, replacing it with

Figure 7. Portrait of Kathy's mother.

melancholic despair. She has been abandoned and left on the side of the road, I think, vulnerable to the ever-shifting winds that pummel her.

Kathy described her mother as having lived a life of pretense, steeped in the fantasies of romance novels and the suburban dreamtime of bridge clubs and trade in recipes. She was the silent "co-conspirator" in her father's double life, having made a bloodless pact with him that would protect her children from knowing the brutal truth of their secret. "My mother," Kathy explained, "lived in the perfect split-level American home. She had a vacuum cleaner and the latest sewing machine.... Having it all, she didn't care to disturb it with the truth of her celibacy. When my father had sex with her at the moment of my conception, it was the very last time."

They are two portraits of the soul, linked by wounding. I hear in Kathy's story a detached fury at her mother's complicity, for having chosen the equilibrium of the undisturbed illusion. My drawn image is a witness to another sort of equilibrium, lived in her soul's hidden landscape. She is merely suspended, I decide, frozen in time and space, with a gulf on either side that a move toward would be unthinkable. Kathy names her celibate; I see her floating portrait as if cut off from the mysterious juices that connect her to living. She has *taken herself away,* and exists in a place of in-between. Its soft, formless illusion protects her from pain until she can begin to trust again, if ever, life's inherent movement into the unknown.

Take what has been stirred and allow it to resonate, I whisper to myself. Let it reverberate outward, like ripples in reflecting waters. Have it affect the comings and goings of your committed life. Let it take you farther along, despite the fear that you will be lost, or that the long night will be forever. Release yourself from the illusion. You will find life lived along the dark edges and in the overlapping spaces. It will be exhilarating to step out into space, shifting the balance, to let go of a day's bitter grief as it sweeps you up and hurls you into space toward some as yet unknown place.

3. Waiting Woman

In the boardroom ... I created an image (Figure 8). It was late afternoon, when the group was feeling sleepy and dispersed, resisting the facilitator's attempt to get them into an intellectual discussion. Someone stood up suddenly and began pacing back and forth. Someone else piped up, let's go on, while others seemed enveloped in apathy. I draw spirals: they dance while two rounded forms of vibrating, complementary colors come together, negotiating the boundaries and interpenetrating influences between them. The tiny, grained spirals collect and gather where they will. The spiraling collective: when the spirals dance, then the two forms come together. They negotiate the boundaries; they

Opening to Enchantment 81

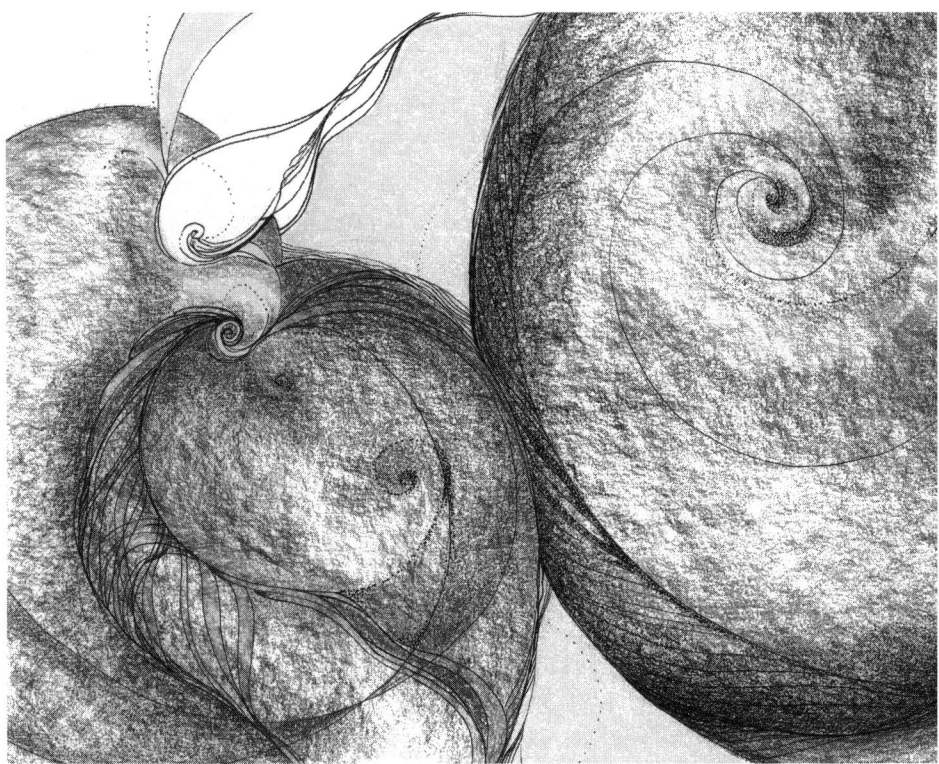

Figure 8. The spiraling collective.

are bounded, they bind into spiraling, dancing forms. What was dispersed becomes gathered into spirals, collected into spiraling pools, pooling ideas, and generating dancing energy. The little grains pass easily from one place to another. They ignore the boundaries of the large forms; in ignorance they gather themselves up where they will.

Now the white gap arrives, the leap of faith, the faithful leaping across while the spirals dance. I see the white place of falling through, falling apart, falling into waiting, loving arms or risk not being caught, not being, forever dispersed. When the white gap appears, the yellow arc forms nearby—like the finger of God pointing across the gap to the primal Adam in Michelangelo's famous painting. The white gap lies at the delicate, single-point, pointed finger of light, the spark where the space opens. The energy of the image rests on that point of contact, where the space opens up, between and despite the intimacy of the larger forms. Spiraling energies, energetic spirals, they are collected most intensely just below the white gap, in the glowing spiral of spinning, threading energies, spinning out their yarns to capture or call others to come together and gather.

I can't help it; I am being drawn into these swirling energies while the boardroom leader drones on, ignorant of my distraction. I look at him with a respectfully composed face, but a vivid corner of my mind is utterly caught up with the spiraling forms that dance and gather together, swirling, whirling, spinning; the spinners of yarns, the spinsters tell their stories. Weavers of the web, websters of the weave, their threads spin, they bind, shape and twirl an elegant form. Between them now, I see the gap reveals the larger pattern weaving. The gap is the space in the threshold between worlds; the golden, glowing space between two intimate forms that rest against one another. Leaning into or leaning away from? Colliding? Gliding, resting, restoring the weft and warp of the tapestry they weave.

After the break . . . I don't remember all that clearly when she entered the picture but it changed everything (Figure 9). What was it we were doing? I only know that the woman in my sketchbook came when the group shifted, taking up the discussion where we had left it. The space had been disrupted; there, a new image was waiting. When the space opens, then she appears. She sits in stillness; she is still. The stilled woman waits, eyes closed. She closes her eyes; she eyes her closeness to the stilled, waiting place. Maybe she is dreaming.

She holds the space of a vast enterprise. The enterprising, dreaming woman is one with the sheltering tree and rocks. In the surround I see that she emerges from and belongs to its primal matter. I call her Sophia, the divine feminine. She is a guardian of the path that opens at her feet. When she sits in stillness and guards the path, then it opens at her feet. But with the path, there are the vast mountains to climb. The calling, waiting, guarding-path woman guards with a fierce heart and calls with eyes closed. Eyes closed, she hears what is within the heart of the one who mounts the path. The one who will climb upward, rising up, gaining new consciousness and the view from the top of mountains.

Sheltering rock, sheltering tree, she gives me shelter. She shields the shielding, yielding heart. She guards the dream where the broken heart beats. She witnesses the beginning, the starting on the path; she is the call. The calling woman says, "Everything is connected. Whatever you can do or dream you can begin it."

Later . . . We are feeling stirred with an ever expanding vista of the work before us. Another image arrives and she wears the face of a trav-

Opening to Enchantment

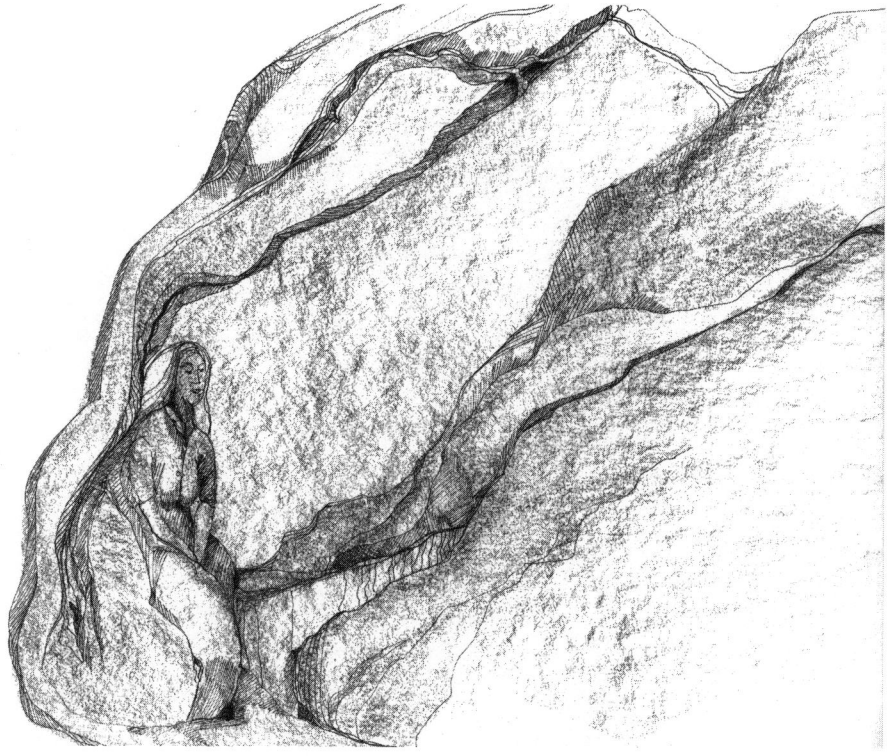

Figure 9. Waiting woman.

eler (Figure 10). She reminds me of my grandmother; she wears loden green, woolen coat and *babushka*. A grandmothering, traveling woman wearing loden green; in greenness she is weary. She sweeps up and gathers; she binds her hair up and gathers it into a flowing scarf. It protects her as it also identifies who she is and where she comes from, whose family she belongs to, what nation. She wears her community like a flowing scarf.

She is looking beyond the picture frame, only now it seems she is looking back; she backs into the past, what came before. Maybe she looks at it for the first time, seeing it more clearly for what it was and what it still has to offer her. Her gaze travels to the left of the picture, to what she left. Her gaze is riveted there; it stops her movement forward, up into the hills and mountains. Only when she looks to what is left, then her traveling movement is stilled. What do you see, traveling woman? What is catching your attention so vividly that it stops you in your perpetual movement?

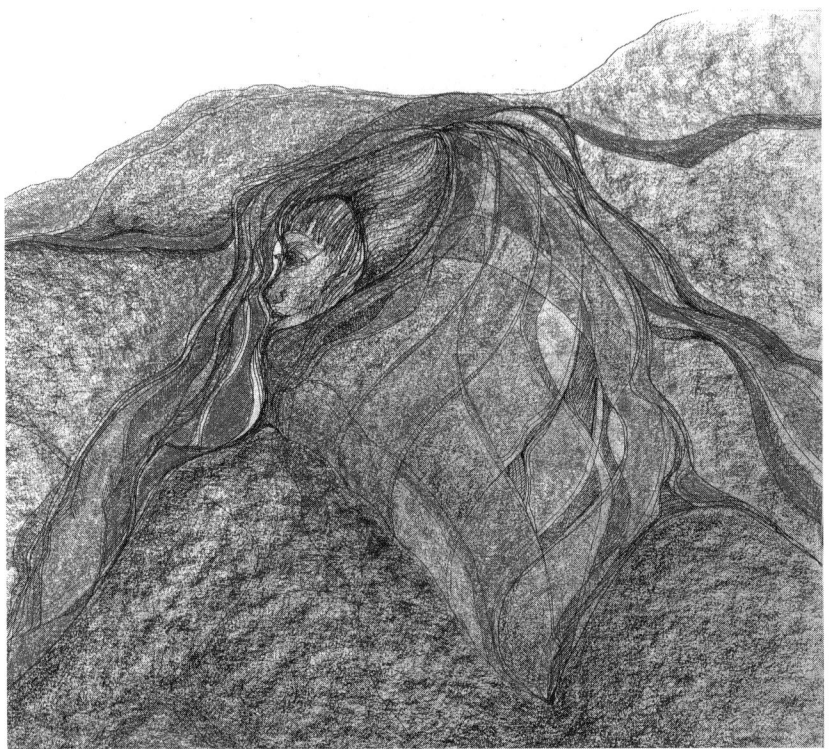

Figure 10. Gazing terra woman.

The gazing woman blends into and is one with the elements of her surrounding terrain. She is *terra,* mountain woman, woman of the mountain. She is green and blending, flowing; the molten rock and forces of water shape her terra forms. Her shaping, molten destiny lives on, long beyond her in the very forms of the earth. Looking closely at her gazing eyes, a tiny whiteness of the gap forms beside them and looks beyond to the intense ribbon of blue, like water, or like an opening into the sky. There is flowing clarity just beyond her eyes; just beyond the blue are ribbons of red and orange, like veins in the rocks, fissures and fault lines, and beyond that, the hills she wanders freely. Veining rocks, fissuring faults, faulting, lining ribbons surround you and hold your gaze in timelessness. Your checkered scarf is the farmers' field, the cultivators. You bless the cultivators. Blessings on the mountains and hills, on the rocks and fissures where cultivating change comes in, erupts, causes the masses to shift and move. Shifting, massing, changing woman, she is a volcano in the waiting.

Now I see her no longer traveling into the hills. When stilled, she is an image forming beneath the ground. Her visage is just below the surface of the hills, invisible unless we look deeply, deeply looking into the cracks and ripples of her waters bubbling up from below. Were she to move, the landscape would crack; she is an earthquake in the making. Cracking, quaking earth woman: The earth is always moving below our feet, always that shifting, changing, bubbling from below, we quake at the realization of her power. Riveted, gazing, powerful woman with the strength of mountains. She waits her moment to begin the quaking, cracking, moving change that will disrupt and re-form the very hills we walk on. Shape shifter. Shifting, sifting, shaping woman.

What do you see, *terra* woman? "I look to the past and see the timeless, endless movement of people on the earth. I am older than these hills. Remember this truth and you will keep your own life in perspective. Where you are tiny, I am vast. You stay in one place, believing in the illusion of your security there, forgetting that the very ground beneath you is moving all the time. All is dynamic change, all is movement, the landscape is forever changing beneath your feet. You forget that, forget your real place in the world. You are here only for a brief time, a blip against the eons that belong to me."

Why did you come, grandmother? "I come to honor your boldness. There is magic in it. Trust the leap of faith into the gap, into the river of clear blue sky that is just to the left of your gaze. You fear being abandoned by me in that faithful, fate-full moment. But I am always beside you, older than old, with the strength of mountains, witnessing your life, your purpose on this earth. To repair the world. To re-pair, pair again and create partnership with me, the one who is your Mother, your grandmother. The one who wears your face."

THE ENCHANTED LANDSCAPE

The split between human beings and nature, mind and body, spirit and matter has generated damaging conflicts at every level of life. The essence of the self and the essence of the world, appearing to be separate, are actually two expressions in partnership within one underlying field of consciousness. I sit in the meeting, attending to mundane conversations while my hand draws an image calling for my rapt attention: two expressions of a unified experience where, if I see and hear correctly, one informs the other. The *mundus imaginalis,* or world ensouled, is neither literal nor abstract, but still real.[35] If the world has a subjectivity, as Hillman says, we can feel our congenital ties to the things of nature and of culture, and discover new intimacies with what has been previously dismissed as dead, throwaway matter.[36] The world as a loving partner comes alive with shapes, colors, textures, and expressive forms that announce themselves and arrest our attention, drawing us into it. The begging bowl is offered to the world, and in that gesture, I extend the space within it and the world becomes alive for me again.

We should move through the world as though we belong to each other, says philosopher Morris Berman, convinced that the flesh of our bodies is also the flesh of the earth and the flesh of all our experiences we have come to know in both their pain and joy.[37] We do not. We live instead in a land of Eros transformed into a landscape of Thanatos. We have lost a primary satisfaction our ancestors routinely found living in rhythm with the natural world, out of which they created community, continuity between work and meaning, and spiritual connection. We find temporary satisfaction instead in secondary sources like materialism, drugs, or violence.[38] Collective trauma explains, in part, the insidious reality of addiction and abuse infusing our lives in a mass technological society. Over a hundred generations, we have created a world redefined and formed in a state of psychic dislocation, reflecting the rage, terror, and dissociation of the traumatized state.[39]

According to some theorists, when our infants do not experience life as genuine love radiating outward into a caring family and social environment, we fail each successive generation by creating a world torn with fear, hate, and violence.[40] In the spilt between the self and the other will arise ideologies trying to call us into various types of earthly paradise or in the hereafter, and always failing in recognition of the fact that the importance of security for babies and their mothers outweighs every other issue.[41] If this is not achieved, then everything else we do merely sustains human struggle with violence from crisis to crisis.

I once argued this very point with an economist who was quite amused by the idea that if our society were willing to invest hugely in the existence of a secure world for children and mothers, we would not need to put so many resources into defense, health care, or even new technologies. In societies where babies live closely attuned to the rhythms of the human and natural worlds, and are held in arms twenty-four hours a day for two years, they do not grow up experiencing a discontinuity with the world.[42] They have no sense of an empty space within themselves that must be always filled, and they do not spend an entire life proving they exist or making up for a missing sense of self. I imagined what it would have been like had I raised my infants by holding them in my arms for two years. Surely, I think, it would be impossible. Yet, what if everything in my culture supported me in that ideal, making it not only possible but desirable and welcome?

One beautiful fall day, I decided that I had to consider this question through my feet, and grasp what I know by heart, sight, in memory, and in the imagination. I walked a familiar place where I have worked for sixteen years as a teacher of therapists, and fell into a meditation on how this particular landscape actually holds me in loving arms, generates life, and ensouls my world. In practice, I was being a *theorist*, which in ancient times were people who traveled to strange places and came back to tell what they had seen with their own eyes, obtaining in the process a worldview that balanced common sense with intellect and imagination.[43] My purpose was to open to a larger horizon or "to claim the land," which Campbell says is done by creating sacred sites and investing the land with spiritual powers.[44] The landscape, as well as every phase of human existence, is made alive with symbolic suggestion. It becomes like a temple, a place for meditation. Claiming the land and turning it into a place of spiritual relevance is an ancient practice that can re-enchant a world often rendered dead to us.

To help me with my task, my imagination conjured such a traveler-theorist in the image of a troubadour, who became my imaginal guide and companion on a meandering path, showing me my soul's familiars in the land and buildings that announced themselves and arrested my movement. Only much later did I recognize that the appearance of a protective figure is a common feature in the myths and any journey of transforming consciousness. Protective and dangerous, Campbell writes that such helpers represent the "supernatural principle of guardianship and direction . . . signifying the support of our conscious personality by that other, larger system, [and] also the inscrutability of the guide we are following to the peril of all our rational ends."[45] A soul that is bound to be troubled is also bound to stir up strange helpers whose speech must be learned and whose sudden appearance must be gotten used to.[46]

"I see your spirit is troubled," the troubadour said to me, upon greeting. "There is a great fear and evil lurking about you. You are haunted by visions of mothers and fathers torn asunder, and children left to find their own ways in a cold world. You see people driven from the plagues of war, suffering, and want into the arms of orthodoxy, whose prophets foretell greater disaster unless they submit to those who will be their saviors. You tell me of human souls becoming denatured at the same time their games, technology, and entertainment give soul to monsters, dragons, and devils."

"Well, such was life that befell me in my time, too. Or do your people think they invented everything, including the existence of the apocalypse? No. I lived in apocalyptic times. I made my living traveling from place to place, at great personal risk. Yes, the road was just as hard in my times, the isolation I learned to reconcile myself with. The danger of death stalked me daily–if not from the plague, then from the footpads–those gangs of thieves and mercenaries who controlled certain roads and byways."

As we talked, we came to *a place under a tree,* one of my favorite places tucked into the woods at the edges of the campus. My companion saw, in such an ordinary place, the ancient form of school. In such a place, men or women always told the stories and discussed revelations with a few who were drawn to them, who did not know they were students. "The students were inspired that their children might also listen to such a one," the troubadour said. "So they set out to make such spaces, not to build a school but rather to create a place of consciousness. These structures you see", he said with a sweep of his arm that took in the woods and campus buildings beyond, "they protect the dreamer, to dream in peace. Our daydreaming is what marks humanity in its depths."[47] I told him that in my times, an education that is not immediately functional, rational, and instrumental is seen as completely useless in the quest for becoming gainfully employed. Even though getting a job is an important concern, I know that my students come with a deep longing for a living artistic practice, an identity that transcends a fixed version of a career. "Well, there is nothing wrong with a career," he concurred, "but it is empty and sometimes corrupting if it lacks the contemplative pace of a walk of life."[48]

We followed *a path in the woods* as he told me how fortunate I am to labor in this place of sanctuary. "You have here a bit of golden space scooped from the vast expanse of the world, providing space for your spirit to rest and reside," he said. "To sustain your life's work, you must look beyond the technician's view, and allow your desire to dwell in this place, like the tea master's ladle dipping into the vital waters of creativity." He was saddened to hear me speak of education controlled or narrowed by specialized disciplines, which reminded him of the powerful guilds of his own time. Education should serve the fundamental structures of human life. When these are understood, basic and simple ideas surrounding a professional learning glow with vitality. This life path through the golden woods invites a journey, the first step in the healing of the fragmented psyche. "You are confused?" he gently chided me. "Well, I have learned that if you are not enlightened enough to understand your own contradictions, and out of that initiation artistically create your own destiny, then you will experience your contradictions tragically in the form of an inflicted fate."[49]

Now we saw the dominant structures of the *steeple and the sanctuary* in this charming, gothic-inspired campus. They reflect an archetypal pattern of reaching outward for a higher level of life coupled with the inspiration of turning inward for healing and renewal.[50] The steeple calls the mind to grow in knowledge and experience, while the qualities of the sanctuary—shelter, nurturing, stability, and loving embrace—draw us in. When we see the landscape from an enchanted source, we gaze upon the eternal partners in the cosmic dance—male/female, yin/yang, light/dark, heaven/earth, embodied in these vertical and gathering forms.

"Yes," he mused, "my art is my attempt to return all that I do to the ideal of heaven which each of us feels in the heart as an aesthetic joy whenever something is embraced by love.[51] I began my life in bondage and for many years I resented this, because I suffered so at the hands of my masters. But now I have come to understand the nature of my craft and discipline, which requires me to surrender to and serve its deeper calling. I create my art as an inspiration and witness to our lives in these times and in service to the larger world in which we live. I make but a ritual gesture, a meditative devotion, and offering of service for its own sake, quite possibly unprofitable and pleasing no customer." I hear sadness in his words, and wonder whether the troubadour shares my yearning for the world to reflect back acknowledgement of art's healing gifts.

We have come to a *gate*. The gate is the threshold between worlds, from the external to the internal, at once a symbol of death and resurrection. When we step through thresholds, space opens up and new vistas may be envisioned. He tells me that always, on either side of the gate, there will be pillars that guard the opening to new awareness, embodying life and death, hope and fear, and the other polarities that bind us to a limited existence.[52] But hindering the passage through the gate are the elements of the door and latch of the portal. They are said to represent the veil and challenge posed by rigid patterns of thinking. The door blocks and opens, intimidates and welcomes. Edged in hardened steel, it can only be opened by piercing the darkness at the center of the lock.[53] *The portal,* like the gate, signals the transition from the chaos of the outer world to the peace of the inner one. "Entering the portal marks a new beginning in consciousness, but passing through can feel like a devouring," he muses. "So, often we resist. We fail to step through the portal when we know that everything we once were will be questioned and put to the test of who we will become."

Positioned above the portal, we look up and see a large, imposing form called the *sky door.* What I saw before as only the campus' central bell tower, he sees as another means for hearts and minds to ride the rising energies of the spirit. The sky door's central roof opening connects the hub of earthly existence to the sky's dynamic freedom. He tells me to imagine that it is a ladder let down through an opening in mid-sky. The energies of the sky door support a mythic image of the world mountain underneath it–the mass of experience one ascends through transformative processes.[54] Beneath this spot is the earth-supporting head of the cosmic serpent, the dragon holding the divine life-generating waters of the abyss.[55] Since it connects heaven and earth, the world mountain stands at the psychic center of a place, as the fountainhead of all creative and renewing energies, the source of order and harmony in a chaotic world. In this place, it happens that the bell tower looms over the central administration building on the campus. I laugh and tell my companion that this auspicious place of power is where the Registrar's office is located; for my students, truly a fearsome guardian of the portal and the energies of transformation.

A statue of Mary . . . The imposing steeple dominates the place, but it is balanced by the quiet of sanctuary and the divine feminine. She has many names but in this place, Mother Mary gazes inward and downward on us while her light dawns in all directions unto its own source. "She opens our awareness to the self in all and the all in the self, inspiring the creation of the ground of compassion in those devoted to serving others," he tells me. As we sit beside the still waters of a reflecting pool dedicated to Mary, the troubadour is moved to tell me that in devotion to her inspiration, his life as an artist has not been easy. "I do not have material wealth; I do not seek to be rich materially. I depend upon wealth, yes, and do not despise it particularly–it is usually in wealthy homes that I find a warm stove and more than my usual crust of bread. And you are right, it can be humiliating–my love songs spring from art; they give shape to things I cannot otherwise express. But many times, the people to whom I sing and play are unmoved and do not know or value deeply what I bring to them. They only want a little comfort. Love and art, well, these are other things. They are mostly invisible. But I have come to accept them as such, and I do not seek validation in all the wrong places. Neither should you."

"I am an outsider, a stranger. I do not mind this role, my place there is sacred. Your world seems less in touch with the sacred, methinks: Who here believes that among we traveling companions, homeless people in exile, may be the incarnation of God with whom you refuse to share bread? There is something bigger and more worthwhile than the things we see about us, the things we live and strive for." He gazed at the statue of Mary, and sighed. "You must know that there is an undiscovered beauty, a divine excellence, just beyond us."[56]

We linger a while and then enter the space of the *chapel*. Where the steeple expresses earth and sky, dark and light, and the wounding of the psyche caused by separation from our true nature, the sanctuary represents these energies joining together. It offers safe harbor for casting off worn-out ways of being. It embodies the ancient cave, the feminine consciousness turned inward. In its doors and windows, we find our private lives and the universe overlapping and in communion. My companion is grateful to see an arched window, as it is vibrant with personal and cultural memory, recalling his own medieval times still resonating in everyday consciousness here. The castle, the cathedral, the town – these were the three generating centers of creativity in the Middle Ages, all operating in the same symbolic field.[57]

An archway or *central aisle* passes through the middle of the sanctuary and marks the passage to enlightenment. Lining this passageway, we see arches that imitate the rhythmic passage of time, ticking off the progression of restoration and awakening. One who moves through these arches may be unaware that like them, progress is inevitable through the initiatory stages of the journey, and so one must learn to trust that process. I stop suddenly, startled to see the flaming red leaves of the foliage through the arched passage. Why haven't I seen that red before? Was it always there and I was simply too busy to notice its beauty? We pause to rest upon the rhythms of the passage, arresting movement forward and bringing into focus the enchanting possibilities that always can be found in the most ordinary of daily circumstances.

I am eager to show him the underground *tunnel,* a pragmatic solution to the reality of the campus' cold, northern climate. It is one of the hidden passageways and alternative paths that lie deep in the ground of consciousness and below the visible movement of people through this space. Likewise, when starting out on the journey, we are often surprised when the ground suddenly opens below our conscious mind, and we discover new routes or open up new spaces within our minds. Passing through the depths, the hidden sanctuary takes us beneath the comings and goings of the mundane world.

We arrive at the classroom where I teach. It is located near an intersection of two halls. The troubadour is delighted by this place of the *crossroads,* and reminds me that when the trails of the two meet—whether art or therapy, dreamer or pragmatist, student or teacher—both are transformed. I tell him that in my experience, art rooms are often situated in basements. "Ah, you must welcome that! For art is oriented to the depths. Your pathway here, lined by the artworks of the studio, provides a way of initiation, journey, and a time of transformation. Here your students will gain knowledge and awaken to consciousness, while their long-lost powers will be revived."

Inside the classroom is the *gathering space.* My students and I sit in circles; I teach in circles. Now with the enchanted eyes of my imagined companion, I behold the floor beneath my feet, as I see that it embodies my desire to find stable ground in a world of constant flux. Level and firm, the floors of the place act as a spreading field of information upon which the walls and pillars of education stand.[58] The enclosing space takes on the role of the germinating force within the circle and among each other in relationship. Energies that are depleted and the wounds that are created by the comings and goings of living are replenished and healed at these points of balance. The troubadour says, "You join the spokes of the wheel, but it is the center hole that makes the wagon move. You shape clay into a pot, but it is the emptiness inside that holds whatever we want. You hammer wood for a house, but it is the inner space that makes it livable, the unseen connector of all things.⁵⁹ I sing love songs, but it is the space between the notes where I find your heart is moved."

All the world is a sacred place for those alive to it. "All around you are presences, representing forces and powers and magical possibilities of life that are not yours and yet are a part of life, and that opens out to you. Then you find it echoing in yourself, because you are nature,"⁶⁰ he tells me. As I walk the enchanted landscape, I become newly conscious of an unseen but vividly felt world of information about the people who dwell here, both before and after my time. I see the signs of tremendous creativity generated and stored in the delicate stonework, the arched and lighted way, or in the indented hollows in the center of steps worn down by the feet of thousands of students passing through time. Over time, more and more consciousness is poured into this place through the life experiences that are associated with it.

The link between imagination and place is not a trivial matter. Our places are repositories of ensouled lives, like vessels holding the psychological energy that animate encounters with one another and house the deep dialogues of human imagination from which we gather inspiration. We can move through our spaces numbed and unseeing, aware only of the most mundane existence. Or we can open to the possibilities of enchanted inscapes, making spaces and infusing them with artistic seeing and creative, responsive action. I tell the troubadour that these vivid imaginings of mine worry me sometimes—what would people think if they knew my heart and mind? He smiled and said, "I knew a man once, Shakespeare by name. He said 'the lunatic, the lover, and the poet are of imagination all compact'.⁶¹ This, my love, is a good and worthy notion."

ART THERAPY AS A SOCIALLY RESPONSIVE FORM OF ART

What does it mean to ask whether [artists] are amateurs or professionals?
Do you say of people who are pious and who venerate a saint -
do you ask if they are amateurs or professionals?
It is an irrelevant distinction.
—Barbara Kirshenblatt-Gimblett⁶²

One day, I discovered a curious fact about certain places in my home: everywhere I find little "collections" of stones, buttons, bones, photos, children's pottery, feathers, and other natural objects. The shelf above my computer is piled with an accumulation of little things placed there over the years—objects being saved for some unknown reason, or that seem to have no other place to be. They are like artists' still lifes awaiting some creative attention or use. Taken as a whole, these collections of objects express a personal symbolism intuitively connected to the enchanted landscape. They are ordinary things in an ordinary life space that nonetheless open my consciousness to what is alive and moving in the immediate context.

Various how-to books on "reawakening the creative spirit" have popularized the idea of making a sacred space in one's own home as a special place for meditating or creating ritual. At times, I have wondered where I would place such an altar—all the likely spots seem out of the way from the often chaotic energies of the family of people who live with me and share this space. Looking for a "special place" implies, to me, a place where these arranged objects for contemplation can be contained and undisturbed, a place to retreat to when needed. It reminds me of an art therapist who told me she could no longer "just paint," as she was still waiting for the opportunity to set up a perfect studio for her retreat. The art process that moved in her was so deep and precious, she felt guilty if she did not have the time or space to light candles, play soft music, and keep dogs and children away. So she delayed her painting indefinitely. Another art therapist created a perfect studio but never goes there, preferring to paint "in the middle of things" at her kitchen table.

Perhaps it is true that creativity arises from the *bricolage,* from working with whatever odd assortment of funny shaped materials we have at hand, including our odd assortment of funny shaped selves.[63] I look more closely at the shelf above the computer and see beach pebbles collected from nearby Lake Michigan and far-away Massachusetts. There are buttons from who-knows-what jacket or shirt waiting to be sewn on again. Next to a button is an odd-shaped, rusted object that someone picked up from a walk along the river. It looks interesting but I have no idea what it is. A couple of clay sculptures made by my kids when they were little, a pile of slides, one baby shoe, a safe deposit box key, a ring of keys to my classroom, pennies, faded cartoon clippings, a small coiled basket made in a class, a child's homemade valentine....

Curiously, they are not simply dumped or discarded on the shelf. There is a sense of their having been arranged, but the arrangement is completely organic—a composition added to and subtracted from over ten years of life in this room. The objects have found themselves together, placed in a relationship that has never been scrutinized for meaning. Whose hand arranged them moved them so gradually over time that their movement is barely discernible, as though these inanimate objects are breathing too subtly for me to notice their sentience. There are similar gathering places elsewhere in my house—on dresser tops, inside pots placed on a side table, on the windowsill near the back door. These nooks and crannies serve to gather up the little things that appear in the course of moving along with the daily rhythms of family life. They are not set apart; they are in continual relationship to the spaces and energies of people flowing around and from them. Who's to say these are not the spontaneously arranged altars of a family of artists making a space for the sacred objects of their ordinary walks through the world?

There is so much room for art in the whole larger practice of living, in how we organize and create from our lives, that "the idea of confining art to what we hang on walls is pathetic failure of theoretical as well as artistic imagination."[64] Sometimes art therapists get passionately attached to the forms of their practice. Or so caught up in the notion of the solitary and free artist in the studio that they look at their therapeutic work as a job to put in their time helping others until someday they achieve the ideal of working alone or in private. McNiff writes that it took him years to realize that his desire to live the life of the artist overlooked the riches of his immediate environment, and that every therapeutic group he was involved in demonstrated its potential for nurturing the responsiveness, attention, and inspiration that every artist needs.[65]

I believe that art therapists have enormous potential for creating new forms in the world that are life-enhancing, but we hold a vision of ourselves that is driven by a longing to fit in with existing categories of mental health care as well as those recognized by the art world. Beyond the polarity we've used to define our practice, of "art as therapy" vs. "art in therapy," there is a third position, where art therapy is a form of socially responsive art. There art therapists are known as artists working in the medium of process, the canvas of relationship, and the studio of the community.[66] I align these ideas with Robbins' understanding of art therapy as a conceptual, invisible artwork that we co-create with our clients in the therapeutic studio, an art that is continually shaped and reshaped in the aesthetics of the treatment dialogue.[67] The studio, in this regard, is archetypal: it does not exclude clinical practice, nor demands a special place or particular method, but embraces the multiplicity of possibilities continuously created in the practice of therapeutic artistry. The studio, to give it a cosmic definition, is like the Immovable Spot of the Buddha—a still point around which the torrential flow of creative energies revolve.[68]

While Robbins has articulated the art form that is art therapy from the therapeutic side of the equation, there is also support for situating art therapy simultaneously in the art world. Having so often questioned the place of art in art therapy, what validity is there in naming the practice of art therapy as an art form in its own right? There is abundant evidence that more and more artists, without the benefit of art therapy training, are successfully being employed making art from and in the contexts of healing, mental health care, and the people whom art therapists traditionally serve. What will be our response? Wring our hands and lament that we can't compete because we are not considered artists enough? Hundreds of years of art history has refused entry to women, people of color, non-Western or folk artists, and anyone pushed to the fringes of the mainstream. We are not so special. As Naomi Wolf says, "There is nothing wrong with identifying one's victimization. That act is critical. There's a lot wrong with molding it into an identity."[69]

I think the difficulty comes when we exclude art therapy by defining art as one thing alone, in accordance with the confined dreams of that small segment of the population participating in the national art scene, where art is personal in the narrowest sense, needs to be a salable commodity, and where alienation is one of the requirements of practice.[70] No wonder art therapists, by comparison, have been reluctant to identify themselves as artists. The professional art world, in general, has been hostile to the notion of a kind of art that is socially engaged or participatory in the world, especially if it leads to blurring the boundary between art and life.

Here is a definition of art that opens the door wide for art therapy: "art is that which functions as an aesthetic experience for you."[71] I recall days spent immersed in art therapy, witnessing art created by someone exercising his or her artistic power. And then going to a gallery show: Wine and cheese in hand, I see slick, soul-less images created for hanging in some corporate boardroom somewhere, and I think, what's wrong with me? Why does this art feel so dead and the art of my practice so alive? I reflect on what a schizophrenic experience it is to be an artist in our culture. I am told that the gallery art I see reflects our society and its ugliness is merely art's power to reflect that truth. But it seems a narrow truth, as my heart returns to my day with people courageously painting themselves into new possibilities. I know that if art therapy "works as an aesthetically moving experience for enough people to have consensus," then it is art: "that which we feel worth devoting one's life to and whose value cannot be proven."[72]

Many art therapists carry the disenchanting experience of feeling secondary or second-class artists because of how the worlds of art and therapy have been defined. They yearn to be recognized, their gifts appreciated. They yearn for a special space of belonging, of acceptance. But there is energy in that longing which, if held and embraced rather than blocked with pain and grief, can be used to transform perceptions. That art therapists feel secondary and dismissed is echoed the world over in the experiences of traditional women's art and of craftspeople. Historically, because they were denied access to the art world, women and craftspeople were required to find outlets for their creative drives in art that was not considered "art," usually having to cost little or nothing and having to perform some useful function.[73] Like most art therapy, such art also was private or something rarely seen in public. Women's art traditionally was private, visible only to intimates and within the confined space of the house. Thus, in the practice of art therapy, we have the potential to connect with this source of disenchantment and resurrect our ancestors' activities in the area of "transformational rehabilitation." Restoring and rehabilitating has always been the traditional private resort of economically deprived people—patching, turning collars and cuffs, remaking old clothes, repairing tools—a type of art and craft work that gives life and family public dignity.[74] Like them, art therapists do the transformational work of patching and repairing wounded souls battered in the rhythms of daily living. Even when not actually creating art in the practice, they know that "people are medicine for people," as an old African saying goes, and use their transformative arts accordingly.

We can take pride in tracing our artistic lineage through this unappreciated though vital arena of art making. Perhaps it would be safer and easier to accept a separate and totally non-threatening sphere for our art making, as some have done, than to fight for more power in the worlds of art and health care in ways that acknowledge art therapists' therapeutic artistry. Whether in the studio or the clinic, art therapists may look for a "special place" to retreat to that is contained and undisturbed, but this option should not mean escape to a separate confinement. We may prefer these sanctuaries of private practice, but the subtle sentience of the *bricolage* is also calling us to a participatory creativity right in the flow of life's energy. In holding both sides of the polarities, the reflective, aesthetic self may function with the socially active self without guilt or frustration.[75] In the process, a kind of art will emerge that is significantly different from what art is in the dominant culture.

Art theorist Lippard has identified three "models of feminist art" in which art therapists can consider themselves as active, knowledgeable artists: 1) group and public ritual art; 2) consciousness raising and interaction through imagery, environments and performances, and 3) cooperative, collective, and collaborative art making.[76] None of these feminist art forms has to do with handling the picture plane, arranging space, or new ways of making figures, objects, or landscapes—they are inclusive, communal arts. Art therapists practice a form of art that makes an important contribution to the art world by slowing it down and re-peopling it with communal rituals. Even with the least responsive persons, the art therapist functions as an artist collaborator in the therapeutic encounter, co-creating even the tiniest avenues where new consciousness can appear and disappear. This art is made in the context of relationships and is responsive to real personal needs and collective voices. It is not confined to a client or participant's works alone, but can also be witnessed in the art therapist's entire practice of therapeutic artistry.

The process of forming and reforming oneself in relation to the world is a primary method of artistic practice. I look with alertness to the enchanting realities of my inscapes and landscapes, all the eddying *bricolage* from which my creativity arises. Art therapy is a practice of art that is located in the disquieted places, along a network of many roads converging more territory than art's mainstream expressway. Its images come asking us to awaken them and affirm their existence. Like wandering troubadours, art therapists pass many people's houses, and are more likely to be invited in when this broader view of art's purposes is entertained. Our outstretched bowl brings the divine guest of creativity to transform us, through simple and often unnoticed, loving actions. Whatever image or soul arises in that encounter is alive and seeking transformation. When perception changes, the quality of the art the art therapist gives to the world starts to change. The world begins to listen, to receive this new offering, and interact with it anew.

NOTES

1. *Dar la luz* is Spanish for giving birth; literally it means "to give light," in reference to the mother's gift of light to the newborn emerging from the birth canal.
2. Baldwin, C. (1994). *Calling the circle.* New York: Bantam.
3. Nachmanovitch, S. (1990). *Free play: Improvisation in life and art.* New York: Jeremy Taracher. pp. 32–33.
4. Campbell, J. (1949). *The hero with a thousand faces.* Princeton, NJ: Princeton University Press. p. 258.
5. Remde, G. (1991). Close to the earth. *Parabola, 16,* 3, p. 49.
6. Tracol, H. (1991). Birth of a sculpture. *Parabola, 16,* 3, p. 66.
7. Hillman, J. (1989). In T. Moore (Ed.). *A blue fire: Selected writings by James Hillman.* "Sticking with" means not translating images into meanings, as though images were allegories or symbols. As Hillman says, if there is a latent dimension to an image it is its inexhaustibility. When an image comes with a moral claim it haunts or obsesses until we respond to it in some manner. It may suggest an internal necessity or a limitation, or it may require direct action.
8. Glassman, B. (1998). *Bearing witness.* New York: Bell Tower. p. 32.
9. Campbell, p. 168.
10. Maitland, J. (1995). *Spacious body: Explorations in somatic ontology.* Berkeley, CA: North Atlantic Books. pp. 75–76.
11. Dissanayake, E. (1992a). Art for life's sake. *Art Therapy: Journal of the American Art Therapy Association, 9,* 4, 169–174. See also Dissanayake, D. (1992b). *Homo aestheticus: Where art comes from.* New York: Basic Books.
12. Dissanayake, E. (1992b). Art as behavior, making things special, emphasizes a shift from the object, quality, or commodity to the activity (the making, doing, appreciating). There is no known society that does not practice at least one of what we call "the arts" and in many groups art-making is among their most important endeavors. In small-scale, unspecialized, premodern societies, individuals can generally make and do everything that is needed for their livelihood. While there is no abstract concept of "art," everyone may be an artist, even when some persons are acknowledged as being more talented or skillful than others... the arts are invariably and inseparably part of ritual ceremonies that articulate, express, and reinforce a group's deepest beliefs and concerns. As the vehicle for group meaning and a galvanizer for group open-heartedness, art-conjoined-with-ritual is essential to group survival–quite literally art for life's sake. In a highly

specialized society like ours, the arts are also specialities and may exist for their own sake apart from ritual or any other purpose. This separation, peculiar only to modernized or "advanced" societies, makes art a problem. Art's heritage of specialization and self-proclaimed irrelevance permits it to be dismissed as a frill while its aura of sanctity and privilege remains as a reproach to those whose upbringing has not included exposure to "fine" arts. Dismissal, ignorance, irrelevance, and exclusivity of art are all artifacts of our own peculiar cultural predicament and not inherent in arts anywhere else, pp. 173–175.
13. Maitland, p. 7.
14. Remde, p. 48.
15. Eliade in Dooling, D. M. (1986). The alchemy of craft. *A way of working*. (New York: Parabola Books). James Hillman also has described alchemical principles as metaphors in his theory of archetypal psychology, and references to them can be found throughout his body of writings.
16. Dooling.
17. Ibid.
18. Ibid.
19. Maitland, pp. 122–123.
20. Ibid.
21. Capronigro, P. (1991). Writing with light. *Parabola, 16,* 3, p. 54.
22. Ibid., p. 56.
23. Kapitan, L. (1997a). Consuming art therapy: Paradoxes and perils in a market-driven society. Paper and performance presented at the Annual Conference of the American Art Therapy Association, Milwaukee, WI.
24. McNiff, S. (1998). *Art-based research*. Philadelphia: Jessica Kingsley. p. 187.
25. Capronigro, p. 56.
26. Proust, M., in A. Margulies. (1989). *The empathic imagination*. New York: W.W. Norton. p. 45.
27. Allen, P. B. (1995a). *Art is a way of knowing*. Boston: Shambhala. p. 110.
28. McNiff, S. (1992). *Art as medicine*. Boston: Shambhala. p. 19.
29. Ibid., pp. 14–16.
30. Hillman, p. 46.
31. Ibid., p. 47.
32. Ibid., p. 48.
33. Lorca, F. Garcia. (1940). Poema doble del lago Eden. [Double poem from Lake Eden]. *Poeta en Nueva York, 1929–1930*. (B. Bellitt, Trans.). New York: Grove Press. pp. 64–66.
34. Casteneda, C. (1991). *Journey to Ixtlan*. New York: Simon and Schuster.
35. Hillman, p. 6.
36. Ibid., p. 99
37. Berman, M. (1989). *Coming to our senses*. New York: Bantam. p. 344.
38. Glendinning, C. (1995). Technology, taming and the wild. In T. Roszak, Gomes, M., and Kanner, A. D. (Eds.). *Ecopsychology*. San Francisco: Sierra Club. p. 53.
39. Ibid., p. 64.

40. Guntrip, H. (1971). *Psychoanalytic theory, therapy, and the self.* New York: Basic Books. p. 114.
41. Ibid.
42. Berman, M., p. 44.
43. Walter, E.V. (1988). *Placeways: A theory of the human environment.* Chapel Hill: University of North Carolina. pp. 3–4.
44. Campbell, J. (1988). *The power of myth.* New York: Doubleday. p. 93.
45. Ibid., p. 73.
46. Meade, M. (1993). *Men and the water of life.* New York: Harper Collins. p. 388.
47. Bachelard, G. (1969). (M. Jolas, Trans.). *The poetics of space.* Boston: Beacon Press.
48. Lipsey, R. (1997). *An art of our own: The spiritual in twentieth century art.* Boston: Shambhala. p. 440.
49. Thompson, W.I. (1991). *The American replacement of nature: The everyday acts and outrageous evolution of economic life.* New York: Bantam Doubleday Dell. p. 53.
50. Lawlor, A. (1994). *The temple in the house.* New York: G.P. Putnam's Sons. p. 51.
51. Hillman, J. (1995). *Kinds of power.* New York: Doubleday.
52. Lawlor, p. 20.
53. Ibid., p. 28.
54. Ibid., p. 57–59.
55. Campbell, J. (1949). p. 41.
56. Maybeck, B., quoted in Lawlor, p. 17.
57. Campbell, J. (1988). p. 59.
58. Lawlor, p. 80.
59. Tao te Ching, quoted in Lawlor, p. 88.
60. Campbell, J. (1988). p. 92.
61. Shakespeare, W. A midsummer's night dream. (Act V, i, 7). In W.A. Wright (Ed.). *The complete works of Willam Shakespeare.* Garden City, NY: Doubleday and Company. p. 406.
62. Kirshenblatt-Gimblett, B. (1995). The aesthetics of everyday life. In S. Gablik. *Conversations before the end of time.* New York: Thames and Hudson. p. 419.
63. Nachmanovitch, S. (1990). *Free play: Improvisation in life and art.* New York: Jeremy Tarcher. p. 137.
64. Shusterman, R. (1995). Breaking out of the white cube. In Gablik, p. 265.
65. McNiff, S. (1992). pp 38–39.
66. Kapitan, L. & Vance, L. (1991). Being in creation: Revisioning the artist in the art therapist identity. Paper and performance presented at the Annual Conference of the American Art Therapy Association, San Francisco, CA.
67. Robbins, A. (1998). *Therapeutic presence: Bridging expression and form.* Philadelphia: Jessica Kingsley.
68. Campbell, J. (1949). pp. 40–41.
69. Wolf, N. (1994). *Fire with fire: The new female power and how to use it.* New York: Fawcett Columbine. p. 136.
70. Morales, R. p. 18.
71. Lippard, L. (1995). *The pink swan: Selected feminist essays on art.* New York: New Press. p. 172.

72. Ibid., p. 172.
73. Ibid., p. 134.
74. Ibid., p. 136.
75. Ibid., p. 174.
76. Ibid., p. 179.

Chapter 3

A BOWL OF TEARS: WITNESSING ART THERAPIST DISENCHANTMENT IN THE TOXIC WORK ENVIRONMENT

"We medicine the disquieted places..."
—Shaun McNiff (1995, p. 182)

INTRODUCTION: TRANSFORMING TOXINS THROUGH COLLABORATIVE WITNESS

"But you are glowing with life! You are open, like a vessel incubating new life forms. I see it in your dancing eyes and the smile that lingers on your face. The smoldering fires and clouded apprehension of your mind have lifted. When last I saw you, your spirit was occupied with some dark thing. What has happened?" asked my companion, the troubadour, with surprise and delight.

I could have told him I'd come back from the dead, but that sounded rather dramatic. And yet, and yet.... In the disquieted places where I found disenchanted art therapists, they filled the bowl I offered out to them with dead and toxic matter from the people and places of their work, describing to me that which had killed or mangled their spirits, telling their suffering with flat words droning into obsession, mired sometimes in self-hating voices of judgment and shame. How could I convey the enchanting magic of what happened when broken, wounded, and even toxic hearts are held open and given compassionate witness? The alchemy of suffering and purification, death and resurrection, is in these toxic substances placed in the crucible. This matter is alive and we become alive to it when we allow and obey its fomenting substance. The toxins transform us back to life.

"It was a simple method," I stated, though it was hard to explain. I had invited individual art therapists to a creative encounter I named "collaborative witness." My role was to listen with no agenda of my own and with complete attention as each told me her experience in a toxic work environment. After an hour or so of this telling and receptive listening, a natural pause would occur where we shifted to art making. We each created an art image to capture the story's essence. She looked at the image I made and created another picture in response by silently asking herself, *"How does this image want to be held?"* I did the same with hers. I chose this question deliberately, for it evoked compassion toward the image of her disenchantment. It honored the dispirited image as distinct from she who had created it, and opened it to the possibilities of transformation. Then she reflected upon her first picture and my response to it, and made a third and final picture that completed the series. I did the same. Our art—basically an interactive series of six images—amplified the spoken words of the art therapist's disenchantment and created another avenue for witnessing.

The troubadour listened carefully to my description and recognized the transformational act of dipping into the toxins of the spoken words and creating art from the energies they stirred. "All real living is meeting,[1] is it not?" he asked. "Whatever you call this practice of yours, whatever role it requires you to carry, it does seem to come to an act of witness. You have learned that no knowledge, technique, theorizing, assessment, planning, or expertise can substitute for the encounter with 'the other who is not me and also me'.

"Of course," he added, "it is not that your professional roles, knowledge and skills are unnecessary. Quite the contrary! Only that it seems that what is most wanted by any person in pain is to be listened to and held with love and compassion."

How does the image want to be held? I thought. Whatever image arises in that encounter is alive spatially and seeking its own transformation—the open bowl, the alchemical vessel, the heart that awakens to life and to life's response. It is true that we cannot know that form in advance, not if we are being truly respectful. At the same time that we accumulate knowledge and experience, we need to wipe the slate clean and be in a state of unknowing, for only then can we bear witness to whatever arises.[2] Bearing witness brings us to loving action, the goal of which is to reduce suffering. We have to empty ourselves over and over, return to unknowing and listening, which means seeing what and who is in front of us.[3]

"Imagine what becomes possible," I told my companion, "when the impulse to impose structure on an emerging phenomenon is suspended. What do we do with a world that cannot be known until it is in the process of discovering itself?"[4] Life is inherently attracted to finding order by evolving pattern and form, but to understand this I have learned to suspend knowing things in advance and let go of my expectation of ownership. This is the basic orientation of the phenomenological method in both therapy and formal inquiry.[5] Clearing the perceptual field and opening to the phenomenon as it reveals itself eventually creates transparency and more spaciousness, with fewer attachments and preconceptions about what and who I am encountering.

"Yes," he mused. "When you are ready to live a questioning life, without fixed ideas or answers, then you are ready to bear witness to every situation, no matter how difficult, painful or offensive it is.[6] Out of that process of bearing witness comes the right action of making peace, of healing. Making peace means making whole."[7]

With my collaborators' and my allowing presence, we opened the spaces where disenchantment resided and this itself was an act of artistry, standing in readiness for any possibility that would serve to transform the toxins of disenchantment into living gold. But it must be understood that the art created from such an encounter also functioned as a living witness to that relationship. The art image is not a simple projection nor graphic illustration; it is a material object that mediates the consciousness of its creator. A pure phenomenon of expression not amenable to conceptual interpretation, it is a form of knowing.[8] Such artistic acts, in the individual picture and in creative collaboration with each other, are often misunderstood by therapists, especially those who use images in naive or over-determined ways in treatment.

"Images allow us to think silently; they are like 'silent word', or as 'word speaking like image',"[9] I said, trying to express a slippery truth I knew to be true. But the troubadour only nodded and softly said, "Yes, the open eye and the open ear have the power to transform the slightest disturbance into a profound experience. Voices are heard on every side. And so the world resounds and begins to 'speak' an increasingly distinct language. Thus dead signs turn into living symbols. Thus the dead comes to life."[10]

"Yes! But that is not all," I said, grasping for words that could capture the exhilaration of the opening—of some threshold I had stepped beyond when I sustained my attentions further, long after the encounter with my collaborators had ended and I was left with their images calling me to contemplate them further. "There are many layers to these images, they opened up spaces in me, captured the stirred-up toxic memories from what I had witnessed, and stilled the spoken words by bringing other knowing and perception into awareness. They lived on in me; they seemed to want more. Beyond verbal thought or mere description, they, too, wanted to be restored—re-'storied' into a new life form. Something new was still emerging from them. It felt as though there was a doorway in them that invited passage from the mundane to the mythic. I tell you, it was as if the *art was dreaming a story* that was coming into form and needing my further witness or presence to make the essence of the phenomenon visible."

"There are stories inside stories, and stories between stories, and finding your way through is as easy and as hard as finding your way home.[11] Stories move in circles," said the troubadour mysteriously, "so they need you to listen in circles. Perhaps they showed you another way to hold the disenchantment—offered you another bowl."

The appearance of the dream-story emerging from the art works we created should have been no surprise given that in the state of disenchantment, as Meade notes, people are starved for a sense of meaning that comes only from grasping the mythological level of living and participating in a ritual for exploring neglected symbols and emotions.[12] Campbell writes, "the wonder is that the characteristic efficacy to touch and inspire deep creative centers dwells in the smallest [personal] tale as the flavor of the ocean is contained in a droplet."[13] Such mythic imagery is not manufactured, ordered, or permanently suppressed but is the spontaneous productions of the psyche. "In the absence of an effective general mythology," Campbell states, "each of us has a private, unrecognized, rudimentary yet secretly potent pantheon of dream."[14]

I was eager to share these art-dream-stories from my collaborators, but now I struggled to explain how they had been created. I had applied the skills of art-based research, first by surrounding myself with the image series from each witness encounter and soaking up the words the art therapist used to describe her experience of disenchantment. I read and re-read them aloud and listened with an open and inquiring mind, finding certain resonance between the words and the silent presence of the images, and taking great care not to impose my own ideas, form, or structure. As a disciplined, phenomenological inquiry, it required me to "listen into" the dream space below the surface of their images and words where a larger mythic-dream story existed. To find it, first I had to clear the perceptual field of the specific content from the everyday descriptions of disenchantment told to me in the encounter. Having faithfully recorded each interview exactly as it was told to me, I went through the transcript of the exact words of the interview and substituted 'x' for all the particulars. For example, when one art therapist, told me,

> "Our health care system is having an effect on everything and is in disarray, and things like art therapy with less solid grounding are going to be in a very tenuous place...."

I simplified yet kept its essential structure by writing:

> "The 'x' is having an effect on everything and is in disarray, and 'x' with less solid grounding is going to be very tenuous."

An art therapist wanting a pay raise became "raising the 'x'"; griping about a nurse who interrupted an art therapy session to dispense medications became "the 'x' came in to dispense the 'x'." Free of the everyday particulars yet faithful to the underlying form and structure, the dynamic phenomenon of the art therapist's disenchantment gradually came into visible form, affirmed by the art images created. With compassionate witness of the art and spoken words of disenchantment, a mutual vulnerability flowed in the space between us that allowed mythic imagery to appear. As these images in turn sought expression, new life came to the imagery of deadening disenchantment in the voice of the dream story. Once I "heard" this mythic voice, I could bring back the particulars of what had been told me, now in story form:

> "The drought is having an effect on everything. Everything has fallen into disarray. The garden beds on less solid ground were going to be very tenuous."

What fascinated me about this method was that once I found the deeper story coming forth, everything–from the myth to the images to the exact order in which elements appeared in the content of the interview–all clicked together and corresponded precisely. Yet it was a delicate process. It was hard to hold the creative tension in this act of witnessing the inner landscape of disenchantment and I was especially vulnerable when my own creative impulses or associations to the imagery were stirred. I could easily imagine "better" endings to the dreamer's stories, especially early in the process when it felt as though I was swimming in the toxins of their despairing words and wanted a quick escape. But any time I tried to impose my own ideas or imagery of what I thought the art was dreaming into story, it would reject them. Nothing would fit and the story would start to fall apart. Then I would have to clear my perceptions again, start over, and listen more carefully until I discovered the right elements and mythic images. Then everything would fall into place. It felt as though I were listening to a voice before it was spoken, making a space for it with alert awareness, without rushing to fill the space with my own version of truth. The accuracy of the mythic story to clarify the art therapist's expressions of disenchantment was verified by the collaborators when they reviewed it against the art and transcript, and reflected on its meaning.

The art therapists had filled the bowl of my witness with words that described stultifying experiences in a work environment that was toxic to their creativity. The witness—whether therapist, art, or dreaming image—holds the creative encounter in such a way that continuously opens to the phenomenon of what is, suspending the desire to form it prematurely. It will come to form on its own provided the witness is clear and present. Therapeutic artistry requires this ethical balancing between formlessness and form, and an ability to freely oscillate between these two poles. As one of my collaborators described it, the method of collaborative witness reminded her of the practice of sitting meditation. The inquiry became for her a spiritual encounter that gave her disenchantment greater meaning and a new lens on which to view her suffering for, as she remarked, "we have only a fraction of knowledge of what God is." Putting aside the ego, and being led by the art and the story renewed her awe in the creative, transformational process that is always there when we seek to find it.

DISENCHANTMENT IN THE TOXIC WORK ENVIRONMENT

In these acts of collaborative witness, I functioned as an *animadora* for the latent life energies bound up in toxic, now-dead matter that seemed to fill the disenchanted inscapes of art therapists whose creativity had been killed, maimed, or dishonored. The *animadora* awakens mythic resonance below the surface of their lives, believing that the myth will live them against their will if they do not give themselves consciously to that greater possibility. In disenchantment, the art therapists I witnessed often relinquished personal power rather than endure its alchemical ability to shatter carefully constructed illusions of safety, belonging, and immunity in their workplaces. When the roiling energies of creativity are blocked, gradually all possibilities congeal into an unmoving, sterile or toxic landscape, accompanied by a desperate longing to be free. The enchantment of their creativity has been laid waste; they labor in a wasteland. As the myths tell it, the wasteland is a place where everyone lives an inauthentic life, doing as other people do, doing as they are told to do, with no courage for their own lives.[15]

In the stories that follow,[16] I witnessed seven art therapists who identified themselves as toiling in disenchantment and wanting to understand more clearly what had killed their creativity in their workplaces. They were all women working in diverse settings: in general psychiatric hospitals, a residential geriatric care facility and a day treatment center, a drug and alcohol abuse agency, in private outpatient practice, and a community art therapy studio. As the poet Whyte would say, "they had entered the field when life was full and the moon was waxing; they were powerful and successful. But then something began to die or fall away into darkness and they began to fear that something was terribly wrong."[17] Obstacles appeared on every side; those in the workplace who had invited their unique gifts as art therapists now rejected or disowned them, robbed them of their spirit, or squeezed them into roles that did not fit. Always moving in and out of clarity, focus and presence, so too, their creative vitality ebbed and waned as they lost their connection to it and longed to get it back again.

"Death stalked them, is it not so?" the troubadour interjected in my thoughts, startling me with his apocalyptic vision for something so ordinary found in many art therapy work environments. Perhaps death is more of a constant companion in art therapy than we realize. It is true that my collaborators all struggled with forms of psychological, physical, organizational, professional, and creative death appearing in their work lives on a daily basis. These signs of death and decay signaled that what is not growing is slowly dying. Yet their stories clearly show that they have forgotten or don't notice that their suffering always offers them a choice: to continue to experience "slow death" in the toxic work environment or to make a deep change[18] that would transform the toxins and make themselves clear, grounded, and creatively alive again. "Perhaps," I mused aloud to the troubadour who listened in silent complicity, "were we to invite death consciously to be our companion in all the various realms of our work, the costs of taking a healthier path would not appear so dear."[19]

Turtle Dreams in the Cavern of Jewels

Cautiously now, I hold open the space of stories, asking my companions to suspend what they think they already know so that they may contemplate the art that stirred in us and listen reflectively to how dispirited images dream themselves back to life. The first art therapist I witnessed sat with me at her kitchen table. For a long time now, Danielle (a pseudonym) had been out of work. At first she welcomed the change of pace, for it gave her precious time for her family. But as weeks turned to months and years, she felt herself slipping into a murky confusion.

The dream space of Danielle's disenchantment took the form of withdrawal to a dark cave where life energy had gotten very still. How had she come to be living inside a cave? she asked. She always had been an efficient caregiver, someone everyone could count on for making things happen and getting the work done. It didn't matter that she was no longer working for someone else, she knew she could always fall into her old competent organized self from all those years of endless work. She was in charge, she told herself, so come on! But probably what happened, she thought, was that at some point she just went on autopilot and did what she had to do. And so she started to lose track of time passing. Living just day-to-day, she started to forget. "I don't know," she sighed, as murky formlessness entered the space between us, "a part of me was missing—but I couldn't remember anymore what it was."

Danielle had never been in this cave she'd withdrawn to so deeply or so long. At times she found it frightening as all the time and spaces of her life were filled in. It got so she could hardly move; everything pressed in on her, wanting her attention. It was as if she were moving more and more slowly, through fog or softly textured vegetation. It started to wrap around her ankles and hold her in one place. "I was being held by my own vegetating," she reflected. She dreamed she was riding the back of a ponderously slow turtle leading her into the cave: she struggled to be still and let this slow movement of her instincts guide her.

When she put out her hand and felt her way along the dull, clammy walls in the darkness, she was surprised to discover that precious jewels were embedded in them. Seven jewels in a dancing circle, like pearls on a string (Figure 11A). As she reached out to touch their iridescence, the jewels started spinning a hypnotic trance. Their pearly orbs held long streamers of color that expanded and pulled her inside their dancing circle (Figure 11B). They were singing and she could hear the music of tambourines. Six of the seven dancers held the tambourine aloft while one, with pregnant belly, stood still (Figure 11C).

They were calling her from deep within the cave, so she had to go further until it seemed there was no way out. It was so easy and comfortable there; it gave her such softness and protection, she started to believe she could stay there always. She settled in and made it her home. All movement, it seemed, had ceased.

From time to time, she thought of searching again for the dancing jewels as the memory of them haunted her. It would pop into her mind when she gazed into the dancing flames of the hearth fire. She could almost see in the flames the jewels of her vision, forming and reforming into different figures that looked like goddesses.[20] They danced around a center, with their spirals and colors coming out from it–they reminded her of an artist she remembered who, when invited, always took Danielle to a different place. "It seems so strange, I can always feel that quickening spirit when I'm dancing or painting, like I'm juggling with fire. But it's funny how a part of me just watches my own procrastination, ignoring the dancing figures and telling me that I can just–I don't know–do it all in my sleep or something."

"Yes, they're trying to lure me out of the cave. Telling me that I don't look as frantic around the eyes anymore, so maybe it's time. But I'm thinking 'Are you nuts? I don't have time to do this' while the rest of me is saying 'Well, maybe . . . you don't know until you try' . . . "[21] She told herself that she could go for a long time without having to answer that call. But then she'd remember what the paints felt like in her hands, thinking, God, how could she *not* do this? "It's too gorgeous! Just look at it sitting there and all those colors. And they're juicy! Juicy and wet,

112 *Re-Enchanting Art Therapy*

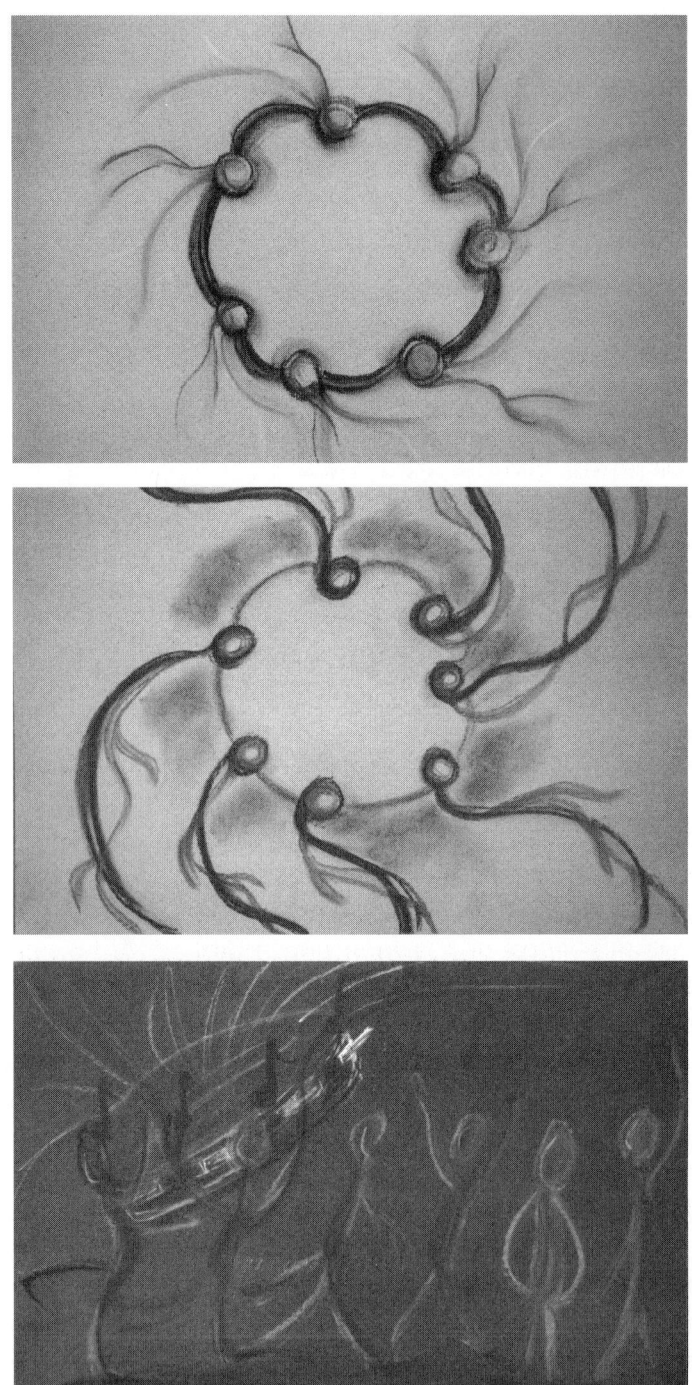

Figure 11A–C. *(A–Top)* Danielle's image of her disenchantment; *(B–Center)* Lynn's witness; *(C–Bottom)* Danielle's response.

and the rest of my life is dry," she remarked. "And then I think, oh, I *have* to do this." But then the idea of sustaining something over several hours, over weeks and weeks— "Oh, I don't know! I don't know if I know how to do that anymore!"

"I mean, there's just so many things that take up my time, it's so overwhelming. I have all these good intentions: I could get this or that done. I am not in a cage; I'm not a prisoner here!" Yet there was some pull to stay right where she was and fight the smothering impulse to get out of the cave. "It's like I *have* to be here. Like it's telling me, 'you are staying here until you accept this! Forget it, you are just going to do this. There is nothing else to be said'." She felt spellbound, stuck between two uncomfortable alternatives. It was a sign to listen more carefully for other voices.[22]

"Where are the jewels?" she wondered one day, as her hand blindly groped along the walls in what was now a familiar gesture. Something had subtly changed in the dream-space and she realized that she was looking for a door or maybe just a window to look out of. She found, instead, a mirror, buried in the dark vegetation (Figure 12A). A rustling sound alerted her to the mirror's voice. It was her mother, saying, "Shame on you, you shouldn't be doing this. Get out, get moving!" She gazed into the mirror and despaired to see that she was living her life inside a tiny, constricting circle. She tried to think about the last time she actually felt enchanted, but there was nothing she could recall until she remembered when her daughter was born, when all was new life and excitement. She peered into dark mirror and saw the dancing figures again, now swimming toward her in a twisting passageway—like sperm navigating the birth canal. "Well, la la la!" she marveled with a knowing smile, "So this is all about procreation, isn't it?"

The image of the sperm dancers awoke her to a new thought: this could change; this could be different. Alert to the possibility of leaving her cave, now she thought of going back into the world differently. She awoke to the near presence of the dancers who encircled her and pushed her toward the open space in the middle of their expanding, pulsating ring. Their voices were calling out to her in lusty reverberations that rippled all through the space, connecting her to them with streaming, colorful energy. And then she realized that there was something in the center of the circle, when before she thought it could only be empty. She could no longer fill up her life spaces because something was there already, waiting for her. It was not empty, nor was she. The cave of her imprisonment actually had been a protected place for the procreation of her spirit.

As she gazed on the soft vegetation that held her in the cave, she saw that something could sprout and different things would happen. Suddenly she thought, "I need to get some life growing here. These are my leaves and sprouts I'm growing." And so the spirit dancers gathered up her leafy vines and carried them into the sun where they could flourish (Figure 12B). Under the sun's powerful rays, three golden figures grew strong and danced in joy (Figure 12C). She was certainly one of them.

* * *

In the space of her disenchantment, Danielle dreamed with the slow steadiness of her turtle soul, who will create time and space to be with herself if she allows it. The cave is the womb of the Universal Mother whose hearthfire is the fire of life.[23] The one who enters the sanctuary evokes within herself the recollection of the life-centering, life-renewing form. Nourished in this way, Danielle pondered the dilemma of whether the cave now held her from living fully, out of harm's way. But when she used its protection to make herself ready to transition back through emptying, then the space drained away her longing, grieving, busyness, or other accumulations in her life that had filled it. Emptiness is the bridge between the known and the unknown, doing and being, inertia and change, isolation and community.[24] However frightening it is to do so, she saw herself starting the journey back from disenchantment, despite uncertainty, and believing that what is needed will appear. She was giving up her secure identity of a planner in favor of having visions, which pulled her once again into renewal, into the full light of the sun.[25]

With the rewards of cognitive, rational, and goal-oriented work comes the danger of losing vitality from sheer discipline. Danielle's discomfort was caused, in part, by the incongruity she felt between her preferred self-image of an efficient planner and her actual behaviors and unexpressed desires. Like many art therapists, Danielle's years of professional experience built in her a set of proficient skills that gave her "conditional confidence," a form of acting well as long as the situation did not violate her assumptions about it.[26] As she looked into the mirror of herself and confronted her apathy, Danielle began to see the need to reinvent her identity. Painful though it is, the stilling of her life's relentless movement forward allowed an incubation of her cre-

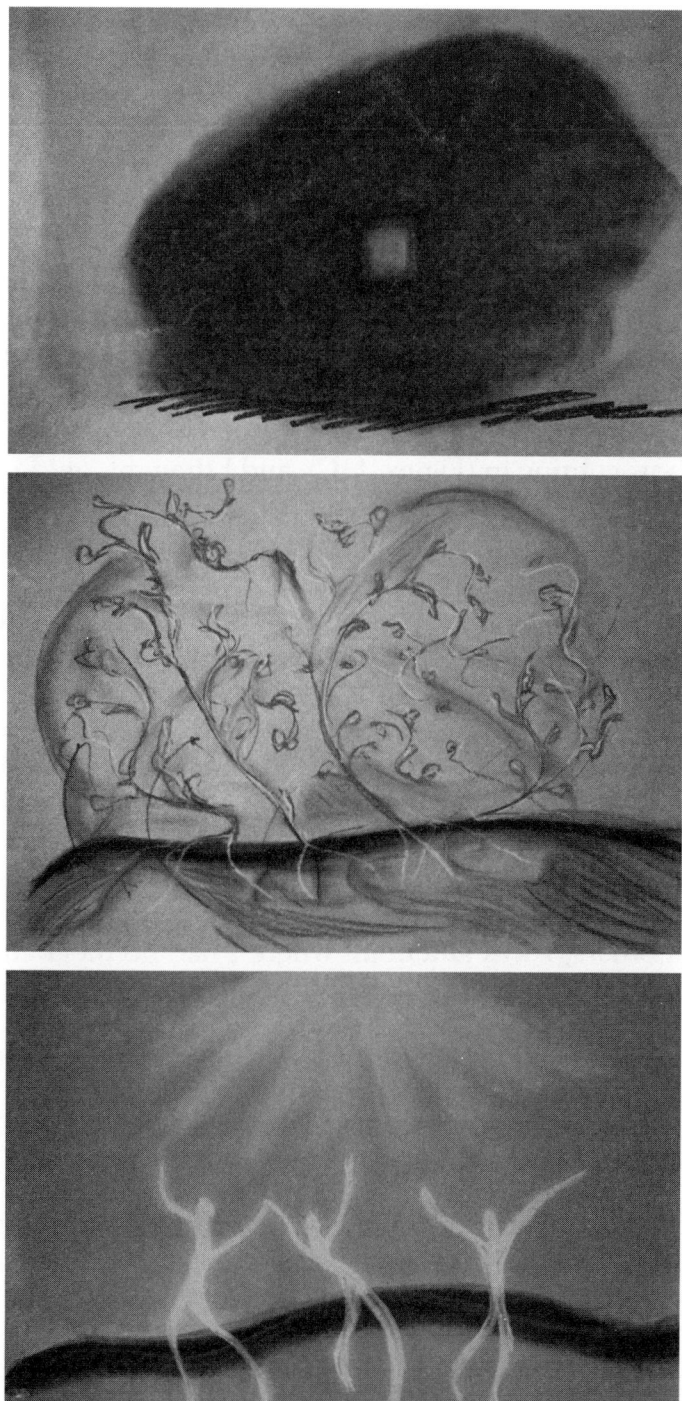

Figure 12A–C. *(A–Top)* Lynn's image of Danielle's disenchantment; *(B–Center)* Danielle's witness; *(C–Bottom)* Lynn's response.

ative vitality, an active awakening that resulted in "unconditional confidence": she was capable of "getting lost with confidence," discarding inaccurate assumptions and ineffective strategies in the midst of ongoing reflection.[27]

The Journey to the Other Place

"I can't remember where I was when I had the dream," Sally began. "It was this little cabin out in the woods, in a kind of wonderful, meadowy country. A hermit lived there and was very happy. The doors were all open and the birds were coming in and the squirrels—and there was a little deer at the window. Little pots of plants were on the windowsill, with a rainbow coming in (Figure 13C), and I thought, oh! I really want to live like that! Well ok, so maybe if the animals weren't there I wouldn't miss them that much!" she laughed. "But the picture stuck in my mind, and came back to me every now and then."

Sally (a pseudonym) and I had found a quiet corner in the Alzheimer's unit where she worked. It was evening and most of her patients had gone to bed except for one tiny woman who wandered in and out of the room where we were meeting. The space between us was as soft and gentle as the hushed noises we heard from time to time coming from the unit. Sally was thinking of her own life rhythms when she remembered the storybook picture of the hermit's cottage. "I knew that my self-imposed isolation, that I had created in order to survive, was essential for me at the time. As much as I had always enjoyed the company of others, I was at a point where I had no inclination or any interest at all. I wasn't unhappy about that. But when I look back, I think I was in some kind of basic shock that I had survived! Yet the wisdom I was getting in touch with was empowering me, giving me a connection with my inner strength so I could go."

"And now, here I am" she quietly mused as she looked out on the Alzheimer's unit, and offered a poem that captured the space where enchantment and disenchantment ebbed and flowed for her:

"At the other end of the spectrum,
The place farthest out where violet turns to black.
The wonder of it is the fact that I am still intact!"

"I love this place; I am so very happy, even though to get here I had to go through a very traumatic, painful time. I needed to go away before; there were people I didn't want to be around and all this noise going on all the time." Sally was telling me about her decision to leave a long-term position at another facility because of her difficulty with staff, but below the surface of her words, the dream voice echoed her patients' confused reality drifting in and out of Sally's consciousness. "I'd hear all this cross-talk going on, very aggressive, very competitive about turf," she went on, "and excuse me, but we had to keep the noise down! They'd just look at me and get louder! I walked over to one who looked like just a thug of a gal. When I put my hand on her arm to say something, she jumped back and I thought, she's going to hit me!"

"Anyway, it was all very, very emotional. I guess when I am really tired or something, the memory of that affects me more," Sally said. "But it is so rewarding when it all clicks, and that is such a relief. And laughter and a wonderful camaraderie. I try to remember those things in detail for the days when things aren't clicking! All I need are just a couple of little snippets of clarity and that can feed me for days! And then having that to share with others who really appreciate those tiny moments of contact. That keeps me going. There are a few people in this world who appreciate me for the gifts I have, but also who know the ruggedness of the journey. They are witnesses to that."

The dream voice now moved along painful edges in her awareness. "I think, early on, instinctively I knew what I needed; what was missing. I would get that wiggly feeling that I had thought was only my negativity. I'd get a little fragment of clarity in that feeling, like the memory of my dad before he passed away." The open bowl of the space between us filled with emotion as Sally said, "I told him how much I always loved being his daughter. With just the few words we had left, he said, 'That's mighty nice, dearie!' There was an old song he had taught me—I think we were the only two people in the world who knew it, as far as I know—and I asked, 'Will you sing it with me, Dad?' And he said sure, and so we sang it. That was wonderful and gave me assurance, but I didn't have faith for a long time. I had been told all my life that my journey would be terrible to undertake. Really needed fire in your belly to do it, they said. It was true, I had to learn to live with fear and pain. I just decided that that was the way it was going to be and keep going along on whatever I could. Otherwise," she said, looking out on the Alzheimer's unit, "I was agitated all the time, wondering if I could keep this act together."

"It took years to get here. I remember the hardest part felt like I was going down a long stairway into darkness (Figure 13A), like I was left with only fragments to make sense of. I didn't want that feeling. I just wanted to put it aside. Then I thought no, but I don't want to do that. I didn't want things to progress like that, but it seemed like where it wanted me to go. I wanted to complete the—the way this vision held me (Figure 13B). Actually, the way I wanted to be held. To take that knowledge it gave me to the next place on the journey (Figure 13C). There was something beyond where I was that I needed to be aware. That's what my guides and mentors always said, that if you haven't experienced that 'otherness' you must journey to discover it. And that is when you become aware that there are these larger forces out there that you have to respond to—with all your antennas up." Whose world was Sally's images dreaming into story? I wondered, listening to her while the tiny woman, one of her patients, flitted in and out of the room again. Sally's long journey in the dark night seemed to be shared by the dying elders whose lives lived on in Sally, just as she lived on in them.

"At the very bottom," she continued, referring to the image of the stairway[28] or maybe of the journey itself, "there was all the mind-boggling stuff that just makes me crazy! I saw that no matter what I planned something else was always going to pop up. For the most part, the rules and regulations I faced all my life had gone. And even when I had been still aware, I didn't give a damn! So it was a lovely place to be. I just had to get beyond the thing about—Oh yes, it's a shame that it can get so messy, not knowing what to do, and to not sound like a complete ninny all the time so people will still talk to you. But there's this wonderful presence that somehow comes through when you don't have those ordinary skills of contact and communication left to work with. I just had to let it go."

Sally now said, "I would never consider it now, but for a long time I thought about dying. I could never get away from that thought because life was so painful. I didn't know how to go on. I lost my rhythm there for a while. I thought I needed to get it back because I knew mine was wacko. I felt like I needed an instruction manual—I needed it in a lot of areas. You'd think I was Kon-Tiki crossing the Pacific, for god's sake!" she laughed. "There were so many directions and I knew I'd never learn them all. I remember others saying to me, though: 'Sally, there's another way that you can take'."

A Bowl of Tears 119

Figure 13A–C. *(A–Top)* Sally's image of her disenchantment; *(B–Center)* Lynn's witness; *(C–Bottom)* Sally's response.

In her reverie, I heard the dream voice below the surface of Sally's words and images describe the transformation from hope to despair and to reawakened life: "I could hold that image just perfectly in my mind, and it gave me a feeling of perfect, enchanted bliss. A space of clear blue (Figure 14B). But then I saw the shadow coming in, close by (Figure 14C). For some reason, I didn't want it there, but I saw how it had been missing before and needed to be here now. I thought I glimpsed my mother there and even though she still looked very beautiful, I realized how wounded she was. I wanted to stay with her, but it was so very difficult to do because she was still so hard. At the same time, I loved her, and oh, my heart ached for her!"

The vision of Sally's mother appeared like an elder agent in what Sally called her "crossing over to the other place," to a new place of consciousness. "I found myself going over and hugging her good bye. I didn't even realize I was doing that–god, after all we'd been through! But it felt like a natural shift and I crossed over. I was coming into life. That's true. That's the way it felt. Actually, to life."

"It's beautiful inside here," Sally now reflected on her work as an art therapist. "Even those very firm boundaries I had to cross are beautiful (Figure 14A). There's something gorgeous going on, and of course, it is going on outside, too. I *know* that I am a part of something gorgeous. I know I am, even though I have restrictions on my life–some people, if they knew how restricted I was, they'd think how sad, how very, very sad. But you know, I am aware of alot of beauty in this place, so I don't expect it. Like these big, uplifted arms and I am inside those arms in the embrace of their love. It is an image just hanging in the corner of my mind. Just sitting there beside me. Yes, I am thankful for being a part of this wonderful thing!"

* * *

Sally's is a story of an empathic traveler and visionary artist therapist whose practice is nurtured by a loving, imaginal inscape she shares with the patients she affectionately calls the "gang that is farthest out there"–people in the end stages of Alzheimer's disease. As she revealed the inner landscape of her disenchantment to me, I was never certain whether Sally was speaking from her patient's or her own reality. But gradually I came to understand that in the fluid boundaries and powerful, emotional intimacy they shared, Sally's consciousness functioned as an invisible holding environment for her fragile patients, exploring

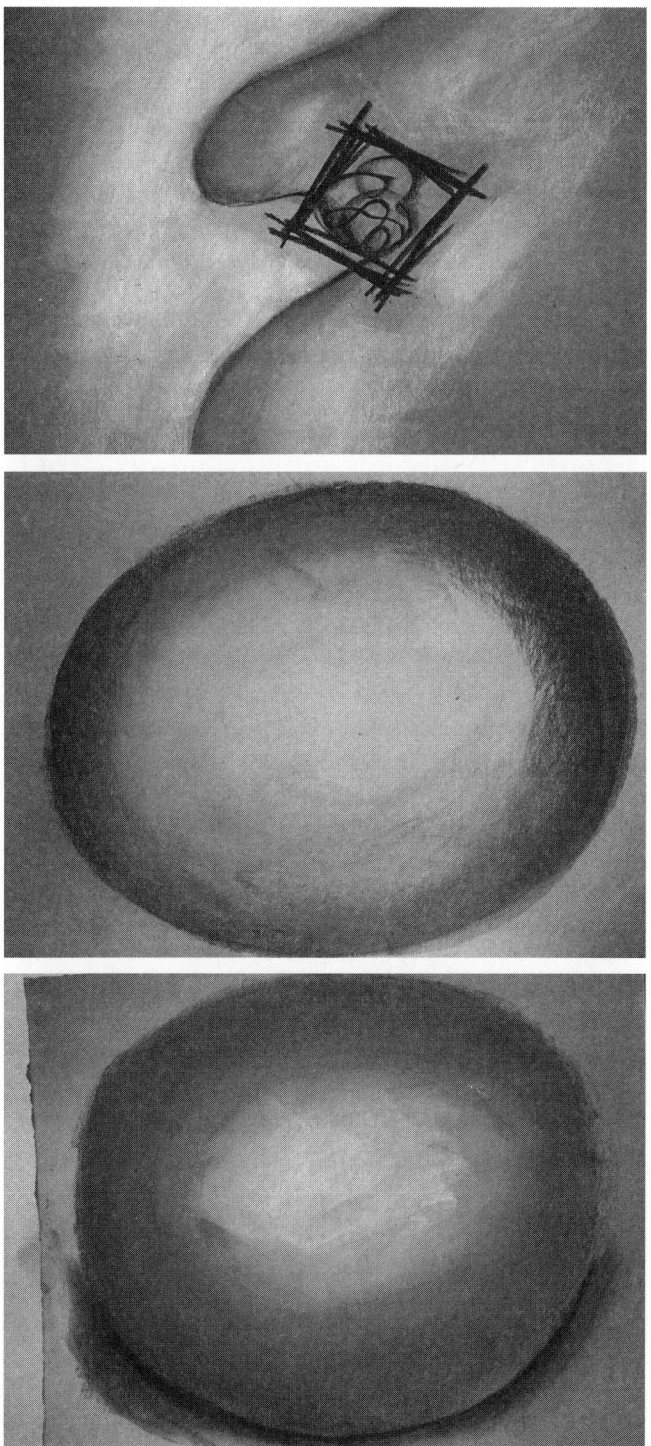

Figure 14A–C. *(A–Top)* Lynn's image of Sally's disenchantment; *(B–Center)* Sally's witness; *(C–Bottom)* Lynn's response.

and enlarging her own inner world as it resonated with theirs.[29] A flow of nonverbal, therapeutic process came from the interplay of these colliding and coalescing dream-states of the self and other and this itself was an act of Sally's therapeutic artistry. While she felt uncomfortable describing herself as an artist, her aesthetically attuned empathy for her clients was evidently a vital source of her own creativity and joy.

Sally's clients of the ordinary life sphere blended seamlessly with the mythic realm of the "strange companions" of the soul who always appear on the hero's journey of initiation and transcendence. In many folk stories, their purpose is to find beauty and release the fullness of life again when the creative sicknesses has befallen the youthful hero. "In that sense, they are the 'elders' at work. They are the knowledge of what underlies our . . . symptoms and the knowledge of how to move toward a cure."[30] In the blending of art and life, in her sensibilities toward her environment and her clients that she experienced in a state of flow, Sally knew that it required maximal openness to hold such a connection with her Alzheimer's patients. In the continual process of letting go of life's burdens, they taught her to trust the cyclical nature of life's generativity.

To hold them while simultaneously appreciating her own needs, Sally needed to relinquish separateness and release herself into the swirling currents of interaction, intense emotion, and meaning.[31] An overarching confidence in a creative outcome is what sustains the art therapist in such potentially toxic, psychological turbulence. When it faltered, Sally would begin to question her own sanity, wondering aloud if she were succumbing to her patients' disease, as her confusion about events or details reflected the other's inner clouding or fragmentation of experience. Well aware of the toxins that could affect her practice, Sally told me how she carefully prepared herself each morning through contemplative prayer, so that her entire working day would unfold from her center. Like Danielle's story, Sally also knew the value of the archetypal cave or times when she needed to isolate herself from others in order to regain her own rhythms.

She was moved to tears several times when later she read the dream story and reflected on its meaning. "There are things in this story I had not quite been able to articulate but knew I that I had lived through and now they were not only witnessed by another but imaged and written about. It documented and further grounded me and my life, my journey, and the ability of images to facilitate this process . . . I think this very uncomfortable split, wiggly feeling comes up in me whenever I experience feeling split, unfocused, fragmented, and overwhelmed. But I have made from it a composition I can live with, taking the green growing things in a beautiful container offset by the purple nervous, wiggly lines. They have been converted into rising arcs of energy that offer balance to the whole (Figure 13C). There is trouble for sure if I lose touch with 'the people who know the other place'–whether they be art therapists or other wonderful souls out there in the world. These are the people with whom you can share those magical, therapeutic moments and snippets of clarity."

The Gardener

When Leah (a pseudonym) read the dream story (below) that was embodied in her spoken words of the collaborative witness and the art we had created, she agreed that it illuminated the essence of her disenchantment, which she said was rooted in her impatience with and intolerance of self-serving health care systems that functioned like walled cities, keeping art therapists and other creative treatment out. Having worked for some time in general psychiatric settings run by managed care systems, she was now striking out on her own and attempting to build a private practice. She saw herself in a painful waiting period, as her practice was not yet viable despite careful preparation. Stepping into the landscape of her disenchantment, the dream voice is of Leah the gardener and me, her companion.

In her story we are encamped on a spit of land surrounded by fog. The garden was not growing. As Leah surveyed the bleak landscape, she reflected on her dilemma, trying to figure out what she had not seen. What had she been blinded by; what was she tackling now?[32] As a gardener, she was well enough versed and had the skills. She should have a good handle on what the plants needed to thrive. But it was also about the whole garden she had been entrusted with. She had to ask herself, "How can I make each part fit into the whole picture? Because when I think I have a fit, then the whole puzzle breaks apart. That's the trouble, when the puzzle breaks apart."

The fog was coming in and that made the situation worse. From our vantage point, we couldn't make anything out—it all looked very chaotic and there was little clarity. It was so foggy we could hardly see the tree line or the water we knew was there on the horizon. The waves of fog were rolling into shore, covering us in a faded, damp gloom. The ground where we stood felt mushy. We could see strewn piles of dead, fallen trees and underbrush lying all around, making it difficult to move to higher ground as there was no clear path (Figure 15A). The dampness seeped into our bones and chilled us, like the sadness of a winter's garden. I heard resignation in her voice as she sighed, "I can't make something beautiful, if I don't think it really is. When a garden doesn't grow," she said, "people have to leave. That's what always happens. Soon they'll forget that it had been their place of birth. The garden would be only a myth, dreamed up by someone or another who was no longer in touch with reality."

Leah's was a small tribe of people living in the rocky uplands between the city and the wilderness where gardens could be cultivated in only an extremely narrow place. Everyone thought that as long as they stayed there, it would be fine. But the drought was having an effect and everything was in disarray. The gardens on more solid ground were failing, which meant those on less solid ground were even more tenuous. Leah's gardens had always grown lush and beautiful, before. Even when she had to till some really hard ground.

She remembered how she had gone to the city for help, two or three times, but it was a futile effort. She kept asking herself even then what it was that she was missing, what she was not doing correctly. She sent them reports of the worsening drought, but they did not give her the time or space for her petition. They told her she'd hear from them about getting more water, but she never heard anything.

Neither of us could make out exactly where we were or where the path was. It was all so disorienting and she didn't like this waiting for the weather to clear. No, she didn't like to wait. She'd say "Ok, now let's just see for myself, what can I do? With all my tools, I knew I could make the garden grow," she said. Others had approached her and asked for help. But they didn't have the proper training, she told me, so they couldn't recognize her unique gifts. They had this idea that the gardens would grow better if they were organized into a rigid system with rows or trenches. She feared these ideas would begin to perpetuate and shook her head in disgust. There is something more there, she told me emphatically, if only we are willing to look at it.

The light was slowly changing as Leah spoke. We could make out a few more details in the landscape now, and see the sky and water on the horizon slowly coming into view. The soft ground where we sat was a sandy beach beside a broad river and we could just barely make out a path to higher ground where a single tree stood (Figure 15B). Before the fog lifted, the lone, sentinel tree had looked ghostly, perhaps dead.

Leah gazed at the tree, saying that she had always been an orphan. She had always been viewed the way an artist was—put off to the side. That was one of the reasons why she had given up before, because she didn't have the energy for it and the work spread her too thin. "The whole problem was just a matter of everyone trying to fit in," she explained. "Those in the city saw my people as not part of their society—not productive members anyway. They only wanted to give us enough space and water to maintain us where we were. It's like when you have plants in your garden that are failing to thrive—you have to make some effort to sort them out from those plants that just need a little intensive care so they can get back to being healthy and productive. Getting them back to being what they want to be."

When the city rationed its water, with the cost and having to pay the bills and all, no one could afford what they were charging. Water was getting very scarce. She recalled how very discouraged she was at this point. "I hit that wall many, many times," she said, remembering the massive wall that protected the city, and the many other walls she faced in her dilemma. "I thought, 'there's no way to get to the other side where the water is unless I can get through it'. Then I saw a tiny crack, which gave me an opening (Figure 16A). I thought I might as well figure out a way to move that space out. I thought I might find the right plant that would grow beside the wall and then tend it so it could get into that little space, which was going to be very difficult. The wall was pretty high."

After several months, she thought that maybe she could make out something different going on. Most of the wall was just the same, but she was amazed to see a tiny green vine embedded in the mortar (Figure 16B). It seemed incredible that it was still living. "I was certain that someone from the city was going to come by and yank it out. After all, how would they know whether it was beneficial or a parasite? And then we'd be back where we started. We were left dangling, just like that vine, trying to get a foothold in the cracks of the wall. We just had to hang on to what we had and not lose hope!"

"And now here I am," Leah said absently. "I had to leave because I needed the distance. I needed my energy so I could tackle what I was

Figure 15A–C. *(A–Top)* Leah's image of her disenchantment; *(B–Center)* Lynn's witness; *(C–Bottom)* Lynn's response.

A Bowl of Tears

Figure 16A–C. *(A–Top)* Lynn's image of Leah's disenchantment; *(B–Center)* Leah's witness; *(C–Bottom)* Lynn's response.

going to do next. But this waiting . . . and to assess now, ok, what am I missing?"

"But what happened to the vine?" I interrupted her. "Did someone come and yank it out?"

"It's funny," she replied, "but there always is this distrust of something new and different, and not wanting to take the effort to explore it. Those people in the city were no different. They were wearing blinders and didn't see what the vine was doing to their wall. The wall was strong, but that vine was getting pretty sizable, and it had a solid base. It had made an opening, like a door that I could just barely see through. Somehow that made it even worse because I still couldn't get to what was there! What I saw were beautiful, flowering gardens—all the gardens inside of the city were thriving!" she said with pain and disgust.

"Because of the drought, I understood, but it still just didn't make sense. Those gardens in the city got much, much more water than ours. It was terrible! So little water, after all we'd done to survive? The water level had to be raised. But they were very firm in saying they could not give more water to anyone beyond the wall. Not unless we lived in the city, but that was not realistic. They were so blind to what was happening in the world. They could have made sure that all the gardens were watered at the same level, ours the same as everyone else's."

"How would they do that?" I asked.

"Well, they could have seen what was happening to us, and start to act! They were so entrenched they couldn't see what they were doing to people outside the walls. I heard all this blame and fault, saying that our gardens were failing because we weren't working hard enough. This really bothered me—their water was only for people whose gardens could survive—in the city—since no one else 'could make it in the world out there' and the water would be wasted. The blame got laid at the hands of those of us who were trying their best to get more water from the system that was closing its doors to us."

She sighed, "I am only one small person and you know, I have an interest and a passion. But, well, I'm getting too old. And right now I am in this kind of waiting place. And I think, should I go somewhere else? I don't really think it's useful to pursue something else." She gazed out over the water to see the tiny whitecaps on the waves as the wind picked up and shifted around us. She began to notice the path before us and all our footprints on the beach, like tiny steps to clarity. There was a little more order in the brightening landscape and that stirred her hope (Figure 15C). The lone tree we had seen earlier was now in bud and our feelings of winter had slowly, almost imperceptibly, turned to the renewed hopes of spring.

Almost as an afterthought, now she told me that in the first spring after the terrible drought, the vine she had planted by the city wall flowered into beautiful bougainvillea. It grew so much that summer that it swept over and tumbled to the other side of the forbidding wall, which had been its chief support. It grew over an archway in the stonework and inspired the people to add a wrought iron gate to the portal it graced (Figure 16C).

"No, I can't just sit on the side; I am not ready for the rocking chair. I have seen the magic. I know it works. It has nothing to do with me; it has to do with the work. My call is very persistent. So I must answer it by trying to find this other community of people who have this vision for where we need to be. And how we are going to heal." As the sunlight danced over the waves in the distance, Leah's voiced trailed off, lost again in reverie. "It's all coming at you and you don't have the energy to be active and to respond," she mused. "You have to make an effort to pick out the colors you want and put them in the garden." I thought about her vine, how gradually it grew into something beautiful. She had said something about how, if she likes a thing–if it belongs– she keeps it in the garden. But when it first starts growing you can't tell what it is going to be. "The thing is," she said at last as we prepared to move our camp, "I don't have much more time and I'll never know where I am going to be."

* * *

Leah's story takes place in a bleak landscape, of drought and the death of growing things in the garden. Such a story makes clear that the dream voice is concerned with her soul's vitality, for the sense of loss is a vital aspect of the soul's connection to life.[33] The garden in the center of the city reaches back to the Garden of Eden where life flows from the center. Within Leah, there is a parched or dying garden seeking nourishment by the waters of the soul that flow at the center of her life. Creative vitality is stuck and draining away from this center. I believe this is not Leah's story alone, that it may be representative of many toxic environments where people labor. But I remained unsettled by her reveries that would peak in tiny bursts of energy only to turn back always to the terrible state of the garden. Or to the estate lords who withheld and defined which gardens would survive instead of "the plebes who do the work of tending them" even as I asked her to tell me more about the growing vine she had planted or to notice the broad river she was sitting beside. The power of that tender plant pressed through rigid wall, was creating the very opening she had sought for so long, and held potent transformative potential. She saw its effect at the same time that she turned away from it, not seeing or embracing it. In the opening she had placed a delicate, wrought iron portal, which she said "was very strong but you can see through it, so it is not so hard to deal with. Yet, seeing through it almost makes the disenchantment harder, because you still can't get to what you can see is there."

Leah seeks escape from a narrow place, and in her story is a metaphor for the narrow places all of us move through in our lives. Of this spiritual journey, one therapist writes, "We come into this world through a narrow place, squeezed, shaken, and battered but we get through. For the next eighty or so years, we repeatedly come to places that seem too narrow, but we keep squeezing through. It is only by negotiating our way through the narrow places that we liberate ourselves from the constraints of our tunnel vision. . . . What keeps us stuck in the narrow places? Fear, pure and simple. We'd rather accept the certainty of the known than dare to imagine what might be on the outside. Fear keeps us from making the journey."[34] As Leah concluded, "The question of where I'll be continues. Getting connected to those gardens where what I have to offer is encouraged and supported is the tricky, difficult, and sometimes disenchanting part."

The Waters of St. Elm's

If Beth's (a pseudonym) art imagery had a story to dream into her awareness, it would surely begin with "Once upon a time. . . . The springs were flowing." "We were full to the rafters with people almost all the time," she remembered happily. "And I loved it! I was working very hard. I got tired of course, but it was a different kind of tired than I experienced later." Her gifts were appreciated by the whole community that was supported by the healing waters.

Healing waters: The mythic element of Beth's disenchantment perfectly constellated her fourteen years at St. Elm's (a pseudonym) as an art therapist working in the hospital's inpatient psychiatric unit, before and during the health care crisis that shifted the very foundation of her work and ushered in tighter fiscal management. Below the surface of her words and amplified in the images we created, it seemed an ancient story coming into form: where guardians of the healing waters lived in community and served the weak and helpless until the evils of the "plague" arrived.

"Yes, things were really booming" she recalled, but then her work was cut to half. "That's when it began. My superior, who was very powerful in the community, came into my rooms one day to observe what I was doing and it obviously had an impact on him." She believed he sensed the power of her healing arts that day and mistrusted it. Was actually afraid of it, as he saw how much it stirred the people. "Maybe I put myself in that place," she considered. "Because I realize that I was probably too challenging—I was constantly getting into situations and being blamed for any trouble.[35] One day, he literally attacked me—in the courtyard with everybody hearing him—just screaming at the top of his lungs. It wasn't just me he was doing this to. I happened to be the target that day. But it was then that I realized it was no longer safe for me to be there."

She paused and quietly said, "Yes, I am just realizing more and more how downtrodden I became after that. How hopeless it all began to feel. And then I made a mistake, which didn't seem like a mistake at the time." The water level of the springs was down by half by this time, rendering their powers ineffectual. "And we knew it! We just couldn't make any bones about it anymore, we were in trouble."

With growing sadness and fear for what was happening to the community's vital source, everyone grew very angry. Their unspoken anger fueled the fevers as the healing waters slowly disappeared into the emptying gorge of chaos. "We weren't very good at delegating and there was nothing to back us up when the springs started to fail," she explained. "I arrived at my post one day and discovered that someone new was taking over. I thought, now what is going on here? And, you know—not that I didn't—I mean, she was excellent. But, I was really angry and hurt, and it felt like they had done something behind my back. I felt they thought that I couldn't do my job well enough anymore, even though nobody was admitting there was anything wrong. There were a lot of things going on that I didn't know about or didn't understand." She paused and said, "Then I became—then I *chose*—to give up my position. As a reaction. Totally. And it was a mistake.

Because then they really treated me like a nobody. Just someone to plug holes."

She was still part of a community of healers but she no longer had any status. It wasn't too bad at first and she justified it to herself as giving her time to focus on other things. But their perception of her never shifted; she was never seen as good enough. "And, when the fevers came...." Her voiced trailed off and she sighed. "I was constantly begging, just literally begging them to give me some of the waters. And they just wouldn't. I mean, partly they were protecting their own turf–taking whatever was still trickling in. And the novices–they didn't even have the knowledge. And here I was just not used, not at all."

As more and more people from the countryside arrived with fever raging, it fell to her to take the most infirm. People came because of the healing springs. When they found out the waters were gone, "well, you know how they felt about that," she admitted, "it was too late. They were dead. They were pretty much burned up by then."

"So they gave you dead people?" I asked her, astonished. "Yes," she replied, "they gave me dead people is what they did!" She laughed, ruefully adding, "and expected me to work miracles with them."

"And when you couldn't?" I asked. She replied, "They had reasons to blame me. Yes." She paused again. "Yes. Occasionally when they got really angry at what was going on, then they wanted me to do more with them. Because they couldn't handle it any more. Didn't know where to go with it. But nobody ever told me that I shouldn't keep trying. We all just got so burned out by then, and didn't want to do it any more."

"You see, I got tired. I just got tired. And my work got a lot harder to do. I mean you could sit with people for hours, you know, but they couldn't get any better without the waters. Much. But there was nothing left, no supplies. Nothing whatsoever." She paused to consider this. She said, "But that's kind of a cop out, because we could have found supplies. Maybe it was just our own tiredness. And disillusionment. And anger. I mean, we didn't voice the anger much–we never really voiced it at all. But we were angry, I'm sure. Angry and grieving. There was a constant grieving process going on almost since the day I got there that never went away."

"We were losing a way of life that had sustained many for a long, long time. There was really nobody left anymore that I was connected to. The tiredness came from being alone. That was exactly what it was.

From the beginning of the change, I was never connected any more. I was working alone." There was a pause as she pondered that. "And that replicated my feeling that I had always been alone. So. Yeah, that was it. There was no—no feeling of connection anymore." I felt her heavy sadness, and waited a long interval for her to tell me what happened next.

She said it was hard to put a finger on when she felt a change, but she remembers going for a walk one night. In the dream space, I glimpsed her moving along the top of the wall of her community enclosure. She told me she couldn't stand being inside any longer and there was no one left she could talk to. "I couldn't even articulate about the shame I felt at that point. I was never very good at talking—that's not my strong suit—especially when I was hurt or angry. I realized that I had lost trust," she reflected. "I was looking to scapegoat others for the whole climate at that point. I felt alone, getting smaller and smaller, until there wasn't hardly anything left of me" (Figure 17A).

Then, in her mind's eye, she saw a beautiful vision. It was an all-seeing eye offering her the possibility of expansiveness (Figure 17B), like a blue sky or an underground river deep below her. "I saw that I wanted there to be grounding under me, you know, like a bridge? First I was just going to surrender to that, but then I thought no, that empty gorge is still there (Figure 17C). It is not going to go away. It's not that simple! I told myself, 'You are not going to get rid of that so simply.' But the emptiness was quite overpowering—my small self was losing power; it was all going away." Once again, she fell silent and I waited.

"The vision held me, even though my life was very hard. There was a possibility in my mind that hadn't been there before." In the dream space, she looked down from the wall and saw a bright, growing vine embedded in it, toward the bottom (Figure 18A). From where she stood, it looked like a red arrow. It occurred to her that perhaps it shouldn't be there (Figure 18B). She thought to herself: Do you want to stay in, do you want out? Do you want to fly out of here? What do you want to do? "I sensed that I did want to remain, but in a different way," she said. "My sadness was becoming transformed; I was looking at it directly at it now, instead of down at it or from a distance. I was already beginning to see my disillusionment was turning into gratitude for what I did have (Figure 18C)."

One night, they had a gathering with the remaining survivors. She said it was affirming to discover that everyone was feeling the same

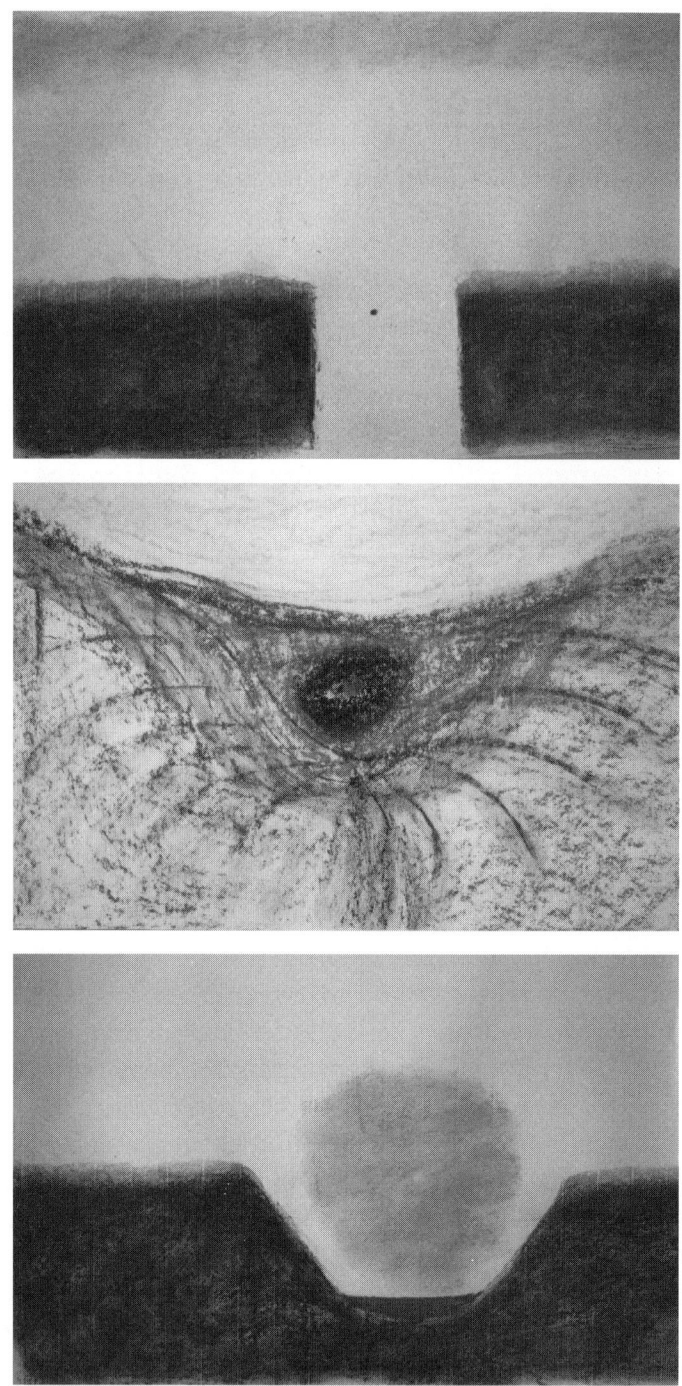

Figure 17A–C. *(A–Top)* Lynn's image of Beth's disenchantment; *(B–Center)* Leah's witness; *(C–Bottom)* Lynn's response.

A Bowl of Tears

Figure 18A–C. *(A–Top left)* Beth's image of her disenchantment; *(B–Top right)* Lynn's witness; *(C–Bottom)* Beth's response.

thing. Everyone was feeling that same loss. "My small self was no different from everyone else's and that changed my perspective. Although it is going to take a while. It will probably take a year or more to assimilate what happened. There is a part of me that wants to stay still and assimilate into the community that is left. And there's another part that says, 'You gotta get moving.' What they will give me to live on is not that much, if I leave. I have to get out there but I am just having a hard time. Yes, I am having a hard time. But then, considering everything that happened, it makes sense, " she said quietly. "It just makes sense."

She turned then and eyed me closely before taking my leave. "I think about those who will come to the waters again some day. I have had a question about that for a long time," she confessed. "Will they will be told what happened here? I have a sense that they will, but if anyone ever comes to me to ask, I will be very, very real with what went on here. Because they couldn't know. They couldn't. But it is important to tell them."

***

The place described in Beth's story is strikingly similar to a description I found in the words of a woman working at a rape crisis center, who wrote "I was struck by how my spirits collapsed the instant I walked in.... At first I thought that the deadening atmosphere was the residue of the thousand acts of violation that had been recounted between those walls. But soon I saw that it was not the traumas themselves that were sucking oxygen out the rooms, but the way in which we pursued the fight against them.... The [depressing atmosphere] was an aesthetic, an integral part of the culture ... staffed by a core collective with its own ingrained ways of doing things: the insufficiency, the misery were almost beloved, for they underscored how much we had suffered, how pitiful were our resources in the face of mighty opposition, and how good we were to [work there] in such conditions."[36]

When Beth reflected on her dream story, she clearly saw how she makes herself a victim and how that perspective keeps souring her life experiences. She would agree that as person who was worn out from the oppressive, toxic work environment, she looked to her victimhood as a source of identity and mastery.[37] She recalled being warned by a fellow art therapist "carrying a heavy sadness and a burden" not to let it happen to her, to make herself a target, a victim. I asked her whether part of that heavy burden might be the toxins she carried for the sake of her clients. "Oh yes, definitely!" she said. "I could feel it on a bodily level, all the time. My whole body picked up stuff from the clients, from the agency. I would take home their images in my mind and couldn't sleep." Seen in the context of her story, I could understand how she held these terrible burdens as an unselfish but toxic act of service and self-sacrifice, making herself vulnerable to her soul's sickness and toxic to others.

She now reflected that the best thing that ever happened was losing that job and having to leave. "Trauma helps kick you out of the unhealthy place. . . . I was so hurt when I lost the only job I ever really, fully loved. I had that job for one-third the time I was there, and then spent the next nine or ten years longing for it, grieving and wanting it back." Like her marriage, she said, it was good at first and then for a long, long time it was bad, yet she stayed under its spell. In her new job, she is confronted rather than enabled by all the stuff she still carries, she said. I asked her what motivates her differently, where is transformation? She said, "It was so painful living in the old story and my spirit needs me to grow past the illusions I had."

The Elixir of Life

Kari's words tumbled out and cascaded over me in a torrent as I struggled to become present to her and the essence of her disenchantment. Unlike Beth, who had worked for many years in one place before managed care arrived on the scene, Kari (a pseudonym) had moved in and out of many art therapy jobs in the past several years. She showed me a drawing she had begun. Like a premonition that opened the space for dreaming, it showed someone's hand punching through a steel door, trying to reach down to touch her. The hand poured water into her own reaching hand, but it just flowed off and she couldn't hold or absorb it. Deep inside, listening to her calling had always given her the desire to keep going. But the steel door slammed shut.

Stepping into the mythic landscape that was her disenchantment, I gathered that she was being held captive and had fallen into "bad company."[38] It is always hard to know what the right place is when a person has never known a right place to begin with. But the wrong places always are those that cause one to feel outcast all over again. The drain of vitality causes more damage as, with each foray into another, hoped-for "right place," new wounding occurs. I could see why Kari had attracted bad company: in the dream space, she appeared as an elfin woman who glowed a beautiful, translucent yellow, her deep blue eyes bright and clear as she spoke. Now her dream voice said, "I glimpsed them through a narrow opening and heard them talking enthusiastically about my future affiliation with them. It didn't sound too good. They were arguing, saying something about wanting 'thirty percent off the top', and 'you gotta find your own, this one is ours!'"

She seemed to be imprisoned in a den, crowded with a ragtag band of ruffians of all sorts, with whom their leader was trying to establish a new alliance. "He seemed pretty hip on their offer," she said, "claiming that he understood my value and how useful I could be, but I guess the others were worried about how I would fit into their plans. I didn't get a good feeling about it. He was real quick to decide, too, even though he didn't really know about me or my kind." A couple of days later she escaped, when everyone was late returning to the den. She made it look like thieves had come and had broken into the place.

I think she caught the incredulous look that briefly passed over my face, because she quickly protested, "Yes, it is true that I was re-captured, but you know, that's the way it is! Once they see what kind of quality work you can do, they slam the door and make you do their bidding. Right away, they ask far too much. I do what I can but I have limitations they refuse to accept. They do not understand what I am worth. At all! I had that door slammed on me three times!"

But she couldn't completely explain to my satisfaction why she fell in with another band of rogues that was eager to put her knowledge to profitable use. In her dream story, the elfin Kari's creative power took the form of a healing elixir that was so special only she could make it. "They made it sound all fine and good at first," she explained, describing the deal they made with her. "But that was just the hook for them to pull me in. Several times when I asked to fill orders for them, they'd just say 'Ok, go ahead, go ahead, make some elixir with this'. That was after someone else had told them how it was made—not the elixir of my kind, but some sort of cheap imitation."

She said that they had no understanding of the delicate process and the kind of pure water she needed, and eventually that got back to the leader. He demanded to know what she thought she was doing and told her she couldn't have any more of the water she needed to create the elixir. By now their operation was one encompassing mess, she said, speaking of the carelessness of her work environment. She told me it was a mining operation that they ran intensively every day of the week for hours on end. They had all kinds of different processes using the available water. But people were having a hard time finding a clear tap because they didn't keep good records. Or, they would tap new places for their own profit and keep it secret.

Now it happened that one day a scout returned from a distant land with a pure sample of her elixir. "It was everything I had been telling them about from the get go! How I could make the same thing, you know, if they would only get me some better water! I could even show them how. But that just kind of flew out the window. And that was hard! Really hard!" They wanted her to work for nothing and lied to her, saying they had no clear taps left to give to her. "'Oh, she can go ahead and do it but we are not giving her that water.' They couldn't see it–they couldn't see what was happening! How could they go on like this and survive? I mean, how many times did I tell them?"

I saw her eyes shine black with bitterness and the elfin glow that surrounded her wavered with rage. She recalled their fear and confusion, their lack of understanding about the water source. Since they couldn't see the poison leaking in, they didn't believe it was happening until it was much too late. "They were so narrow minded–like they had blinders on." She warned them, "You don't get the message! How can you ask me to make the elixir with this? You gotta be crazy! This is absurd." She said that they treated her like they were the masters and she was their little puppet underneath them; all they had to do was push the puppet wherever they wanted her to go. But she refused to comply with their demands. "No," she explained, "I will do whatever I need to do. And I will make sure that it's done properly. But I refuse to send out elixir if it isn't made from clear water. That's how I was taught. That reflects on me and my kind. Of course, they barked at that." They were only focused on the profit.

In the autumn everyone started to get ill. By then there were many problems with the water. The mining operation had to keep switching from one source to another, sometimes two or more leagues apart. Nothing was wrong, they told her, this sickness was just the flu. But she knew differently; she had been noticing the problem getting worse for months. The waters were ruined; that was the legacy of what they had begun. By winter the leader died, making it even more difficult. But the loss was also a chance at last to make the connection that something was wrong. They sent in someone to test the water, but said he wasn't exactly sure what the problem was. "Didn't know what was happening," she sighed. "He just went in and looked at it and shook his head. And here I had been telling them there's something wrong! I knew it all along! But, no, no, no, they told me, it's just the flu."

"I fell sick in the autumn, then again in the winter, and again in the spring. I was sick all the time. The operation wasn't up to speed, not up to a hundred percent. We had all this backlog; the pressure was so great and the demand for the elixir was so high. Just 'do this, do this, do this.' Fifty new people came in sick, expecting a cure. They hadn't been told anything, or if they had, they didn't pay attention. When I told them it was the water, they just didn't hear."

Feeling completely incapacitated, she tried to imagine what the sick people were going through on their end of things. "You know, what was happening to them or why didn't they feel they're improving or even getting something back?" She began to panic, believing there was no way out. She knew it was the stress and the sickness but it was all so overwhelming. "I'm only one person. I have to place limits. I can't do this," she told them. "But in their eyes 'no' means I was just refusing to comply. In my heart, I struggled with, you know, why is this happening to me? I'm not a bad person. I didn't feel I was bad, but I was being treated like that and it made it very hard."

Like in her drawing of the steel door, she said, "wherever I go, it's like I'm banging, banging, banging—it just keeps me stuck in that little hole. But still, I'm not going to quit. I am going to seek out what I need. I have been boxed in. But I am pushing the walls and I'm getting out (Figure 19A). I know that. I have my strength, my integrity, and my willingness to put effort into trying to reach out to others. No matter what. That's my goal. That I'll break through. I will not give up and throw everything away, or sit it in a box or tucked away, with that heaviness pushing down and squashing me (Figure 20A). Because I've gotten stomped on. Where I've given a hundred and ten per cent and I just get stomped on. You know what I mean? Then my spirit lies so far away from me I can't reach it."

She turned to me and her faint glow brightened. "That's why I know I have to move on to a place where they accept me for me (Figure 19B). Coming here to see you, all these things just started happening in my head. I just played it out to the hilt: the fantasy of what it would be like to just open up a little clear place and go from there. So that this wasn't just a terrible struggle for nothing. There are so many people who would want my elixir if they knew. I could tell them, 'Hey, what are you waiting for? Come to me and I'll get you the elixir.' I can picture how to organize the whole operation. But what I haven't found is a clear source. Everything else has just been torn apart and that's why I know I have to move on. I've got to find a healthier, more peaceful environment. A place where I can rebuild—where they accept me for me and work with me."

I recognized her plea for the key that would open the door to the clear pool of the Source, her desire. She described her vision of beautiful blue, clear water, the source of her grounding and power (Figure 19C). The dream she held in her heart felt like perfection itself and was unbearably beautiful. I could feel its power stirring in me as I witnessed her and wanted to see it for myself. I knew not where my sudden desire for healing waters, the perfect embrace, or the promise of transformation came from; it seemed something beyond me, longing to be released (Figure 20B).

Suddenly, I sensed another figure in the dreaming space of disenchantment with us, unseen before and now standing beside her. Another luminous being was holding the pure vision out to her (Figure 20C). She did not travel alone, although she did not see where my eyes now stared, absorbed by the apparition. She was saying to me, "I feel like I've been singled out, like a finger is pointed at me, punishing me for being what I am. But I truly believe that I'm going to be happier and that the energy is going to come from me. It's going to hold me, to provide me, and also give me a lot of hope that I will be more at peace and doing what I know I am capable of."

She paused and told me, "I know that you are behind me and helping me through. That's just incredible for me. You have listened to my struggles and you gave your best for me. And so I want to repay you. I have something I can give you, to help you out." I couldn't be sure but I thought I saw and heard Kari say, "Here, let me show you" as she drew a little vial of elixer out of her pack.

* * *

Kari ardently spoke of her deep passion to bring her knowledge and unique skills as an art therapist into the world. But her frustrations were filled with chronic pain and suffering. Her work was making her sick.

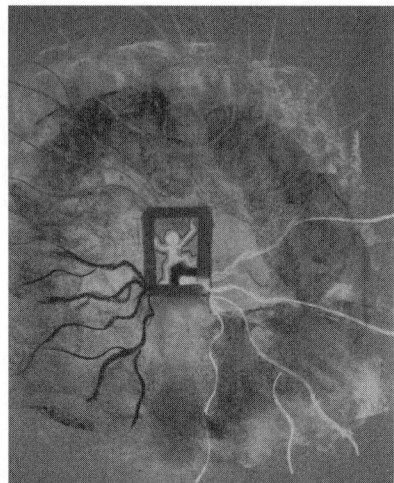

Figure 19A–C. *(A–Top)* Kari's image of her disenchantment; *(B–Center)* Lynn's witness; *(C–Bottom)* Kari's response.

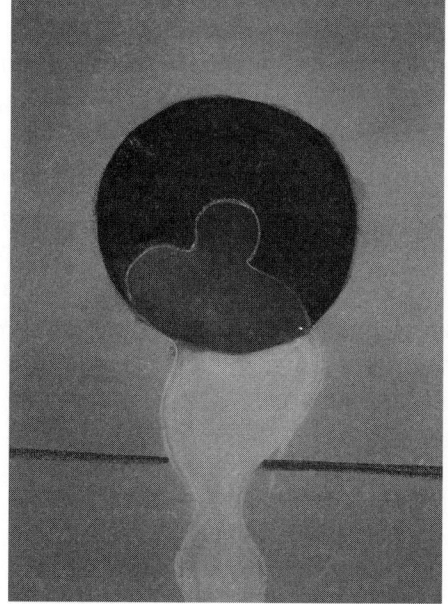
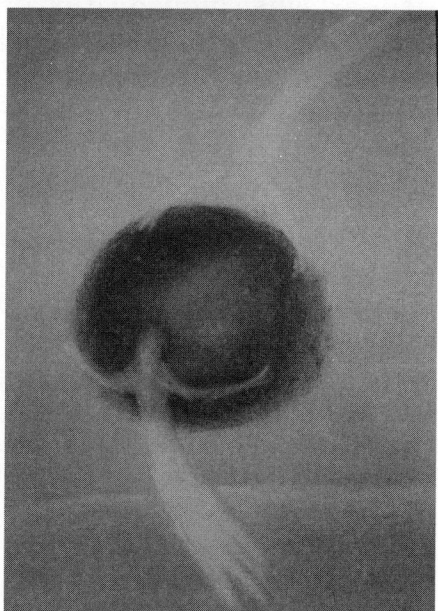

Figure 20A–C. *(A–Top)* Lynn's image of Kari's disenchantment; *(B–Bottom left)* Kari's witness; *(C–Bottom right)* Lynn's response.

Yet she also had split her reality between belief in a perfect place in which to practice and all the evil she saw in her surrounding environment, which compelled her toward illusions of desire, power and escape. On one level, her disenchantment seemed a struggle with what some call the "unwilling-will"[39] or the many ways of not allowing presence to transform perception, such as when we feel driven or crushed by the weight of the past, heedlessly rush toward a hoped-for future, await for someone to magically transform our life, or never resting in the present in order to see clearly what is right there with us, in our bowls, awaiting transformation. On another, mythic level, Kari's story is a familiar one of petitioning the gods for the magic elixir of immortality from the pain of suffering and death. Or wrestling the magic boon from undeserving, brutish ogres.

An experienced alcohol and drug abuse counselor, Kari was having difficulty breaking into a field dominated by government-funded providers and their attendant abuses of the system. The essence of her disenchantment arrived in the image of the poisoned waters, resonating in like manner with the toxic effects of drugs and alcohol on any living system, whether individual or organizational. Alcohol is sometimes called "distilled spirits;" likewise, her story closely paralleled the spiritual searching behind addiction. I sensed a vicious circle in her pursuit and that a process of "detoxification" would be needed to free her creative powers to create the space of sanctuary she sought. After the soul-satisfying vision of fulfillment, the "passing joys and sorrows, banalities and noisy obscenities of life" can be hard to accept.[40] In the teachings of the world's myths, the key is to remember that the realms of the god where the elixir resides is only a forgotten dimension of the world Kari already knows.[41] The glow of her inner light was strong. Her creative vitality came of her courage to maintain this cosmic standpoint in the face of earthly pains and joys, accepting that the enchanting balance of perfection will be lost when life returns.

The Kingdom of the Black River

I was in a comfortable, well-decorated office where Val (a pseudonym) long had a private practice in art therapy. Apart from the soft couch where I could easily imagine her clients gathered, she had a studio table with art supplies and drawing boards where we were sitting now, engrossed, as we tracked the wandering, shifting nature of Val's imagery of disenchantment.

Val was thinking about the well, a mythic image that drew us into a dream space where she was a traveler following the course of a black river. She told me, "It was a fine well. And I liked the energy of that dark river that sustained it.[42] Although some people were anxious about the darkness that flowed beneath us, it didn't feel ominous to me. It was just something inevitable that flowed through and in and out of that

A Bowl of Tears

borderland (Figure 21A)." The space of her disenchantment opened into a pretty place with red brick all around. There were different encampments beside the river—a tribe or huddle of people (Figure 21B).

She didn't realize until later that the structure her people were devoted to creating looked very familiar (Figure 22A). Like a target, they had placed concentric walls in the middle of their commons, where they stored the best of what they had: only the purest of pure water. She marveled at this concentric boundary making they had achieved even as they asked her to tell them about the open lands beyond their enclosure. They seemed to regard her as a sort of extraordinary agent who could see and connect the worlds, when she felt herself a simple traveler. She shook her head, amused. "I have never been driven to make people believe in my ways. I never felt a need to prove anything I do—it worked or it didn't and that was just how it is. If it doesn't work, then try something else!"

Val found it strange to be in the presence of these peoples' prophets, who, by contrast, were so committed to the correct teachings imparted with authority. The purity being demanded seemed an unspoken expectation embedded in the place.[43] "There was this kind of purist judgment," she said, "like everything was taken in with a kind of filter." Then she thought about the well in the center of the commons and added, "It felt to me like they needed something very sensitive to hold their illusions in place. They needed space for their desires that were so beautiful. I wanted to make the world softer for them, like a delicate nest that was coming into being (Figure 22B). I imagined what it would be like if together we could create a nest of nurturing instead of a dominion for our creative, healing work" (Figure 22C).

When Val thought of the powerful dominion that ruled in that place, she felt so disillusioned she didn't think she could even talk about it. It was like being a vassal in a kingdom that demanded too much from her. Divergent views were often subject to intense hostility fueled by repressed anger. Like all unrecognized domination, it was sterile and life choking. The queen of the realm answered her petitions of complaint by shaming her, saying 'You should know better than to even think that you have a problem we need to talk about at court, and anyway, we have more important things to deal with'." All such regimes are overseen by a hierarchy that rewards those who will do their bid-

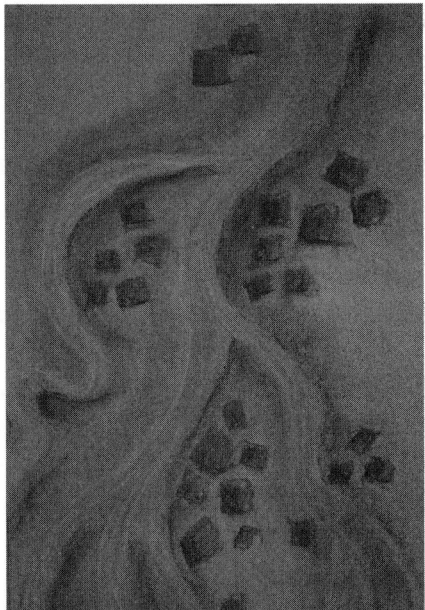

Figure 21A–C. *(A–Top left)* Val's image of her disenchantment; *(B–Top right)* Lynn's witness; *(C–Bottom)* Val's response.

ding faithfully.[44] "But it was all too much. I needed to say to them, 'This is terrible. I am tired of being treated like this.'"

She had been called to bring forth the confluence of the waters that her kingdom celebrated every year. But then they built the dam and that changed the course of the waters in the realm. It required people to decide quickly in which camp they would live. "Whoosh–everyone

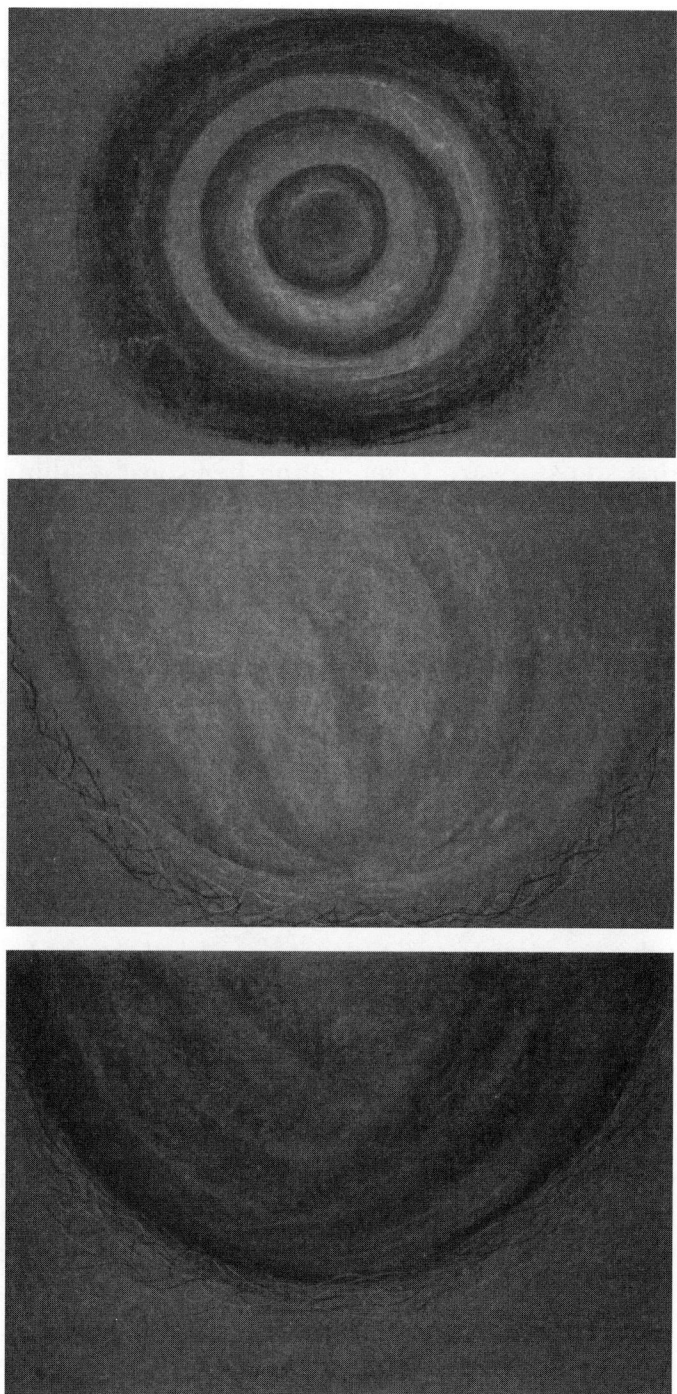

Figure 22A–C. (A–Top) Lynn's image of Val's disenchantment; (B–Center) Val's witness; (C–Bottom) Lynn's response.

had to move or else. 'You better be in or you're out.' That's the mentality that we functioned under; there was only one right place to live from then on, and if you're not in, you're cast out." When people feel they have no options, they cling to the assurances of polarized certainties.[45] "And that is a sad and terrible place for us," Val continued. "I thought that maybe I, too, was not going to be included since I lived far beyond the encampment. So I asked them, 'Why are you so passionate about this dam?' And they said it was about bringing more water to their people. But I think it really had to do with exclusion. For survival people need to diversify so the waters will flow to the many. I think that's what they were afraid of."

She knew the ways of water intimately and trusted that she was now taking the first steps toward regenerating her spirit. Calling forth the confluence in the beginning had been important work that gave her energy. But then she felt it draining her. "It takes too much of a toll. I'd rather be planting flowers in my garden," she laughed. She thought of a place of her own (Figure 21C), next to the trees and beside grandmother willow which gave her a different sort of protection. She drew from the wisdom others were thirsting for. Thus, she was beloved and known for her artistry in the beautiful and sensitive libations she made for the people. She had allies, even among those most different from her—trustworthy people who knew the work, with whom she felt comfortable. The fear in the tribe's heart, she could clearly see, had to do with scarcity.[46] Not believing that the waters will always come. "Yes, I can feel the energy I've created is around me and that things will change. But the circulation of the waters needs attention. I hope some of the energy I brought was enough so that it will keep happening."

Val's energies were shifting and now she was being drawn to other places. The call was so strong in her that having to pay attention to these things was distracting and simply drained her of needed energy. "I feel very grateful for my work and do not regret it in any way, because it was preparation for whatever is next. I learned much and saw clearly that I really do need to have a larger circle, a larger challenge in my life that can feed me." She did not believe, as so many others do, in staying apart out of specialness. "You know, this idea that 'I'm special and you must come to me because I'm special and pay my tribute because if you don't.' . . . Or that 'there's not going to be place for me so I really have to fight to secure my place.' I don't know if that is true; there are many places for me. Maybe I am deluding myself, but I don't think so. I do think it has to do with belonging in a bigger way."

"I kept asking myself, 'What am I doing here?' I never felt I could just be me. Yet that was what I really wanted." She told me how differently the kingdom paid attention to things that mattered to her and even to the black water itself. It flowed from below the well, from areas that had been pushed aside, avoided or overlooked.[47] All rivers want to go in different directions and have these different qualities. Like her, the black river of the kingdom wanted a path with different places to move into. She said, "There was a time when I needed to be in such a family. I do think that belonging is very important. It's not that I don't want to be around people in the kingdom and it's not that I want to go away forever. I love them, I really do, but I don't feel they're at the center of everything important. At first, I did. I'm not so sure any more. I'm part of the circle but maybe I am more on the outside. Maybe that is my place now, where I need to be."

* * *

Val's space of disenchantment was connected to a struggle in both the work place and professional organization for the inclusion of many voices and ways of being in art therapy, and in the sharing of power. Her disenchantment resonated with the tensions of gate keeping, prophet-seeking, and concentric boundary setting in how the field defines itself. The very qualities in the black river that are a source of creative vitality for Val—a darkly feminine, self-organizing confluence of diverse origins—may feel vaguely threatening to those professionals committed to the purity of their discipline. Those who challenge us by questioning what we hold dear are disturbing but also may be right.

The traveler is an archetype for a change agent: someone who has "seen the world" brings unknown and possibly dangerous ideas into enclosed societies. In ancient China, such a person was treated with respect and hospitality out of fear that the traveler might return with enemies.[48] Individuals acting as change agents like Val must suffer the organization's most powerful expectations, see them from a self-authorized perspective, and still care enough to become willing to do whatever it takes to make deep change.[49] Val senses that for her to stay alive and vital, she needs to answer the call that will take her beyond provincial kingdoms. She is contemplating the ascetic road of medieval saints and yogis who discarded the costumes of identity and duty to society in order to break through to their own unfathomable realizations. The road of the exile is, at the same time, a road homeward to what is soulful in her life and dwelling in the center. There she has discovered peace and gratitude.

Jewels in the Stream

Joy (a pseudonym) began the collaborative witness encounter with a confession: she was not disenchanted. She apologized, hoping I didn't mind and that she wasn't "contaminating" my research. She'd simply thought the topic was a very interesting one to explore. Certainly from time to time she felt "un-enchanted." She supposed that most art therapists went through short or longer spells in which their sense of creative wonder disappeared. Perhaps it was more a matter of regaining enchantment when it had been lost, had simply disappeared, or had been taken away.

"I wonder what's upstream?" It was her first question when she imagined stepping into the dream space of the images we created. She saw the jewels in the stream, crystalline at first (Figure 23A) but later softer and more organic (Figure 23B). Where would they be coming from? she wondered. Wouldn't it be the source upstream? Sensing the power of the current's flow, she felt a tiny waver of resistance, thinking, "But I don't want to give all my gifts away." The answer came to her then, "You always have more."

"If it is struggle we are talking about," she reflected, thinking of disenchantment, "then I would describe my experience as such. But I went into this field with my eyes open, with my own notions about what it was going to be about." Joy was working to develop her practice, a community model of art therapy in close collaboration with artists and professionals from other disciplines. She shared studio space with a local dance company and frequently went into schools and retirement homes to create art performances and programs. Joy was describing the formative stages of her practice when she said, "I had a sense of what shape ought to evolve. But I was not curious about the finished form as much as helping it become." The dream voice below the surface of Joy's words whispered, "What was I going to become? I do not know. But it doesn't really matter, does it? It's going to be more incredible than I could ever imagine."

I could feel the energies of the space ebb and flow between us as Joy spoke of her work as an art therapist and as we created interactive artwork to capture its essence. Later, when I re-lived her words and images and 'listened' them into a mythic dream-adventure, I discovered that conception, gestation, and birth were the basic rhythms of this still-enchanted art therapist's story of evolving her practice. In Joy's story (below), she is a witness or midwife to a newly conceived and created being that is herself in the process of becoming. Her dream-voice takes form as a spark of creation inviting me, her companion, into a dance of life:

Joy did not realize at first that she was starting at the bottom of the heap. Or that she really had no blessing. But the struggle—my gosh, she had to become stronger and stronger. Because at first, as a tiny seed, she had to retread a little in order to move forward, like swimming against the current. I don't know why it was that way, except that I think she knew at the core there was something she wanted to become. Of course, she also wasn't just going to throw it all away, because her commitment was huge. It was going to disrupt everyone's life in her constellation. You know, you do something and everything else around you changes, too, if you are really committed to what you are doing. She wasn't going to give up—whatever this amorphous force was that swept her along. It kept changing.

You might wonder why she took such a risk to go this way, instead of a more conventional kind of route. It just seemed so huge to her and she was exactly in a stage of life where she could take these kinds of risks. Evolving her own dream was really important to her, but it was also important to know that this—*she*—was going to be viable. I mean, she could get a sense coming from the others who were more purist, who told her "you should be this kind" or "why aren't you that kind?" Nothing that direct, of course, but she certainly felt the implications of her moving so far out from a center that was known.[50] On the fringe of something, she worried that she could be mistaken for many things. I don't know why except that she didn't believe in what the others were working themselves into. She was going full steam ahead anyway, approaching a point where she was thinking about finding the right place to settle. Soon, she realized, she would be moving to a bigger space. "I wonder if maybe something is wrong with me since I've coupled with outsiders? I don't know if it's important that I'm not coupling with my own kind."

She wanted a partner she could make music or dance with, to be more attuned to what she was becoming. That was the plan. And I suppose it was a healthy way to approach it. The essence, she knew, would be found at the place of crosscurrents, where all the differences and commonalities, of all expressions of creation, are found. I mean, in order to create anything there has to be lots of stuff going around that could be used to create the core, a coming together as a new community (Figure 23C). She understood. "We are a work in progress, but we're still creating and it is so wonderful. Just with what we have, we can start there and say, where else can we go with this?"

In the great force of this process, she didn't have much down time; she didn't feel the need. She felt once removed from that. "Every time I enter into a creative act with another to create the community we are becoming, I know it validates myself and the other, but it also validates the work of creation. When I do have time to reflect, I ask myself, did I do the right thing? Because my journey is uncharted. Because I don't know what that next thing is. You may never know—Who ever knows?"

There was another thing she wanted to add, to complete that thought. She sensed that she *should* be somewhere at the bottom because the bottom is usually the foundation. I agree, but there are others who refuse to recognize this. When you choose this path, you have to realize that you are choosing the foundations of civilization. You can't expect to be much more and not struggle, because you've chosen to climb the rungs from the very bottom of the tier. The way of foundation—it's where the prophets are. This is what the work was all about and she loved it so. It felt like being a voice in the wilderness. "The ones who came before will say, 'Oh, thank goodness you're here to speak'." She got the chilly bumps just thinking about that—that whatever comes, comes. It is powerful. But it is even more powerful to be connected to the other forms. And that was her mission, Joy decided. That was why she was coming into being.

Now she realized that she didn't have a voice and or any solid background yet. That was why she needed to collaborate, in fact, because she knew there were others and they would divide, develop, and claim their prospects. It was like they owned her creation now. She could hear them mimicking her model. She recognized her style, but thought, "How great that now there's not just one of me, there's two of me! And there are others, too." She sensed the incredible community they were all in the process of creating, built up so big that their expectations ran

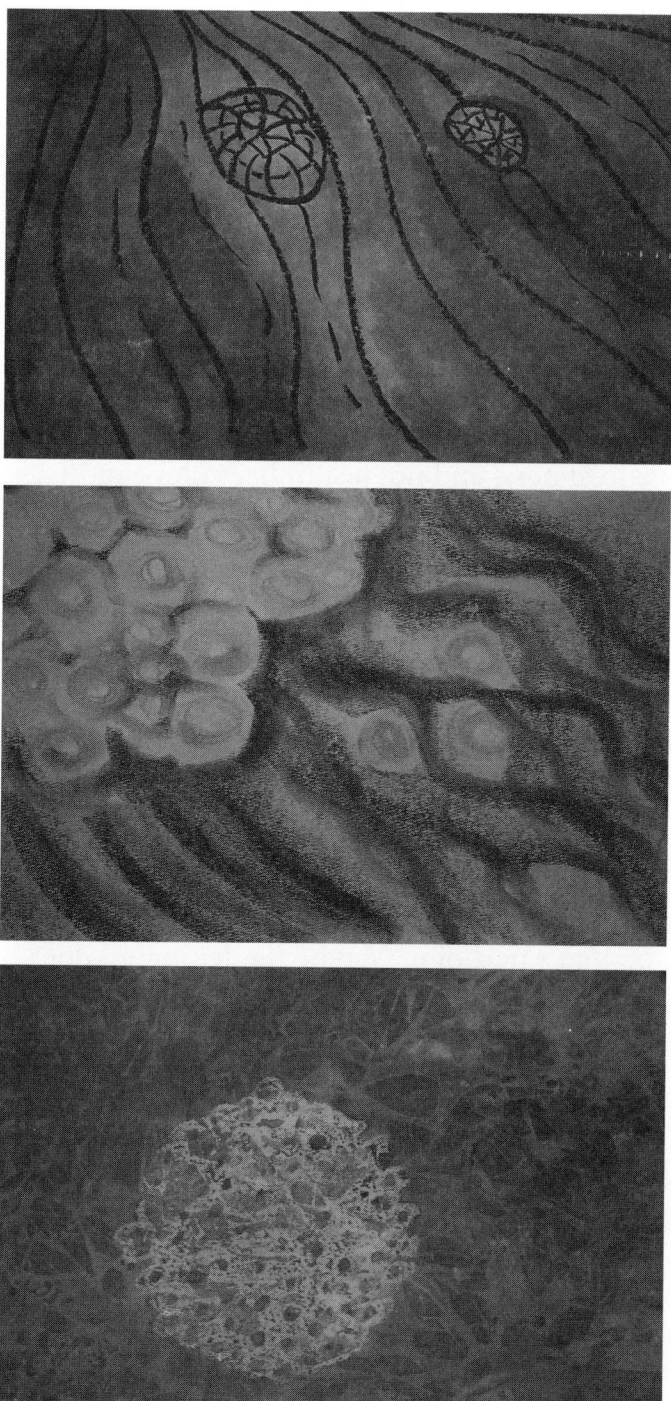

Figure 23A–C. *(A–Top)* Joy's image of her enchantment; *(B–Center)* Lynn's witness; *(C–Bottom)* Lynn's response.

a little wild. She thought, "I don't know what we are delivering but you only get what you get! But oh, we are going to look so good. And the forces that propel us will be powerful, you know, from the inside out."

"Do you believe in magic? It's the root of creation!" And I think that was to be her mission. To keep the magic, the ancestors taught her to imagine. What their art and stories awakened in her was the memory of this potent, creative time for later. You know, to remember something that you're going to have to recapture for the rest of your life, if you lose it? "Do you believe in magic?" seemed to her to be the whole premise. Truths were revealed in the creation stories flowing through her and what she was forming reflected those truths. There was a certain sense of freshness, a part of her that was being nurtured. Her spirit would have freshness, and not just in her colors and lines but in the primal, indigenous expressions of the community she found within her. I think what she was identifying in the stories and creative work was that piece of herself that she wanted to stay alive. It's that magic, that enchantment.

When she considered the difficulty that comes with the magic, a memory of an old story came back to her just then. It was about the child who had decapitated the queen. Yes! The queen's tragic death had been a traumatic but necessary lesson for the child to learn from and remember for later. How else would she have ever separated and become her own person? That violent seed was there at the very start of her conception. But it could be so very traumatic, she knew that. Many get stuck or fear that cutting of the umbilical cord when the time comes. Maybe that's part of it. Maybe the letting go does not happen for some. The separation does not happen completely and some remain stuck and suffer. But others use the very same trauma for their own birth, to become healthy and alive. Sometimes it depends on where we come from. It is not even farfetched to think of tragic deaths happening in some places as being connected to this dilemma. You hear them say oh, everything is fine. Except that what you see are people walking around like zombies, living in soul fatigue. People who are just surviving—or who survived to the finish but never got their energy back together. At one point, she did think her soul was fatigued because it felt like having the pressure sit on her too long. She felt she was losing all her energy. She thought "Oh! My *chi* is gone! There's no point in any of this!"

But living past the trauma for her soul's restoration is the important lesson. You can tell people the facts a thousand times, but what if they refuse to see it, because they think they will forever be in the space of enchantment? Then, when the illusion breaks, what do they do but blame somebody because, you know—because they didn't assimilate the purpose of their suffering. You lose your soul because of an event that happened that you didn't cue into. We do have to die to certain parts of ourselves in order to be in the world.

Thinking now of breaking illusions or bursting the amniotic fluids for her birth, Joy tried to picture what the queen looked like without her head. She was supposed to be fearsome but what Joy conjured in her mind looked more like a perfume bottle (Figure 24A). She had a sudden, silly thought: What kind of fragrance would come out, now that her head was chopped off? She thought of the story of the three wishes, and also the genie and the magic carpet (Figure 24B). "I think that's what's inside," she pondered. "Now there is an opening in the vessel and there's magic if you look inside it. I wonder—am I making my three wishes?" (Figure 24C) Maybe people always think there will be someone like the queen to do the magic for them. But if you open that bottle and make your three wishes, you have to remember that they all have to come out." All belongs in the circle.

Was it bleeding she sensed now? She saw red. She wasn't sure, but it felt like something primary in what was happening to her. It had to do with believing that she could do it. What this work was about—that the process of creation is a healing act in the community. You know, you come with this wonderful vision that you can heal the world. But I do not want you thinking it wasn't too hard. To be able to say "Aha—This is right! This is really, really viable" took blood, sweat, and tears. And that's part of the birthing of her. You don't ever finish it, either. There will always be those moments of disenchantment—because we struggle! Do you see the connection? I just know that there's a place for her. Of course, the prophets always were the minority. They always were the women! *Ha!*

* * *

The surging energy of Joy's mythic story describes the sense that she is birthing herself into the freshness of life forces. These are so powerful, they sweep her up and carry her along in her work to create vital communities for others in need of healing and restoration—people who

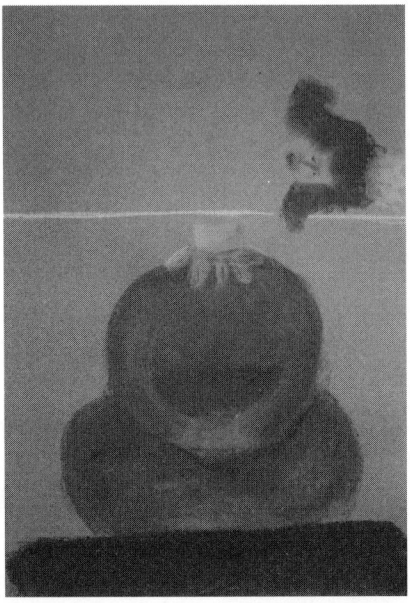

Figure 24A–C. *(A–Top)* Lynn's image of Joy's enchantment; *(B–Center)* Joy's witness; *(C–Bottom)* Lynn's response.

A Bowl of Tears

"can stand this healthy environment," as she put it, which she is creating with her therapeutic artistry. She is unsure whether her lack of interest in collaborating with art therapists, her "own kind," is the result of their lacking a vision of multiplicity or vitality, or is simply the pull of her own need to expand into new possibilities for her practice. Her story offers much wisdom to others seeking to restore their sense of the magic that brought them into the field to begin with, as it also explores the responsibilities and consequences of the identities we birth.

THE WATERS OF CREATIVE VITALITY

There are many common and universally recognizable themes that wind their way through the stories of these seven art therapists, all of whom identified themselves as disenchanted in some way, though to varying degrees. But most striking is the primordial image of the waters that must reach their souls or they will die of thirst and hopeless despair. Gasping for creative energy, they know something has gone wrong at the juncture between the source and the tributary they depend upon. Yet for those whose connection has not been severed, they are swimming in the waters, coupling with "dancing sperm," following the coursing energy, or using its power to navigate its many passageways.

In the encounter of the collaborative witness, there was no actual discussion of such themes. In fact, having rigorously put aside all preconceived notions in order to witness with complete presence, to embrace the as yet unseen phenomena before me, and to impose no inappropriate structure of my own, the unifying theme of the waters in the phenomenon of art therapist disenchantment came as a revelation. Only gradually, as all seven dream-adventures came into story form, did the great underground river make its presence known as an essential aspect of the art therapist's relationship to disenchantment and creative vitality.

Afterwards, I verified this finding in art therapy literature as I re-discovered references to the waters of renewal and creative life that are threaded throughout Allen's work.[51] She describes the "river that surges below my observable daily life, the place of the soul," saying she'd "gotten so busy being an art therapist, [she'd] forgotten all about the river."[52] Elsewhere, in an article that identified the frustrations of art therapists having difficulty with changes brought on by licensure and managed care health systems, Wadeson chose "wetlands" as a metaphor for a shrinking habitat and the "draining away of art therapy."[53] Although she does not link the image of longed-for waters with the behaviors of disenchantment, she decries art therapists who "no longer do art therapy or [who] plunge into the studio approach and the danger of being caught in a vise with art on the one side and therapy on the other and art therapy squeezed into nothing in the middle," saying that art therapy "may be forced to become land or water and forsake the fecundity of the transition space that is both land and water." Both references suggest that the search for connection to a lost river is a compelling or essential image of disenchantment among art therapists.

Throughout the world's mythologies, the creative force of life is described as a flow: a circulating substance, a streaming of energy, or spiritually as a manifestation of grace.[54] The torrent pours from an invisible, divine source, its point of entry being the center of the symbolic circle of the universe. The research of Pinkola Estes verifies the connection between the mythic image of water and creative vitality particular of women. Of the river, she says:

> The creative force flows over the terrain of our psyches looking for the natural hollows, arroyos, the channels that exist in us. We become its tributaries, its basins; we are its pools, ponds, streams, and sanctuaries. We don't have to fill them; we only have to prepare the place that induces the great creative force to advance. Creativity is not a solitary movement and that is its power. Whatever is touched by it, whoever hears it, sees it, senses it, knows it, is fed. For this reason a woman's creative ability is her most valuable asset for it gives outwardly and it feeds her inwardly at every level. The river pours out endless possibilities, acts as birth channel, invigorates, slakes thirst, and satiates our hunger for the deep and wild life. Ideally, this creative river has no dams on it, no diversions, and no misuse.[55]

Like the flow of a wild river, we can expect our creative lives to fill and empty, to rise and fall in seasons and cycles, over and over again. As one art therapist said, after reflecting on her dream-story, "I love how the creative process, like the river, shifts and turns along the way. I am reminded that the power of creation opens me to a larger energy. This creation is a gift of love."

While it may be true for all art therapists, and further inquiry would be needed to verify it, these seven stories of disenchantment were limited to a woman's reality. In the daily, complex rhythm of many women art therapists, being admonished to go to the studio and make art rings a little hollow. She knows that there will be many times when she dearly wants to respond by creating aesthetic works but there is no time or energy and so she makes art wherever and however she finds it alive in her.[56] At times, the river of creativity disappears underground for a while. She incubates. She goes into the cave, listens to the stories or sits beside the willow, drawing up waters from her roots; she waits and rests so she can return to the work and regain her focus or energy for later. We all may lose the flow of creativity at times. But this is a very different sensation from that of a soul dying a river's death, found in the images and mythic stories of the parched or poisoned wasteland.

When I pause to reflect with deep sadness on the possibility of soul death, I feel the begging bowl form again in my heart and mind and recall the art therapists who placed the materials of their disenchantment there. The bowl of our shared witness held the waters of their tears. Placing them in the vessel of transformation, the toxins could become cleansed and the vessel made clear again. I am reminded that wounds need to be washed as well as exposed. Old wounds, it is said, often have to be dipped into the waters of the ancestors. Grief gets moved by water, by the tears and laments that wash the memories of loss the way rain washes stones.

A soul dying like a river is no slight thing but a true psychological and spiritual crisis. Facing this implication for art therapists in my research, I reach for the comfort of my imaginal companion, the troubadour. "Yes," he gently tells me, "When creative life dies because we are not tending to the health of the river, we feel the loss of energy; we feel tired. There is nothing creeping, roiling, lifting leaves, cooling off, warming up. We become thick, slow in a negative way, poisoned by pollution.... Everything feels tainted, unclear, and toxic."[57]

Alarmed, I tell him that the souls of many art therapists may be in crisis or dying in the toxic wasteland of their work environments, health care system, and culture. Their stories recounted the pollution and sealing off of their creative functioning, disabling their ability to create or act with clarity in the world and making them toxic to others.

"But certainly, in the witnessing of the art and resonant spaces you created together," the troubadour reflected, "you learned that creativity can never be lost. It is always there, filling us or colliding with obstacles placed in its way.[58] What are these barriers between the water and the dying soul but the result of your own negative inner state or the toxic environs of people, places, and organizations that surround you—or both?"

"Yes," I told him, "I have read that 'if the culture in which a person lives attacks the creative function of its members, if it splits or shatters any archetype or perverts its design or meaning, these will be incorporated in their broken state into the psyches of its members in the same way'."[59]

Another figure in the art therapists' stories was that of the alienated soul who lived in exile from the village. "Well, indeed, this is a terrible state to be in," my companion remarked. "But there is some value in the experience that should not go unnoticed. It is sometimes worse to stay where one's soul does not belong than to wander lost for a while, looking for the psychic kinship one needs in order to feel life and power."[60]

I confessed that at one time I thought it was the desire to escape the realities and limitations of living that motivated the flight of many art therapists out of the dispirited places where our work is so needed, as though we are children searching for parents who would unconditionally love, accept, and protect us. While this may also be true, I have come to better understand and value the longing for spiritual and psychological freedom for our true nature and the search for or construction of a culture to go with it. We should not have to accept that our work lives are life-depleting deserts. My collaborators told me that trauma can act as a force to move us to a better, healthier existence. But we have work to do: We must detoxify ourselves to become clear, current channels once again. And we must broaden our understanding of our artistic therapeutic practices in order to become activist community, culture, and peace makers. Coming home to our own souls, we can create homecoming for each other.

NOTES

1. Buber, M. cited in Palmer, P. (1998). *The courage to teach*. San Francisco: Jossey-Bass. p. 16.
2. Glassman, B. (1998). *Bearing witness*. New York: Bell Tower. p. 73.
3. Ibid., p. 78.

4. Wheatley, M. J. & Kellner-Rogers, M. (1996). *A simpler way.* San Francisco: Berrett-Koehler. p. 75.
5. An excellent discussion of the comparison of two introspective methods of investigation, phenomenology and psychoanalysis, can be found in Margulies, A. (1989). The uses of wonder, in *The empathic imagination.* New York: W.W. Norton. (pp. 3–18). He states, "Both processes have as their goal the opening up of possibilities. Both demand the suspension of preconceptions in the service of discovery; such suspension is characteristic of descriptions of the creative process. Further, the processes are unforced and unselfconsciously creative; they are not planned." It is his contention that therapeutic truth is a dialectic, a creation of the relationship itself, a continuous coming into being of possibilities requiring further exploration. The working methods of phenomenological inquiry and psychoanalysis are alike in their relation to the creative process: both are "methods that optimize the potential for novel perceptions and thoughts; they permit surprise configurations of the new arising from the old", pp. 11–12.
6. Glassman, p. xiv.
7. Ibid., p. 41.
8. Schaverien, J. (1992). *The revealing image.* London: Tavistock Routledge. p. 7.
9. Lipsey, R. (1997). *An art of our own: The spiritual in twentieth century art.* Boston: Shambhala. p. 52.
10. Kandinsky, W. quoted in Lipsey, p. 222.
11. Bender, S. (1996). *Everyday sacred.* San Francisco: HarperSan Francisco, p. 10.
12. Meade, M. (1993). *Men and the water of life.* New York: HarperCollins, p. 10.
13. Campbell, J. (1949). *The hero with a thousand faces.* Princeton, NJ: Princeton University Press, p. 4.
14. Ibid.
15. Campbell, J. (1988). *The power of myth.* New York: Doubleday, p. 196.
16. An edited paper containing four of these stories of art therapist disenchantment entitled *Dying rivers, depleted wells: Loss and restoration of art therapists' creative vitality* (Kapitan, 2001) was presented at the 32nd Annual Conference of the American Art Therapy Association, Albuquerque, NM. Denver, CO: National Audio Video [Audio tape 108–1036].
17. Whyte, D. (1994). *The heart aroused.* New York: Doubleday. p. 285.
18. Quinn, R.E. (1996). *Deep change: Discovering the leader within.* San Francisco: Jossey-Bass, p. 25.
19. Ibid.
20. Meade describes the bead girdles that Gisu women wear over their wombs, which is reminiscent of the seven jewels in this story. Clearly associated with the intimate parts of a woman's body, they also represent the generativity, creativity, power, and sacredness of women. The beads remind the women that they are the creative womb of the people, a source of strength to endure, and each one a bead in a strand of beauty that goes all the way to the ancestors, p. 270.
21. Quinn, p. 85. He says that trusting our vision enough to start our journey into the chasm of uncertainty, believing that the resources will appear, can be very difficult.

22. Torbert, quoted in Quinn, p. 77.
23. Campbell, J. (1949), p. 42.
24. Peck, M. S. (1987). *The different drum: Community-making and peace.* New York: Simon and Schuster. pp. 94–97.
25. Campbell, J. (1949), p. 42.
26. Torbert, quoted in Quinn, says "most professional knowledge results in conditional confidence–that you will act well as long as the situation does not violate your assumptions about it. The active awakening attention described here results in unconditional confidence–that you are capable of discarding inaccurate assumptions and ineffective strategies in the midst of on-going reflection," p. 77.
27. Ibid.
28. Margulies, A. (1989). *The empathic imagination.* New York: W.W. Norton. He describes the stairway in the darkness as symbolic of an indeterminant, psychological space in which the presence of the other can be found only through sound, groping, and touch. In contrast to the clarity and safety of light, a symbol for insight or enlightenment, here one has lost one's way in the dark. "Steps create a way in and a way out . . . they are both separations and connections, lower to higher, between two spaces. They are in between, transitional, a change; one passes through a staircase to something else. Jung saw them as symbolic of the spiritual . . . for small children, steps are exciting and dangerous, a physical challenge to master. Interpersonally they are also a warning and a hope–children listen in the night for our steps," p. 79.
29. Natterson, J. (1991). *Beyond countertransference: The therapist's subjectivity in the therapeutic process.* Northvale, NJ: Jason Aronson, p. 212.
30. Meade, p. 388.
31. Natterson, p. 57. These ideas support the theoretical orientation that defines psychotherapy as an intersubjective dialogue in which each participant is influencing and being influenced by the other. Intersubjectivity is seen as the basic process of psychotherapeutic action, from the standpoint that consciousness is always co-consciousness. Naturally, there are hazards in emphasizing the therapist's subjective involvement in the therapeutic experience, such as overidentification with clients and acting out of unconscious countertransference projections. Natterson notes these hazards but states that "paradoxically the more ample the therapist's awareness of his or her subjective experience and its extended meanings, the less the likelihood of destructive developments. . . . In my experience, any subjective elements of the therapist, no matter how extreme or unconventional, can constitute valuable input. The outcome depends on how the therapist processes his or her fantasies and feelings", p. 210. For a complete discussion of clinical approaches to intersubjectivity, see Stolorow, R. D., Atwood, G. E., & Brandchaft, B. (1994). (Eds.). *The intersubjective perspective.* Northvale, NJ: Jason Aronson.
32. Hammerschlag, C. A. (1993). *The theft of the spirit.* New York: Simon and Schuster. He tells a story in which the protagonist says, "The message becomes clearer to me. I think I see, but I am blind. I have sight but no vision. I'm always looking but not always seeing," p. 105.

33. Meade states, "when a story starts with sickness, death, weeping, and the garden, it makes clear that the issues are those of the soul, for the sense of loss is a vital aspect of the soul's connection to life. Reconnecting to this sense of loss is one of the main tasks of an initiation by water. The gardens in the center of city within its walls reaches back for the Garden of Eden where life flows from the center," p. 298.
34. Hammerschlag, p. 42.
35. Gustafson, J.P. (1992). *Self-delight in a harsh world: The main stories of individual, marital and family psychotherapy.* New York: W.W. Norton. He describes the "psychology of captivity" in the following scenario: "playing up to the overpowering is dangerous but what else to do if one is to eat? With the use of this servant often comes the abuse. Long enduring these humiliations, he finally loses his temper and brings shame upon himself. He vows to serve better to make up for his transgression so the playing up is resumed," p. 33.
36. Wolf, N. (1993). *Fire with fire.* New York: Ballantine. pp. 52–53.
37. Ibid., p. 141.
38. Pinkola Estes, C. (1992). *Women who run with the wolves.* New York: Ballantine. p. 183.
39. Maitland, J. (1995). *Spacious body: Explorations in somatic ontology.* Berkeley, CA: North Atlantic Books. pp. 204–205.
40. Campbell, J. (1949), p. 218.
41. Ibid., p. 217.
42. The well frequently appears in myths as a point of entry or "world navel" connected to the earth-supporting waters of the abyss, where divine life-creating energies and substance of the demiurge is found. See Campbell (1949), p. 41.
43. It is interesting to note this art therapist's outsider view looking in on the enclosed encampment of others, where she feels somehow debased or estranged because she lacks their ideological purity. Wolfe has observed the theme of contamination warnings about corruption throughout feminist discourse. She says, "Indeed, we cannot understand . . . the fear of corruption without understanding women's millennia-old relationship to prostitution. . . . For centuries, in almost every Western culture, virtually every woman who was not an aristocrat had to uphold the ideology of respectability and chastity that distinguished her from a prostitute. While she was given the benefit of her 'decent' status—protection, shelter, a position in society—this came at a heavy price." After centuries of acculturation, this mentality's legacy keeps some women in organizations "on the 'correct' side of any given issue, even at the expense of a fruitful embrace of intellectual ambiguity or worldly power," pp. 111–112.
44. Gustafson states that "since all niche spaces are held by regimes, and since all regimes are overseen by a hierarchy, the hierarchy will select joiners who will do their bidding, which is to be overpowering to rivals of the regime, or to steward its resources faithfully by careful, diligent, bureaucratic procedures, or to be subservient and cook and clean and fix up the place," p. xii.
45. Wolf states that once a group feels it has been pushed to the margins of the culture, "it will tend to treasure and hold on for dear life the identity it has. The nor-

mal push and tug of mainstream life, which polishes ideas as the ocean polishes glass, feels threatening," leading to inflexibility of thought. "Either/or thinking is the natural mental reaction to a perception of scarcity. When people feel they have no options, they cling to the assurances of polarized certainties. It is only when people feel rich in confidence and space that they dare to pursue the subtleties of both/and thinking," a psychology of plenty, p. 107.
46. Wolf describes the psychology of scarcity, in which there is only so much to go around, so one woman's gain is another's loss. If there is inequity, a strategy of "equalizing downward" is used; for example, giving up beauty [or art] instead of expanding its definition, p. 137.
47. Meade says that reviving the flow of the Water of Life within an individual or culture requires change that moves what is stuck; water comes from below, from what has been pushed aside or from areas usually avoided and overlooked, p. 303.
48. Palmer, M., Ramsay, J. & Xiaomin, Z. (Trans.). (1995). *I Ching: The shamanic oracle of change.* San Francisco: Harper Collins.
49. Quinn, p. 127.
50. Pinkola Estes: It is not uncommon in punitive cultures for women to be torn between being accepted by the ruling class (the village) and loving her child, be it a symbolic child, creative child, or biological child. This is an old-old story. Women have died psychically and spiritually for trying to protect the unsanctioned child, whether it is their art, their lover, their politics, their offspring, or their soul life, p. 175.
51. Allen, P. (1995a). *Art is a way of knowing.* Boston: Shambhala. p. 55.
52. Ibid., p. 65
53. Wadeson, H. (1999). Commentary: Where are the wetlands? *The Arts in Psychotherapy, 26* (5), pp. 345–348.
54. Campbell (1949), p. 40.
55. Pinkola Estes, p. 299.
56. Kapitan, L. (1999). In Wadeson, H., Junge, M., Vick, R., & Kapitan, L. *Why do you make art?* Panel presentation at the Annual Conference of the American Art Therapy Association, Orlando, FL. Denver, CO: National Audio Video [1565].
57. Pinkola Estes, pp. 305–306.
58. Ibid., p. 300.
59. Ibid., p. 309.
60. Ibid., pp. 186–187.

Chapter 4

TRANSFORMING TOXINS IN THE CAULDRON OF COMMUNITY

We dance round in a ring and suppose,
But the Secret sits in the middle and knows.
—Robert Frost[1]

INTRODUCTION: BRINGING ALIVENESS BACK INTO OUR WORK

At the heart of my journey through the landscape of disenchantment is the elusive experience of aliveness itself. Some say art therapists turn to the studio to strengthen artistic identity and give their work lives greater meaning. But I am beginning to think that is not what we're really seeking. I think that we are "seeking an experience of being alive, so that our life experience on the purely physical plane will have resonance with our inner most being and reality, so that we actually feel the rapture of being alive," as Campbell once said.[2]

Aliveness is the opposite of numbing, mindless, heartless work. The toxic landscape is a flat, featureless place or state of being experienced as "no place." The stress of working in such places leaves many people feeling isolated, depressed, anxious, devalued or angry. In fact, only ten percent of North Americans report feeling really satisfied with their work.[3] A telltale sign that work has become toxic is when people describe their work with the symptomology of physical complaint: the schedule is a backbreaker, the paperwork is a headache, the new manager is a pain, there's no room to breathe. People describe feeling fragmented, pulled apart or pulled in too many different directions, as though bodily cohesion or wholeness is no longer possible. Work is toxic when, for whatever reasons, it causes protracted distress, emotional suffering or physical symptoms, heightened by the perceived inability to stop the pain and move on.[4] Toxic work saps energy and lulls one into a stupor. Eventually the insidious eating away of energy and self-esteem causes a sense of paralyzing powerlessness or collapse.

The terrorist acts in the United States in 2001 against a population of workers in their own daily environment destroyed any illusion of security or immunity from impinging forces of violence in the world. In our longing for a protective sanctuary from assaults on our work lives we become conscious to the cold reality that work environments will never be stable in the old predictable ways again. Both the traditional patient-therapist relationship and the employee-employer covenant have been shattered by permanent changes in the shape and speed of work. One must be able to act swiftly, change gears often, and constantly learn new skills and technologies. We work "not [by] choice but on demand; not for ourselves and our own reasons, but for others and their reasons; not for the sake of the act itself, but for the sake of money or security or approval or the prestige it will bring."[5] When thrown into continuous, rapid response that is unconnected to reflective thought, action may turn into frenzy and result in "a frantic even violent effort to impose one's will on the world, or at least to survive against the odds."[6] We see this on the micro-level of individual lives and the macro-level of escalating violence in the world.

In the midst of such frantic work, I have often stopped to wonder: What am I doing? How did I get to this place? Sometimes what I do in service to others feels alien to my nature, and at times I have been resentful of its control over my life. I realize now that as I am catapulted into a constantly changing world, if I do not find the means to ground my work in the deep connections that engage me I risk losing sight of inner truths that compelled me to action in the first place. The culture in which we live and work will provide us with ready-made patterns that pretend to give meaning to our lives.[7] But these patterns wear thin and increasingly fail when we don't acquire genuine meaning and life vitality through them.

If we can't find ourselves in the new version of the world we create, we will be unable to change.[8] We will both suppress and crave aliveness; thus, art will recede even as we long for its reappearance more intensely. Life will fall into a pattern of reactive impulses that generate standstill or numbing denial, as actions become linked to confused motion and psychic pain. Once flexible and trusting, people and organizations adapt to the increased anxiety with over-control or self-protection. In the need to control or protect from pain, systemic actions that lead to predetermined outcomes or precise destinations will be valued over the risks of experimentation and surprise. "Yes," I think to myself as I recall my own suffering in organizational life, "such environments feel unapproachable. They know the way the world works. They stand in their certainties, suppressing disturbances, shooting messengers. They see through a self that admits no difference, no doubts. They don't wish to be disturbed."[9]

Even though we may be required to act out of the external demands and undesirable constraints imposed on us, it is critical to realize that we still possess the capacity to transform our original desire into something that transcends "the illusion of enslavement and claim[s] upon one's own inner liberty."[10] Palmer insists that we will never be fully alive if we hold back any action that might fail or deny evidence of failure when it happens.[11] An art performance I witnessed perfectly expressed the paralysis of an art therapist stuck in toxic work but unable to see her way through to restoration: Buried up to her neck in sand, when passersby asked if she needed help, she looked down at the huge mound that held her motionless and said, "No, I think I'm all right: I can still wiggle my toes."

She could break out of this self-imposed isolation were she to let go of the image of the autonomous, self-determining individual that believes has to carry the whole load alone.[12] She is a product of our contemporary, democratic ideal of the self-made individual, the invention of the power-driven machine, and the ascendancy of rational, scientific research that have "so transformed human life that the long-inherited, timeless universe of symbols has collapsed."[13] Living images that nourish meaning have receded into the remote past, temples have become sterile museums, and the myths people used to ground their reality are now seen as little more than a clutter of absurd anecdotes. All meaning is in the self-expressive individual and there the meaning is mostly unconscious. The art therapist, buried under a mound of paralyzing powerlessness, does not know toward what she moves and so, perhaps, it seems better to stay stuck.

It is no wonder that resurrection is threatening for it forces us to abandon the idea that we alone are in charge of our lives. When we are willing to let go of life as we want it to be and give over to the larger reality that lives through us, vast areas of half-dead iconography disclose again their permanently human meaning. The life we then find is that of the self embedded in community, created wherever we find psychic kinship needed to become alive to life's power. We find a home and create homecoming for others in our "resurrection into community" which arises when we receive the gifts of grace that sustain our lives, turning from disillusionment to life's magic once again.

THE REFLECTIVE CIRCLE OF PEERS: A COMMUNAL PRACTICE FOR RESTORING CREATIVE VITALITY

Throughout many months of inquiry, I wanted to grasp "the questions that meet the eye" known by other art therapists and myself in our hearts and spirits, in memory and in imagination. I had traveled several different paths into the phenomenon of disenchantment and its transformation. I brought my questions to individual art therapists and heard their collective voices in the professional organization. I had sustained personal artistic reflection; I witnessed and co-created images and stories with dispirited others; I listened deeply to their dreaming. All paths directed me toward a crisis of psychological and spiritual soul loss in those who identified their creative source as drying up or becoming polluted like a dying river. My journey to this point revealed no singular truth as to the cause of disenchantment and diminishment in their work lives, but it did implicate the larger dilemmas and violent effects of the modern, disenchanted world in which we live. I decided that transformational rehabilitation was necessary and so I created a communal studio for disenchanted art therapists seeking creative renewal as my intervention.

I recalled a painting I made several years ago of a circle of people, huddled on a sloping, barren hillside. They were gathered around a crackling fire, their faces illuminated by the coals and moistened by the steam rising from the large stew pot placed at the center. It was a night landscape and I could easily imagine the howling winds that pummeled these people on the hill. But their backs were turned away from the cold, toward sustenance and each other. They stirred the watery substance of the simmering bowl, their cauldron. How strange that this imagined, painted scene would come to back to me now in real, human form, made alive in the medium of a communal studio of art therapists seeking restorative sanctuary from work lives that were becoming toxic to them.

This persistent image in our collective imaginations, of a coven of people brewing, stewing and cooking up spells, is potent with secret power, ambitions, and cackling revenge.[14] To paraphrase Pinkola Estes: What relief this magic circle offers those who are trapped in dubious definitions of their creative selves! What permission it gives—to feel rage and envy, to accept our wishes to defeat others while triumphing ourselves! What license there is to turn one's toxic partners into toads! To not to have to debate them, or out-argue them, but so effectively silence them! In the communal studio we can help each other to "dig deeply, fructify the wild and natural aspects of our return to creative living, and practice having *more!* More head-tossing, more brimming, more sniffling intuition, more get-down-and-dirty, more solitude, more nocturnal life, more fire, more cooking of words and ideas. More deep song, more howling and cackling, and more terrorist sewing circles!"[15]

Our circle formed the bowl; we held the rim, explored the edges between us, and the silent presence of the generative center. We were seven women art therapists[16] who spent our days putting up a good professional front; our daytime voices spoke in the measured tones of rational, well-educated clinicians, our well-honed management and technological skills clearly demonstrated our competence and threatened no one. Families and employers, clients and student interns—all were assured of our sanity and rationality. But as members of a "radical sewing circle" we also had a secret life where we permitted the wildish woman who lived in the recesses of our creativity to come out and play. In our ritual art and people making, the bowl became a cauldron of creative power from which we cooked up new possibilities for ourselves and our practices. We dedicated ourselves to a communal process of re-enchantment, aligned with a form of art making that focused on questions of personal and social transformation.[17] We were art therapists creating art together, not as aesthetic objects but as social action, applied not to a traditional category of identified clients but to the creation, care, and transformation of our art therapy culture and community. This was art that called us into relationship.

We took turns leading the circle, beginning each weekly gathering with informal conversation and an invitation to release anything in our awareness that might otherwise limit our presence for that evening. We lit a candle and called for several minutes of reflective silence. The focus for the evening usually came in the form of a meditation, poem, prayer, and music, drawn from reflections of what had emerged in our gathering the week before. The rest of our time was spent in reflective art making. Each of us created artwork inspired by the opening focus, usually in silence and always in the presence of the other participants in the studio space. Usually we ended art making by writing a brief response to our work and sharing this with the others. Some discussion followed, but mostly we were inspired to use our words as aesthetic reflection rather than explanation or mere description. Sometimes this created storytelling about the artworks; sometimes it led to vivid, emotional responses in the group. The gathering ended with a final ritual: After a few minutes of silence, we ended the night by taking turns around the circle to state what we each took from the bowl for the week to come and what it was that we wanted to leave behind.

I had named our communal studio the Reflective Circle of Peers, but we liked calling it the "radical sewing circle" which harkened back to our mothers' and grandmothers' own participation in transformational rehabilitation among their kind. We established patterns for meeting and interacting based on continuity, interpersonal trust, psychological freedom and safety.[18] Our studio was committed to creating itself out of an open flow of interactions and to supporting one another's stated intentions rather than planning a set agenda in advance. We committed to follow basic practices of council meeting.[19] We tried always to speak with intention, meaning that reflective thought went toward contributing only what had relevance, heart, and meaning. We listened with attention, attempting to suspend judgment, memory and ego that might otherwise filter what was being said through preconceived thought and feeling. We self-monitored the impact and contributions of our words and actions upon one another, asking "What is the intent of the circle in this moment? Is what I am saying or doing helping it or distracting?" Because we shared leadership, with every individual agreeing to lead one of the gatherings, the circle helped us form new alliances as peers, modeling equality and democracy in our community.

While people use the circle in many ways, ours was shaped by well-known art therapy practices and years of experience with the studio as a form for gathering and interacting. We cherished the long and ancient history of the circle as a form of council among many people. We were familiar with the techniques of focused conversation, reflective dialogue, and silence, and knew how to use a talking piece to slow the pace, create reflective listening and responding, and touch the group's consciousness. Respectful speaking and listening to the images created in the artworks was a mutually understood group norm. We regarded the images created as sacred forms that needed our humble attention, not graphic indicators to be analyzed, dissected, and thus, killed.

The art and reflections that arose during and after each weekly gathering were placed in an artistic journal that was passed from leader to leader as an object for reflecting on what was arising in our circle and needing further response. Each gathering would open with the leader's reflections on the shared journal from the weeks before and a focused intention. In this way, the artistic journal acted as the aesthetic voice of our group from which each week's structure was created to further our community consciousness. While it began as a record of our communal history, almost immediately the group journal of art and reflective writing assumed a living power that influenced and directed the circle's life in subtle ways. Created in a very specific culture, such works can approach the embodiment of an intense, emotional experience and so become a living form.[20] Cassirer tells us that all image magic rests on this same idea that the image is not a dead imitation of an object but is sentient, a collaborator in the creative undertaking.[21] In the image is found the essence or the soul of the object.[22]

The magical perception of the world in which objects are made to cleanse and carry away what pollutes our source is a universally accepted practice found in the scapegoat concept of various religious practices.[23] A hallowed place always is set apart for such rituals, where sins or disease can be split off and vested in some form of object. Transformed into an embodiment of the suffering, the scapegoat is then ceremoniously cast out. In the practice of art therapy, the studio space and the art object become empowered, like the scapegoat, and used to transform inner conflict so that an altered sense of self can emerge.[24] Often motivated by suffering, one purpose of the studio is the making of soul, for the artist as well as the community. Our reflective circle practiced a timeless pattern of re-enchantment that depends upon a believing community, in this case, a small and committed group of artists. Creating the magical space, through rituals and ritual objects, where emotions are awakened, felt, and expressed frees up rigid, repetitive attitudes and perceptions that have fossilized from lack of creative, life-affirming energy. Approaching the toxic wound with actual and symbolic support and safety allows energy to flow again, returning the individual to the sympathies and empathies that connect people to one another.[25] Thus, the provision of a communal sanctuary awakens in the individual a renewed relationship to the community, which is restored in turn.

What happens when we attend to the transformational energies that exist in communal healing practices and spaces? If it is accurate to trace many of our present dilemmas to the "disenchantment of the world," then how do we break the spell and circle of routines of our violent world and begin the transition into a different stream of experience?[26] I called the circle of peers together to address these questions from the place of my own core values as an artist and art therapist in community with others. My purpose was supported by my goal of nurturing healing in ways that help us regain what is lost, support one another, and find ways to sustain deep change. I hoped that in the process we would come, as a community, to better understand of the roots of disenchantment and the process of re-enchanting our work and life spaces.

In the disenchantment, I encountered a longing to reconnect to the sources that sustain and nourish art therapists, generated within the spaces of their inner and outer lives. The studio is a deep structure in the imagination of art therapists seeking sanctuary, a resting place. Sanctuary is an image that invites peacemaking, and making peace means making whole. The gathering space we created was a bit of space sculpted from the expanse of our lives that provided sanctuary for our wounded spirits to rest and reside, to be cleansed, or to knit themselves together again. The circle, an ancient form, held our longing for the studio—not so much as a physical place but a place of consciousness. The germinating force of the circle's open yet enclosing space, we believed, would replenish our depleted energies and heal wounds created from the comings and goings of living.

On the first night, I placed in the center of our circle of chairs a large, handmade ceramic bowl as the tangible symbol of the transformational vessel I hoped our studio would become. I invited my peers to consider that whatever we place in the bowl, our circle, calls for our attention; it is the material from which we would create new, nurturing forms.

The First Circle: Walls and Victims

I imagine that had our circle included men (not that we had excluded them but they simply didn't answer the call), our art and people making would have taken on a very different character. I don't know what that would have looked and felt like; I only know this particular group's shared life in this particular time and place. It began with the image, on our first night's gathering, of walls. Walls surround us, we said, keeping us out. Keeping us in, domesticating us and robbing us of our creativity, and contributing to a special sense of victimhood. In our shared journal, Melody reflected on her reaction when, at the group's closure, someone in the circle said that what she most wanted was to leave her sense of victimization behind. "I believe that I jumped in," she recalled, "with uncharacteristic disregard for her feelings because I felt so strangely connected, protected, comforted (all odd to me) by my own image of 'Victim.' She's been with me so long! Why is she so hard to release? I know she serves me well and with important purpose, or at least she did. I really do wonder about that strong reaction of mine and am curious to learn more. Especially because I feel so tired of art therapists seeing themselves as victims. I am beginning to notice now where I embrace 'Victim'; where I reject her."

"And the walls I've been banging up against! The immovable ones! The totally frustrating, impenetrable walls often in the form of stubborn people—people whom I believe will not or cannot change or bend. They have helped me as I begrudgingly turn toward myself and ask, 'Where does this damn wall live inside me?' When I bump into it again and again, I must at least praise the wall for how it has clarified and defined who I am, what I believe in, what I need. To be in a space where I can say 'I am. I exist,' and to see loving faces all around me there. Don't we need that reflection to strengthen us? What makes it so difficult to embrace my own needs? Perhaps that is the power of community I seek: to affirm that I exist as who I am—as who we are—in one another's loving embrace."

In the circle, we asked one another: Doesn't the well need the constricting structure of the wall to hold its deep, replenishing water? Yet when the walls are high and formidable, as they are among disenfranchised "outsiders" wanting their chance to share power with those on the inside, our disenchantment pulls at our sense of separateness and tells us that we must adapt at any cost. Be like water and find a way to seep in under the walls or through its cracks, we tell ourselves. That is a possibility, yes, we think. "But I have been so much like water, so able to flow and shift and adapt to their liking, that I became utterly invisible," one of us said. Made invisible, how do we know we exist?

Is it not a delusion to pretend that these walls don't exist and that as women or art therapists we aren't treated unfairly in the marketplace? We so desire to withdraw to the cave to replenish ourselves from living in the world of walls and dominance. But in these very walls we discover power is being stored. Our walls enclose a protected space, a place with an inner, spacious opening. We remember the feminine principle of the cave and the ancient time when a tribe's women retreated to a cave every month at their time of menses. This was always seen by the world outside the cave as a most dangerous time of women's power. Isolated, domesticated and victimized by the walls, our disenchanted spirits want to re-connect with the power of enclosed, set apart, interior spaces but we sense the danger in that act. Thus, we courageously begin on the first night by making the cave our retreat at the same time we nourish the procreative, interior spaces within our women's bodies.

The Second Circle: Lovers in Dangerous Times

> . . . when you're lovers in a dangerous time
> sometimes you're made to feel as if your love's a crime.
> Nothing worth loving comes without some kind of fight
> got to kick at the darkness 'til it bleeds day light.[27]

The danger of our power evokes, on the second night of our gathering, an uncanny feeling that being art therapists in this world is like being "lovers in a dangerous time." Sometimes, we think, we're made to feel our love's a crime and we "gotta kick at the darkness 'til it bleeds day light." Creating art is a passion that feels criminal at times, especially when we feel the harsh judgment and suffering of the world that looks upon us. But perhaps that is simply another illusion that binds our power, for we know as art therapists that making art is an act of self-empowerment that "kicks at darkness" and suffering. In the irresistible flow of life energy, we get in touch with life's tough implacability without forsaking our human responses. On this night, we gathered strength to look more equitably at life's suffering and survive what we see, giving what we can, wholeheartedly and warmly, precisely because we do see more unflinchingly what life costs us.[28] As if recalling the mythic dragon of power that has eaten up all the creative energies of the cosmos and needs the sword of intuition to shatter it, our circle evokes the images of destruction's force as a place to begin the process of our re-enchantment. We gazed at a picture (Figure 25) of "a woman of authority who holds back in a dark place" and heard Melody's reflection: "I thought about kicking at the darkness 'til it bleeds daylight and this guardian appeared. Are you keeping me from the light or holding me back? I surround you with my fears. I feel them tighten my chest; they sit on my shoulder. They are mostly about love. What if I don't know how? What if I am blind to its presence? I'm looking from this dark place. Why am I afraid to enter a place of such beauty? What keeps me here?"

"Like a blanket, the heaviness of victim lies over her," Michele echoed in response to her own art piece (Figure 26). "Unable, unwilling to move, to open her vision, she stays the victim.

–Unsupportive!
–Unloving!
–Un-everything! she shouts.

And many rally to her call. Like a cool breeze that flutters the edges of the victim blanket–they offer support. Why does she stay with victim, what would it take for her to stand, throw off the blanket of victim? Why would she want to? Why would she not?"

How do lovers survive with so much danger around? How do we, as art therapists, survive in a toxic world? We people of passion who seek to keep alive our art making in our lives beyond our work with others? "How do we communicate the essence of our work to those in authority over the health care of those we treat?" Min asked. "We must tell the stories for our clients' sakes–of their art, their insights, their awakenings, their pain, perceptions, their development, hopes, fears, passions. And we do this through verbal language. But the power of the art is diminished in the telling. The images our clients make–some hang on the wall, or are piled up in stacks. The ones who want the information

Figure 25. Woman of authority.

extracted from the art do not come to the studio! They do not see, do not have time."

"Life pushes the art around. Like the brown colors in my drawing (Figure 27), I lean away from the browns and purples, the reds of life's push. Yet I hold onto my treasure, the gift of visual image—a feast for the eyes, heart, and soul. On the inside, I close my eyes and stay with grace of what I know. Through the grace of art we will educate the value and effectiveness of art therapy. Not through griping, complaining, or being victim to a verbal world. The art speaks with grace and our clients are receptive to showing their work. It is time to be steadfast and show the healing power of art."

Transforming Toxins in the Cauldron of Community 177

Figure 26. The blanket of victim lies over her.

Figure 27. Leaning away from life's push.

"But oh!" Min wrote later, "How can I handle the push of life with grace?" How much we love—with passion and depth of expectation—our art, our calling, our work. Despite and within the killing spaces we are called to. The emotions that stirred in me this night recalled to mind a true story of two lovers in Sarajevo who died on a bridge trying to escape the city at war. I wondered, how was it possible for them to love one another—he was Christian, she was Muslim—much less find some small place of normalcy to go on living? As the bombs fell all night? As all the stately trees lining the boulevards disappeared for firewood in the cold winter months? As the sniper fire was always, always there in the background, never knowing what victim would be next? Their love was impossible in the best of circumstances, a miracle in times like those. Too dangerous to leave, too dangerous to stay—what kind of life can be lived in the limbo of between?

I once contemplated how world history might have changed if Hitler had been accepted into art school in Vienna. Had he been able to access art and creativity within himself, his destructiveness might never have been manifested on such a monumental scale.[29] Like other serial and mass murderers, he was a man in the grip of *thanatos,* the death force that counterbalances *eros,* or life energy. Feeling so dead and lifeless inside, he stopped at nothing less than the annihilation of all that he found unbearably alive. Most disturbing is that his culture gave him sanction to do just that.

"The bodies of the lovers lay on the Sarajevo bridge for days," I said, as I told the story to the circle and felt the deep connection to art therapists being like lovers in these dangerous times. "No mother could retrieve her child's wrecked beauty; no brother could avenge his brother's death; it was too dangerous. So their bodies remained for several weeks for the whole world to see their shame. Their shame for killing children and lovers. Lovers who said 'yes' to life and faced their deaths in open defiance of the forces that controlled their destiny and made them victims and martyrs. I do not know how to respond to this—my story feels bottomless to me—where is comfort? Where is courage? Can it live in my life, in my art?"

The imagery of violence permeates our life and workspaces and anesthetizes the senses, eroding the conscious awareness needed to deal effectively with its impact. But when we make art, we experience a felt connection to the world despite its suffering. Art can help us differentiate what is right from what is wrong and serves the human need to achieve and maintain freedom and justice.

Love, of course, is the force that transforms the violence. On this night we remembered that without love, life is crude, cruel and empty. To see the truth of love, we must be free of the imprisoning processes that destroy individual human life and disintegrate the world around us.[30] It is not enough to say that we need more love, and less shame and guilt. It takes great effort, whether that means having to fight, or having to be still, or finding some other place where life's vitality can flow again.

As we concluded our circle, we recalled the rhythmic image of push, push, push, push and rest, taking breath. Suddenly, we beheld ourselves in labor. We remembered the labor it takes for us to give birth. It is a cycle of effort and rest. Knowing when to let go and rest is a challenge. And knowing we a part of a community of others making this effort also gives us permission to rest. This understanding empowers us and affirms the need to have a resting place, a place of the sanctuary. In the studio we replenish ourselves from the pushing, pushing, pushing of our passionate labors. We kick and "hammer at the walls," our loving is killed by sniper fire, and in the suffering or "bleeding" of being pulled apart, we despair of whether we can find peace and wholeness. In our ambivalence for the power of our creative work, we sometimes lean away from life's push, glimpsed in the circle this night. Then we realize it is none other than our birth rhythms calling us. We must not shrink from them.

Afterwards, in the middle of the following night, Michele took out the group journal and recorded her dream: "I awoke with the image of a broken cup in my awareness. It was shattered, shards and splinters were scattered in all directions. 'How do I repair it now,' I despaired, 'even if I could find all the pieces? Could I fit the hundreds of bits—flakes—back together to make a functional cup again?' At three in the morning, why was I absorbed in this dilemma? My logical self thought to sweep up the mess and throw everything in the garbage. But it was a short lived fantasy as I desired to fit the pieces back together. I realize now that it will never be the same cup again; it has changed forever."

"What are the possibilities for all this brokenness? I think of our circle of possibilities, our potential space. I saw so many possibilities reflected in the art, especially our diversity and the ability to create our own perceptions. But if I truly believe that, then how does 'victim' fit into the picture? Maybe it is my unwillingness to accept my own responsibility in the dance that leads me to being a victim. Or is it through being a victim that I actually come to this place of acceptance? I do know now that the cup did not fall off the counter by accident. I pushed it off; I could not stand to look at, or use that cup one more day. So I smashed it! I smashed it! It was no longer functional; it was useless; its original beauty stained, scratched, and unseeable in its present form. Now I am left with all these pieces. What do I do with all the pieces?"

The Third Circle: Feminine Wisdom and the Generational Roots of Violence

With the pieces and shards of the toxins, in the necessary darkness where we sometimes dwell, on our third night together we began to cook. The suffering of the clients whose stories tear at our hearts and minds, the disempowering realities of our work lives that convince us of our victimhood—these are simply the materials with which we creat our art, both apart from and flowing back into the various spaces where we live. Leading us, Debbie described our circle "not only as an enclosure but, paradoxically, also an opening. Thoughts fly in and out, comfort, sharing, victim, pain, walls, power and passion! I try to stay open to any possibility and find it is hard work. So tonight I offer up images that lead down many paths. Let's stir the pot, see what comes up."

We began with a poem—"an unspoken hunger we deflect with knives, eating avocados with sharp silver blades, risking the blood of tongues repeatedly"[31]—and a story of a woman who dreamed she walked toward a grizzly bear and embraced it. A man she told her dream to replied, "Get over it." "Why?" she asked. "Why should we give up our dream of embracing the bear? For, it has everything to do with exposing and embracing a commitment to the wildness within—our instinct, our capacity to create and destroy. It is an embrace of paradox. Paradox preserves mystery, and mystery inspires belief."[32]

A powerful she-bear lived in the cave of our communal studio this night, going into and coming out of her restorative cycle of hibernation. We would do well to listen to her and remember that creativity always has such an ebbing and flowing of energy. We listened to a story of a grizzly mother with two cubs which suddenly bolted through the trees as a female elk ran to other the side of the clearing, stopped, and swung back toward her. Within seconds, the grizzly emerged with an elk calf secure in the grip of her jaws. The sow elk, only a few feet away, watched the grizzly mother devour her calf. "She pawed the earth desperately with her front hooves, but the bear was oblivious. Blood dripped from the sow's muzzle. The cubs stood by their mother, who eventually turned the carcass over to them. Two hours passed. The sow buried the calf for a later meal; she slept on top of the mound with a paw on each cub. It was not until then that the elk crossed the river in retreat."[33]

"We are capable of harboring *both* these responses to life in the relentless power of our love. As women connected to the earth, we are nurturing *and* we are fierce, we are wicked and we are sublime. The full range is ours. We hold the moon in our bellies and fire in our hearts. We bleed. We give milk. We are the mothers of first words. These words grow. They are our children. They are our stories and our power."[34] The bear is the guardian of that wild, feminine power and it rose mightily in our circle. In the fullness of her force, we could barely hold our ground and felt ourselves confused, questioning, shrinking, "What now? What next?" we asked. "Where am I in this power and passion—when do I run from the chasing man," as Melody mused in another dream she shared, "when do I decide to give up the chase? And to choose to end the chase by lying down, being vulnerable and opening to him. But if he sees me lie down, why then does he give up the chase at that moment? Why do I risk lying down only to find myself alone? What does he fear?"

In Melody's image (Figure 28), the bear takes off her pelt and reveals a woman in her primal state of being. She stands on the curve of a red crescent moon, like Venus rising from sea foam or like Christ, standing with arms spread, beseeching heaven, one hip thrust out, head surrounded by the halo of the moon's light. Will she know when to stand in the fierceness of her heart and when to chase the chasing man? She can't only be "Earth Mother"—she needs this man, too. Masculine and feminine are the dual forces and she can't be one, alone, ever. "So I have a few questions," Melody reflected in response as she gazed on her painting. "Let's start with the two mothers—the elk and the bear; one sustained the other, offering such pain and loss. I wonder about my children, like the cubs in the scene. I wonder at the violence they've witnessed. Do they understand that love is like meat to their mother, not a choice? We have to be nourished. Yes, I want to throw off my

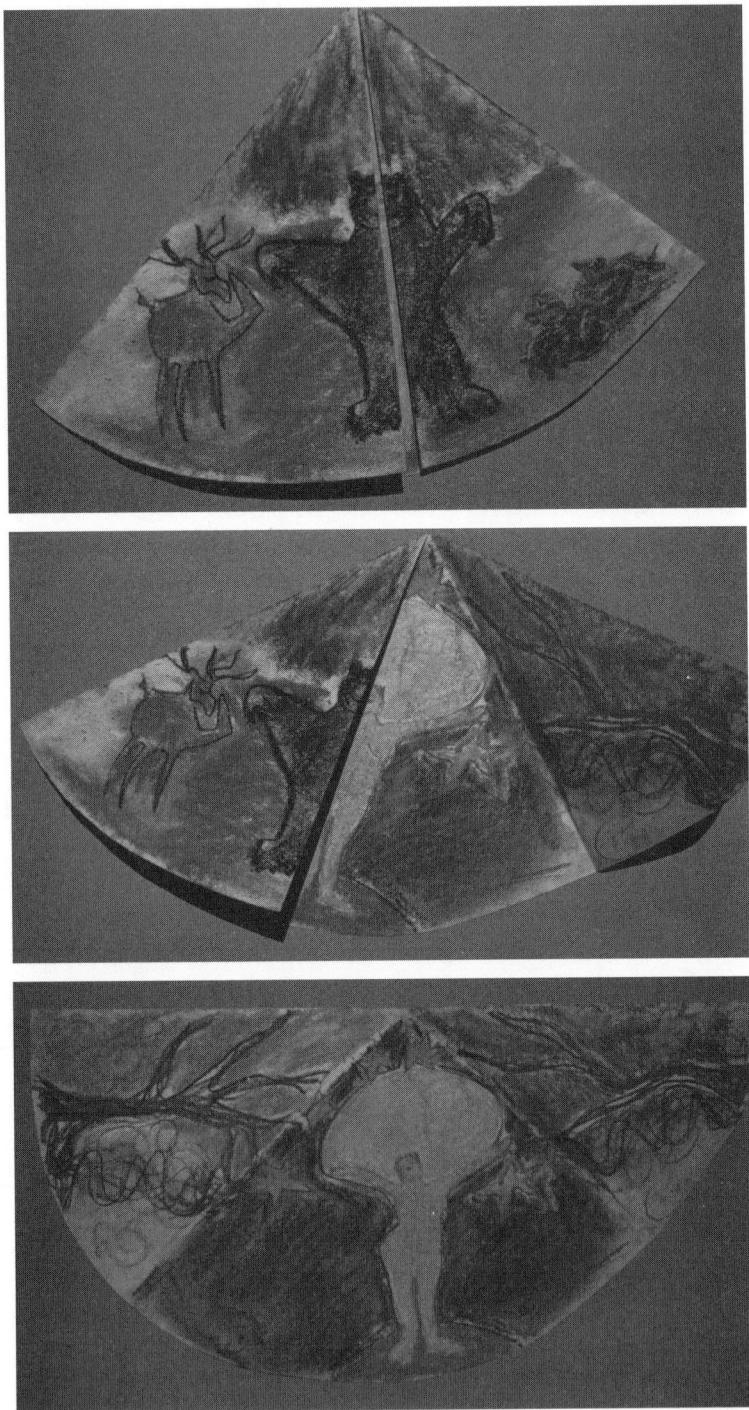

Figure 28A–C. (A–Top, B–Center, C–Bottom) Bear woman triptych.

pelt. I want you to see the spirited woman that is me. I'll go out on a limb

> Raging rivers I'll swim
> Courage to share
> I have one last question, though—Is anybody there?"

But not to deny her power, it lives in Michele's art (Figure 29) as a bear-cloaked woman, born and living deep within the inner recesses of the procreative womb. We see it bleeding. It is the inner, emptying space. She stands balanced on the head of the penis, honored and sanctified. "We must get to know this power!" we laughed. We do not know it, as our ancestral women forbears did. We want it—we are redefining it, even now, living as we do in these times of changing woman-power. The bear woman is so powerful that we get afraid. Sonnie's art image (Figure 30) wears the bear-toothed pelt; she opens to her naked self. She is big bellied, holding to her chest the bear cub that has not yet been tamed. She recalled a man who used her, who took his power over her, and perhaps still does, metaphorically, in the toxic work environment—"he shaped and formed who we are, too," she said. "Made us, in part. Years and years later, we can say 'I forgive him.' I cherish the aggressive bear power that helped me get out into the world after years of hibernating in my safe den."

> Bear mother, sky mother,
> mother of wings.
> Winged woman
> of the wild, deep skies.
> Carry my soul, my spirit.
> I do believe in you.

Belly full, in my art (Figure 31) bear mother comes with magical, beating wings. An enchanted image, she is a guardian protector of the wild. Before, I believed that if I loved and opened myself that much to the world I would forever want to weep. But this night I remembered that even in such depression and disenchantment, all I really have to do is look up at the sky and see this winged, bear mother. Another lesson for our dis- or unenchanted spirits, we agreed, was to remember to look up from our cooking pot from time to time and gaze upon the resplendent cosmos that lights the darkness on our barren hillsides. We are alone only when our perception narrows to the task before us. The

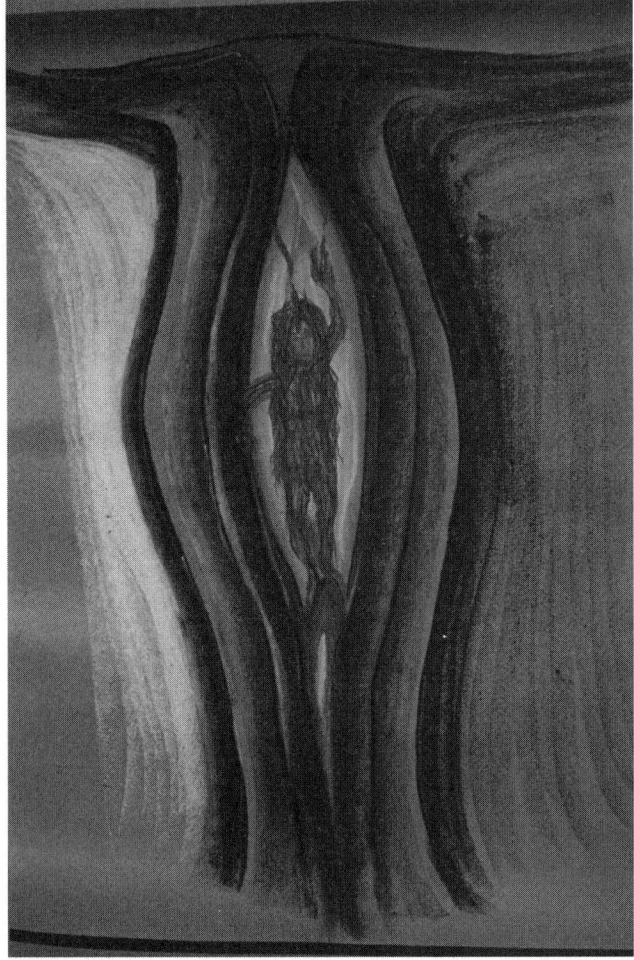

Figure 29. Balancing on the head of a penis.

isolated art therapist often feels disempowered in his or her small corner of the workplace. But within the enchanted landscape our perception changes: we are properly small in relation to the vastness of the cosmos, yet we are not alone. Our work places us at the crossroads of the soaring sky spirits and the molten earth energies always in dynamic change and motion. This hallowed place is the fountainhead of renewing energies, connecting our pasts, present, and future.

The last image of the night is from Min who holds the empty space, the lost mother (Figure 32). She said the stories took her to a place and time where she first learned what being a woman was about. "The sto-

Transforming Toxins in the Cauldron of Community

Figure 30. Taking off the she-bear pelt.

ries told by my aunts, the meals prepared, the focus on a woman's life task: raising her children. This was her purpose. In my art, I saw the story of my mother's life and my own, our similarities, our differences. Her life: much strife, struggle, traditional. Mine filled with my own strife yet living in a time when the choices are mine. I wouldn't have it any other way. I love being a woman who has choices."

In her later reflections Min wrote, "I showed my vulnerability and I wept before my peers. Did they misunderstand and do they see me differently now? I let it go. I have had many losses in my life and the feelings come out when they need to. I must have felt safe to be so much

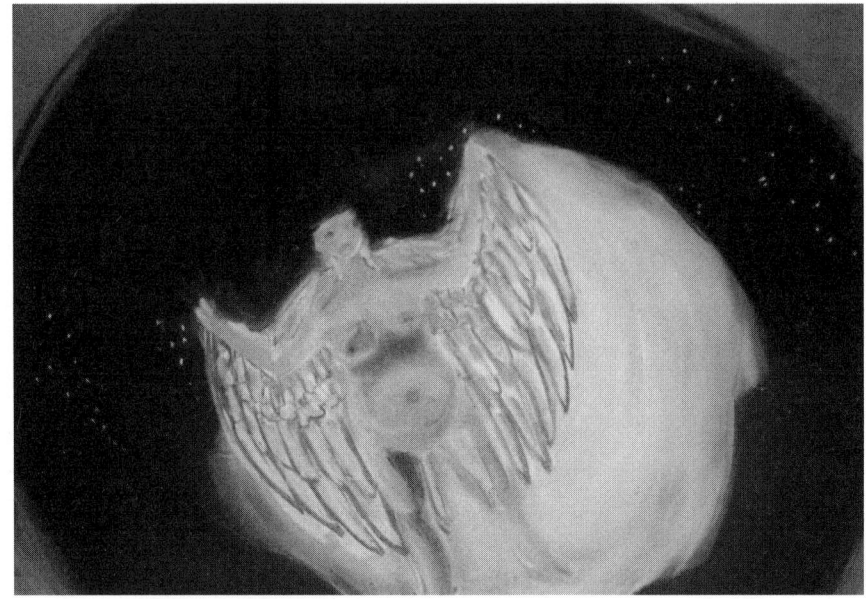

Figure 31. Winged sky-bear.

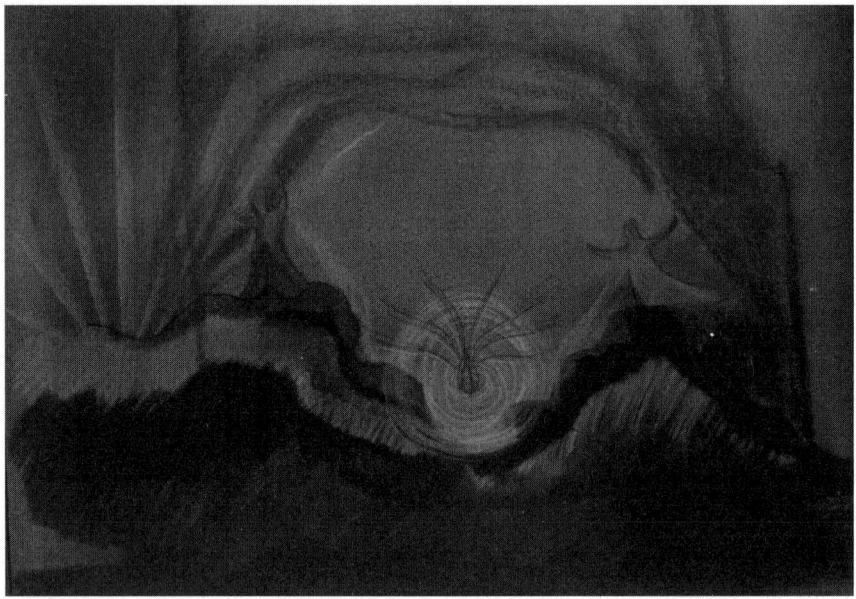

Figure 32. Lost mother.

my authentic self. As I moved forward into the workweek, I looked to my past to understand transitions in my life. I live in the present to enjoy my life. But what is not clear is what the Bear is for me? Perhaps it is courage facing fear. Strength facing adversity. Both gentle and hard, being understood and misunderstood. I do not know. What I do know is that I am becoming, changing, expanding my knowledge and my senses. I am listening better, and being gentler with myself as I try to be with others. Perhaps the bear is both my story and my knowing. Perhaps the bear comes forth when needed."

Reconciliation must include a profound understanding of the toxic roots of violence, carried through the generations, which must be seen clearly before they can be dissolved.[35] Krishnamurti, the late Indian philosopher, wrote that the wars we witness are never the accidental result of an irresponsible society, but merely the spectacular, bloody expression of our daily actions in relationship to things, to people, and to ideas. As long as this relationship is not fully and deeply understood, there can be no peace and violence cannot be transcended. "The real causes of war," he said, "are hidden in our unwillingness to keep inwardly, psychologically free. As long as we are not ready to abandon our various compulsions which are merely the chains provided by society, the problem of violence will continue."[36]

Min's lost mother is an angel who looks over the layered earth; the earth that is in motion, below the empty space she protects. Layers of molten rock, of earth shifting and forming. Reforming. She stands on the high place as an angel who looks over us, protecting and witnessing. The mandala, spider web-like place of power, we see, is the center of the soul, the womb. Surrounded by the empty space that is not empty. For how else can we have creative renewal? We bleed each month to prepare the space, the emptying. We need these empty spaces—we think our power is in the doing, the filling of the space, but it is not.

Magical night of women's power. So much to bear witness to in between spaces. We do not know; we do not have answers—only questions. We are still shaping and forming who we will be as women of power being recreated. Our circle soothes the wild hungry cub in us, while the mother bear teaches that love is like meat: not a choice but a primal need to be nourished. The landscape is bloody, but of course it is, since blood is life. Birthing—the creating of new possibilities in our practices, our creative work, our personal and professional lives—

always is accompanied by blood, gore and mess, by tears and vulnerability. Powerful artist women, on this night we dance on the head of a penis; we create a circle that celebrates the juicy and resplendent. But still the question, Where am I in this power and passion? When do I run and when do I decide to give up the chase? Why risk surrender if it means finding myself alone?

The Fourth Circle: Bring Back the Peace We Are All Aching For

> . . . Is it true that you've come back, is it true that you're here
> Is it true after all this time the cycle's complete
> And have you brought the wisdom that we had then lost
> Oh have you brought the peace that we've been aching for?
> . . .[37]

Acceptance and tolerance, Michele offered us, as images for our fourth circle. By night's end we were in a state of grace, in the presence of magic stirred and moved, and feeling a profound sadness. Min told us a story of grace from her art therapy practice: sitting in the presence of fifty family members, a circle she held so they could tell each other what was deep in their hearts, asking them to imagine "what if their lives were different?" Sharing their tears of pain, sadness, relief, love and joy; she made magic. With gratitude, she said, for being an art therapist. She delights in that risk-taking because she trusts it. Her enchantment is fed by her community and her art, and that allows her to step out into the unknown and feel held by others. Her art expressed opening: holding out her hands through which wind and spirit swept into her like the spirit of the bowl that was near her as she painted. Debra recalled her labor, how she needed to rest sometimes and to fight and struggle other times, just to feel the pain of contractions as she brings something new into being. Sonnie beheld an otherworldly image of a woman who came to her in her art (Figure 33). Paraphrasing the poem offered to begin our circle that night, she wrote:

> You're here—the cycle is complete
> you brought the wisdom, the peace
> You've been waiting
> for your chance to come
> You're like a song on the wind

Transforming Toxins in the Cauldron of Community 189

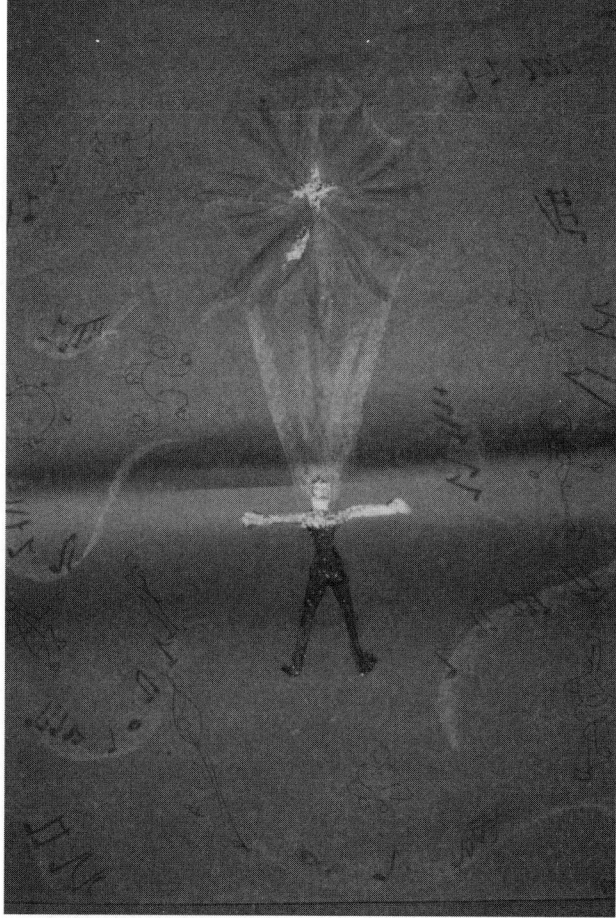

Figure 33. You're here–the cycle's complete.

You brought the wisdom,
the peace as balm for our wounds.
You knew the answers no one
in this land who couldn't hear
Bring back the wisdom,
bring back the peace
Our souls are fed.

Whether we are accepting
the diversity within ourselves
or the great diversity among us
there is a reassurance,

an other kind of love, a wisdom and a peace
that passeth understanding
and all the way there are hints
like songs on the wind.

"A process was started," Min told her, "and it is not yours alone to complete." Melody, too, labored to bridge timelessness and space. She had forgotten her art supplies but found an old unfinished image to work on, saying "She looks like a dried up crone–like the desert so parched. Why do I push away the rain? The drop by drop –I think of Chinese water torture. Oh, the aching! What is it that I can and cannot accept? I ask my art. I have guesses. Tolerance seems like settling for something–I will fight for what I want

what I need
what I deserve
Will I accept less? Is that tolerance? How do I have arms big enough to accept it, to hold it?"

"I inherited you from another time," she told her drawing, "another picture left unfinished. How do I accept you into this one? What is the new picture? It shows a sad-faced juggler who says I cannot give up the fight, that I must keep these balls in the air. Another figure is holding the empty space, a place of loss. I accept that. But there is something beyond this picture I do not yet know. I see the hungry sticks of figures guarding the inherited one who looks far into the past beyond my knowing, who's mouth just says 'oh'–a circle of nothing more to say."

Michele held the rim of the circle from the place of leadership tonight, but shook with the emotions of betrayal that fed her disenchantment, having felt shamed in an incident that week. When she projected this feeling of not belonging and regarded her artwork as different from the rest of us, we tried to hold her gently without judgment. Her art showed a chalice: holding blood, bleeding, driven through with a sword (Figure 34). "What is this image?" she asked. "The spilling of blood to feed the parched soil? No. No grail for me," she asserted. "I bring to the circle the themes of acceptance and tolerance–but I'm not there," she later wrote in the group journal. "I've tried to skate around my anger at what has been said, implied, suppressed. Such betrayal: it hurts not to be accepted when everything I know tells me I am right. Where is the tolerance for me? Where is the

Transforming Toxins in the Cauldron of Community 191

Figure 34. No grail for me.

peace? Just when I feel centered about what I am doing, I allow myself to be pulled out of my center and into anger. I brought this issue to the circle and risked exposure for my insecurities, my need/desire for approval. I swore that I would resolve this on my own, in my own way. But I brought it here anyway in hopes of finding some acceptance and peace."

Her creative spirit is killed by such martyrdom, by the soft submission of acceptance women are told is theirs. Maybe the acceptance called for comes from a place of fighting energy, of taking a stand and saying "NO! I will NOT give up or give in to you! I am a fighter! That is what I am here for. I will not go softly, I will fight. I take up the fight—it is my place here." Angry women in the circle, where is rest and reconciliation in this space of our many-sided selves?

Debra heard the call to take up the fight and asked, "Is this my call? No! I have only just ventured out. I need to find my true way and listen to my true voice." Her art showed ridges and waves, moving into three dimensions, finding a way—like Michele's conviction that the passage through obstacles is like water finding the chinks in the wall to flow through. Leah's response showed the heavy burden of Eve and the apple, being blamed, as women, for original sin. She had drawn a keyhole in the apple that reveals a passage. She saw it as a key to finding the way out or through the burdens placed on her. She wrote:

> Keys to acceptance, tolerance—
> What do they look like?
> Earning wisdom
> Discovering peace
> external peace among peoples
> internal peace:
> what does 'I am who I am'
> really mean?

Krishnamurti would remind us that our own transformation is of the utmost importance in discovering peace because we, ourselves, are the cause of the confusion in the world.[38] We have the power through our daily acts to immediately transform the surrounding world or to cause more sorrow and confusion. We beheld in our circle the fear of losing love and respect, or of being rejected, and it is runs to our core. But reacting out of protection closes off the life force by isolating our pain and vulnerability. Fear and protection often prevent us from inquiring very deeply into the truth for we may discover something in ourselves or in the other that will leave us feeling more vulnerable and insecure.[39] But when we choose to learn from conflict, we open ourselves to a shift in perception. By becoming aware of the protection and examining it from as many angles as possible, vital energy is released and the experience is made more spacious. The conflict may never be resolved, yet the key is that if we actively explore with one another, it can serve to promote growth, intimacy, and trust. What is freeing is the exploration, not the resolution of the conflict[40] that, like Eve's apple, may exist forever or across many generations and cultures.

I have created an image of the parched desert (Figure 5, p. 64). Like Sonnie's woman of another realm who comes blowing in on the winds, I beheld an image of a grandmother approaching. She walks toward me over the parched, hardened earth where no rains ever fall. She carries a bowl of water. Is it to drink from, to parch my thirst? Or is it blood, the sacrifice of ancestral martyrdom that she brings across from the other place? I am waiting, silently, patiently. Acceptance for me this night in our circle was this still, waiting patience. For grandmother's arrival, for my time of meeting. At the night's closure, speaking of what we will take from the circle and what we will leave for the week, my heart felt filled with sadness. Not in pain, but just as it was, the sadness accepted. Then I realized that my grandmother's bowl, her sacrifice, was not water but tears. It is a bowl of tears that she brings across the desert to replenish me.

Michele had led the circle that night with her reflection on an isolated raindrop hitting the surface of a large, dry desert plain. "The single drop of water soon evaporates. The dry earth remains hard, cracked, unable to support all but a few types of life. But," she tells us, "I imagine now a gentle steady rain of drops falling in a small area of this desert. The earth dampens and softens. Soon, a puddle forms and small birds and animals drink from this unexpected treasure, and life expands. As this small puddle accepts more drops, the water begins to flow out into the dry cracks of the earth, finding its way into lost and little known crevices, and filling them with life supporting nourishment. But what is the danger here? Could there be too many raindrops? A raging torrent? A flood? I don't know. I do know there has been a dampening of the dry earth tonight: our 'radical sewing circle' is such a puddle that feeds the pool which supports life."

"One drop cannot do it," Michele said, speaking of how to bring creative vitality back to the desert of our disenchantment. "But what about another one, and another one? Soon the earth will be dampened; soon something will grow there." Something transformed. "There are art therapists who are not in these circles," she now said, "not in the state organization or going to meetings, or in any way attending to replenishment by our community. They are burned out and dried up. They do not see the value of the community; do not feel the urge of passion stir in them anymore."

Yes, together we make magic. We make the rain. With a gentle rain, the desert—dormant for so long—bursts into sudden bloom where there was dried earth before. Seeds were sown long ago, waiting for the rains, however long it takes for the rains to come. The circle revealed its hunger for such a landscape. On the fourth night, we explored the hunger and longing for the creative source to always be within reach, in images of the moist earth soaked in the blood of life and the clear waters that cleanse and replenish us. So often we work when we are bone dry and toiling in the desert, our sweat being drawn inexorably out of us. Our imaginations brought us right to the gruesome places we know where nothing grows. Art therapy tries to take root, often it seems, in facilities and institutions that are like hard, cracked, dry earth unable to support all but a few types of highly specialized life forms.

We put our many paradoxes and contradictions in the bowl this night. We asked for water, we waited for guidance yet guiltily realized we must do the work together, ourselves. We asked for peace through tolerance and acceptance but raged at the injustices we witness. How can we accept less? we asked. Giving up the fight—is that what tolerance means? We plunge the sword into a proffered cup of blood sacrifice and we say, I can't accept this chalice you offer. We open our hands, asking to give and forgive; we connect to the many, diverse parts within ourselves. The bowl of our communal cauldron held the softness and forgiveness we think is wanted, but also the energies of pain, loss, betrayal, and anger. We remembered that when we choose to hang onto feeling betrayed we give away our badly needed power. Neither maturity nor wisdom can be purchased except through making hard choices and learning from what most greatly challenges us. No matter how difficult, we can learn to use the offending reality as a catalyst for change and creation.

The Fifth Circle: Searching for Home

Leah guided us on the fifth night, saying "It seemed to me as though the whole world, all its space and time, as well as a sense of history somehow occupied our small circle last week. Our heritage, our ancestry, crossing a desert land, being stuck inside the forbidden fruit trying to shake off guilt, not really wanting to accept certain so-called truths—a blood-filled chalice and piercing sword, songs of peace and wisdom riding on the wind, conflict, tears and turmoil over acceptance—such are our images of the struggle. Each of our paths go their own ways, then converge for sacred time in this 'room of our own' where the light of candles flicker against the bowl's round walls."

"What I'm left with is a sense of searching in the midst of transitions—searching as we try on different identities and try to define who we are in our non-static selves. We come out of the cave and go inward again, meeting up with world moments, then with self-moments. It is a back and forth swing of the pendulum." As inspiration for the circle, she offered the words of David Wagoner's poem "Lost":[41]

> . . . The trees ahead and the bushes beside you
> Are not lost. Wherever you are is called Here . . .
> You are surely lost. Stand still. The forest knows
> Where you are. You must let it find you.

We come to the fifth gathering searching in the myriad of images released in the process of re-enchantment. The mixture of the paradoxes we gave the cauldron to hold starts to take a mysterious form we've not seen before. Secretly, we realized that we are making magic. We looked inside the opening of the bowl, our cauldron, and see an image of a yellow, spiraling orb that pulls us into a spell of enchantment but spins out too many paths to know which one to follow. We see an old oak tree that radiates magical sparks, promising new vitality to the frail and unsteady. A face appears in our cauldron (Figure 35). It is so fiery hot that it melts ice, and we gather up the melted water like a cool drink in a hot, sweaty place:

> "Oh Dear—
> as I heard stated earlier—
> the beginning outline of a heart,
> that then needed a face;
> a face of heat,
> brightness and passion.
> She was left with a hole
> on the left side of her brain.
> The hole filled with a soft, cool blue.
> Spilled out
> and surrounded her
> in coolness.
> I don't have a clue about her."

Figure 35. The face of fire and ice.

Michele said the word "passion" came to mind as she painted this image, recognizing that her passion for her work was so great that she could feel its heat consuming her. There is a vital aspect that smolders inside us, not caring whether we have an outlet for it or not.[42] We considered our burning passions and ambitions, the fires of love that can break out but also break a person down. "How do you know it's time to cool it?" I asked her. "Maybe it needs to burn up the old in order to bring in a new space for the new."

"No," she said, "it doesn't feel good anymore. I need to let go of some of these things, to clear a space." Her passionate woman's face holds a lush heart aroused. "I know absolutely nothing about this picture," Michele said. "But she has something to do with being lost," Melody replied. The woman's face was a crazy quilt of hot colors, "like a landscape," Sonnie told her. "I am attracted to her shiny, black lips."

Curiously, there is a space or hole in the left side of the face's head that Michele filled in with a cool, cool, blue. She said she didn't know why, just that the face couldn't seem to complete itself and wanted that blue color. Now we could see that she looked like "fire and ice," like a face that emerges from the ice, melting it as she comes forward in the encounter. There was a sense that we were pushing beyond revitalized energies, awakening our passions to the point of self-consumption. We explored how it is that we could contain this heat yet keep our hearts open. Can one be too passionate? And need that drink of cool water in the hot, hot place? Now I thought about enchantment as permitting the wild woman to be greedy. We sometimes want to be in the magical space all the time and get frustrated, as Melody said, "when the rest of the world is clueless about our magic and our hot passions." Debbie remarked that last week when her energy had been so soft and relaxed, and she wanted to tell the group, "Come on! Cool it! You need to relax!" Tonight it seems we did "cool it"–Melody, Michele's and mine were images that were similar in their cool, subdued, and dark colors; Debra's, Sonnie's and Leah's seemed to show the other side of the polarity. All were held in the circle.

"We seem to be searching," Leah remarked, "for who we are and who we choose to become." She looked at her picture and said that it expressed the lost forest that was the soul, and that she was searching for herself in the soul place. Sonnie's (Figure 36) was a most magical piece, with a large oak tree holding the figure of a woman, as though contained or trapped in it, or perhaps emerging from it. In the crown are the raven and the wren that know where they are. They are "home." A frail, bent over man approaches the tree, drawn towards its life-giving magic in a swirl of glitter. Maybe he is the magic-maker, a wizard himself, where we only see a frail, bent over man.

Debbie mentioned that this was the first night she didn't come "empty" to the circle. "I took the time for some nourishment first. Was that the difference? Today I am full enough but agitated." Melody's art (Figure 37) was beautiful and tender in her expression of feeling disenchanted. Her picture was of a young boy lured into and left in a cave, and forced to find a new family. The boy is hunkered over in self-rejection but Melody saw the gesture as humbled. The cave and the deep

Figure 36. I made this place around you.

dark woods are backlit by vivid reds and oranges that give a feeling of transparency and luminosity to the whole painting. It is as though the woods are not really so terrifying and dark, the boy is not really so lost, and the feeling of being trapped and stuck is not really stuck at all, since there are access points all over. "Today I, too, feel trapped in the cave," she wrote. "The rock is rolling in and my mother didn't sing to me. There was no music or I've forgotten the song. It seems too long since I've felt that shelter of warmth and strength. Walking to the studio tonight, I was lost in my private despair. Feeling like I'd failed or been failed everywhere today. So heavy. In your company it lifted," she told the circle, saying that it was a place of being held by a group that

Figure 37. Trapped in the cave.

sees more deeply within her. We see her light within her sadness and we draw that light out.

Finding life in the balance requires not control but dynamic connectedness. We may not be able to control the events that cause us to suffer but always we can search for the impact of our feelings of discontent on the rest of our life. Often, in the disenchantment, we believe we are surely lost and will never find the way back to peace. Yet, the third way, beyond fight or flight, is purposeful reengagement in the disenchanting reality, a true belief that "wherever you are is called Here" which "makes this place around you." "If you leave it you may come back again, saying, Here." What matters is how we interpret what is happening and whether we can see life's upheavals and dissatisfaction as catalysts rather than catastrophe. Standing still, we awaken to the sure knowledge that the world itself knows where we are. No longer lost, we find our way home.

The Sixth Circle: Necessary Soul-work

"I've been dreaming that I've lived in another world. I hope I do not miss it too much" we heard Sonnie say as she opened the circle on the sixth night. Could our disenchantment have to do with being out of touch with our soul? we asked. Is this the source of our deep longing for "home"? When the energy of the soul is recognized and valued, it begins to infuse the life of the personality and when the personality come fully to serve the soul, that is authentic empowerment.[43] Sonnie read: "Our soul is not a passive or a theoretical entity that occupies a space in the vicinity of your chest cavity. It is a positive, purposeful force at the core of your being. It is that part of you that understands the impersonal nature of the energy dynamics in which you are involved, that loves without restriction, and accepts without judgment. If you desire to know your soul, the first step is to recognize for yourself that you have a soul."[44]

What is soul? What do our souls want? "Truly in my innermost soul place, being an art therapist is a bit of holiness, a bit of heaven to be shared" one of us told the circle. Another showed a picture of a soul quilt made out of all the fragments of lives she has come to know as an art therapist, "all those feathered fronds asking of me simply to be held and noticed." Buried under desire, under the demands and responsibilities of day-to-day living. Buried under societal pressures, family needs. One cannot simply "be" with nothing beyond the being. "It chose me, called me in my youth. I have climbed and reached the top," said one of us who saw a landscape set before her. And at the top is yet another landscape to walk upon. "I will always climb the mountains set before me. I do not know the place beyond the high mountain. But I trust I will be part of something that is good—that is hopeful—that perseveres. It is not with ease, but with belief and trust I move to the mountains."

"My soul is a young child appearing at the opening of the cave, asking me to come out and play," said another (Figure 38). "The image is inspired by a dream I had many years ago when my daughter was a little girl," she said. "I dreamed that I was in a cave. I was waiting for the wise woman to appear. I had smudged and prepared the space. Reverently I awaited her coming. A shadow darkened the doorway and I looked up, expectantly. It was the face of Erica, my little daughter. 'Come out and play!' she demanded. She was a wise soul even then. Tonight she appears—as my soul? Have you come back, been awakened, decided it was time to push me out of the cave?"

"My soul is a black Madonna, with earthy, wet hair standing in moonlight," said one of us, telling her dream that she was pregnant despite certain knowledge that she could not have more children. "I

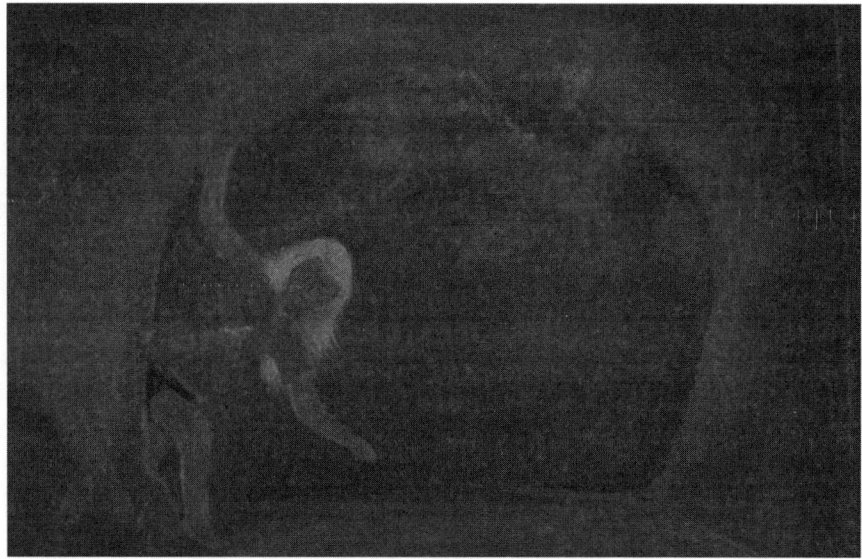

Figure 38. Come out and play with me!

knew it was a miracle child and that I was ready for it. I felt warm, safe, and ready. My soul-Madonna is earthy, wet, black with some chocolate colored hair. She has seed/fire/baby in her belly and greens under her feet. She makes me think about how I have long felt opposite to her unpredictability."

Another said, "My soul is encased in my personality, with its soft petals, sturdy stem, and protective thorns, aching for deeper connections with everything but mostly with myself." She showed us her beautiful, alive and luscious flower on a thorny stalk, backlit by a luminous moon or globe. She spoke of when she first started to make art in her life "just for me—not for the galleries, not to sell, not to give as gifts, not for the professors I needed approval from, not the portraits I made for my family," she said. "No, just to make art for me alone." Art therapy brought her to that place and she became acquainted with her soul for the first time. "It is not like a religion," she said, "but art therapy is something filled with my spirituality. Making art is like praying."

"So why don't we want to make art more often?" I asked. "If we know that it connects us to our soul, our center? If we know it is going to feel so good for us?" Somehow we have to walk a path between the worlds. "Our job is to balance the energies. It is like the shaman who can't be in the world because she would lose her power. And the city dweller who can't be shaman. But we can walk between the worlds, we balance the energies between them. We can't be in one place or the other for too long." "It's a rhythm, like making love," Sonnie said. "You love and let go, love and let go." "Or like an orgasm," Melody told us. "You know how hard you try to get to that orgasm and then it is there and it is gone? You can't hold onto it forever but you keep wanting to go back there." There's an ache, a longing for it the moment you let it go and in that moment you are filled with soul.

Melody said she wanted to explore that line between her lives to see if she can't blend it more–instead of her "oh-so-wonderful art therapy work and her totally unfulfilling, clueless and ordinary rest of her life," as she put it. Because art making is like that, too. It becomes so special that we feel we can't do it at all unless we make a special place for it– everything has to be just right, just perfect–space, timing, materials, everything. Or, as Michele said, you put so many hours into something you make and you don't want to let go of the grandiosity it makes you feel. She, too, wants to commit to making art wherever she is rather than only at "special" time and places. "That's the ego part," Leah said, "the personality that thinks it has to set everything up and make a grand plan. When all you need to do is pay attention."

Yes, we decided. It is so much about paying attention to what is already there and giving it space instead of having to set things apart. It is as though your ego sees how special art is to your soul and so your ego has to be in control of that oh-so-special contact with it. "Why not just make art–make life?" I said. "Wherever you are and with the materials at hand?"

There was much correspondence around the circle tonight in our images spontaneously created. Melody noticed this and remarked, "that is what is so convincing to me, that this circle is about spirit and that the spirit moves through us and is larger than us. We had to make a sacred space–it is here, so very here with us!" Min's still woman facing the mountain, Michele's still growing and alive flower, Melody's woman tree, rooted in the ground and reaching into five stars. Red roots flowing into Debra's rooted woman with the wet, black skin and the chocolate hair–a baby, red flame, a being growing inside her, like Melody's red roots. My cave with the luminous child peeking inside– just like Min's colors and a piece of Sonnie's soul quilt. Leah's tree, like the others, looking as if it were growing right through a page from her sketchbook: "Like we are deep inside the earth," Debra remarked, looking up at a tree with its crown touching the paper from below. "A very rooted tree, very central, not fragile at all," Melody said. And Sonnie's quilt–many, many squares like many lives, with the background fabric of her soul shining through it all, linking it all together and creating something whole from the fragments.

All the images were vibrant, strong and beautiful. We make such fine art when we give ourselves the opportunity to get back in touch with our soul or core. We carried these images and each other's words and presence throughout the workweek. Sonnie said that from time to time, she imagined a darkened room with our lit-up faces and voices, as she replayed the circle in her mind during the week. "I love our Radical Sewing Circle! We take our piercing, crocheted intellects to penetrate the fabric of our lives, our experiences," she wrote in the group journal, "and we weave together the parts that seem appropriate to our weekly compositions. Every little piece and feeling is worthy, as we sort, sift, search and re-search our experiences to bring forth the composition we will highlight for the evening and as a springboard for the following week. This process is such a creative joy for me–and it is a wonderful feeling to belong here. To be a member of such a thoughtful, spirit-filled group of talented women who possess such a bawdy sense of humor!" Once again, we felt grateful to be in each other's presence and to be part of such a giving community of fellows. We were filled with spirit and with lush images that were so radiant along the rim of the circle, as the bowl and our souls lighted the center.

The Last Circle: Making a Space for Dreaming and Returning Home

Min's words guided us in the beginning of the circle, saying, "We are women who are artists, we are therapists, and we are women of passion and love. This is our seventh week to gather and to offer support and acceptance of one another in personhood. We took time from our busy lives to gather once a week and to bring our whole selves to the circle." From gathering together we now shifted our thoughts to making a space for dreaming. "Blessed are dreams," she said, "for they help us create our lives beyond the confines and walls of predictability and structure. We must dare to dream and to have faith in our dreams. And so I believe we must dream about the future of our profession and dare to create beyond the limits, each of us at a pace that is right for ourselves. For tonight we go to the realm of dreaming—about our light, our soul's call, our hopes. Our enchantment of what can be for art therapy, if we would believe."

We had arrived at an understanding that what was needed was a space for dreaming. "After all, we go through our work days with everyone telling us 'you can't, you can't'," one of us wrote, "and if we take that in and make it ours, then we won't." We will lose our dreams, we said. But if we hold our dreams, we will influence and make our reality. Our art making is society's dreaming. It truly is the center of what we bring to the circle and take from it, as the circle closes and we carry its energies further into our lives. In our last gathering, we dream to give ourselves hope. A wild plethora of natural materials fills the studio space, strewn between and among us as we work. We tell silly stories while our hands shape our dreaming into material matter. We make dream catchers and prayer sticks, wind chimes, and talismanic objects to place at the threshold, to protect the dreamer to dream in peace.

Michele reflected later that in this small community she had peers who dream with her, held her in ways that she was not held elsewhere. She named her dreams—to have a loving relationship and to have a space of her own. "And I dream of the studio," she smiled. "I do dream, often and with great passion. I dream of a giving partnership, of images not yet born, unlimited laughter, love, and acceptance. My dreams are so vivid I can still feel them when I awaken. I attempt to weave them into the fabric of my waking world. Some dreams are actually tangible now; they are reality. Others keep that soft ache alive in me, letting me know that I am not done dreaming. Everyone must dream. To stop dreaming—well, that's like saying you can never change your fate."

"Dreams . . . dreaming . . . giving soul space, room to see with wisdom according to the dreams of the true self. The unconscious is slow to move—it needs reflective time, dreaming time—the open heart to allow enough love for the dreaming time to happen." Sonnie described how she couldn't get what she was making to hang together. She wanted very much to leave and go to her corner in the studio room but tonight she decided to stay with it, to stay with us and make art in our presence. She said her piece was like her life—it only barely hangs together with her humor. If she lifted it, it would fall apart, she laughed. But she created it anyway, grounded by laying pieces on the floor rather than desperately trying to tie it all together. Melody also struggled to get her dream catcher to hang together. She realized that all her fussing over it was simply a part of her creative process; instead of thinking, once it came together, "now why did I have to fuss so?" Leah's prayer stick, she said, "was so easy—all the right pieces were there and they all just came together." It seemed a great contrast to the difficult effort Leah had put into trying to make her art therapy practice a reality. "Yes. It is like that," Leah agreed. "Both are there—the times when it all comes together and the times when you can't do a thing to make it happen."

In the group journal I later wrote, "I dreamed, just before I woke up this morning, that I was running along a road that fronted Lake Superior. It was winter and there were places where ice tunnels had formed. I passed a place where a row of houses faced a huge levee or wall with icy water—the water level of the lake was far above the houses—slopping over the wall in waves. Night time, starry skies, just like you see in the North. It was just me and the expanse of the northern coastline, following the edge of water and wall, and running, running, running." My dream catcher had turned into a threshold guardian and I realized that I had come full circle, having started this inquiry long ago with a deep desire to create a sanctuary. I had an insight that what art therapists were seeking was a protected, sacred space to come together for their own healing. And so tonight I crafted a guardian of the threshold space, the sanctuary, created from the energies, passions, and most importantly, the dreaming of this group of seven women peers creating in community. Seeds were sown here for these energies would be carried into the world by these remarkable women who created this space together out of their own lives, out of their attentions to each other and to what was being formed in the circle of the studio.

Debra's piece appeared very small, but when you looked at it carefully, it looked expansive, even explosive. Tiny shells and beads, and seven flecks of gold, embraced in a spray of a curved stick bundle. "Dreams—I know I have those nocturnal visitors. Some grand, some not, but I have not had waking dreams of real life goals for a long while. I got to a place of contentment and held there for a while. Then, petty everyday things accumulated into mountains I did not want to climb anymore. Still, I grieve—how I grieve. I thank the circle for your willingness to see me, to witness my current formlessness, my quest, the wrestling with the unknown, perhaps the dark. My dream of the future may come clearer with time—but it may not. I might just learn how to live in the present. I am an art therapist at the center of my being, looking for paths to bring something meaningful into being."

As the weeks passed, our circle became ever larger. We made more room for ourselves and for the joys and pain we all carried inside; we made more room for the person sitting next to us. We discovered the many ways to express a broken heart: tears, bawdy humor and laughter, silence, and even rock music and lullabies. We scrutinized our inheritance of suffering and re-awakened our deep gladness as a vital life sign. We discovered that we could make art together—during the evening and throughout each interim week—without even having to make art together, as we felt our community's presence continue on in us, together and alone. In the presence of each other we gained the simple joy of feeling at ease and at home, trusted and becoming once again able to trust.

A return to soul as a community intervention has ancient roots in the shamanic practice of traditional medicine. Early in the profession's history, McNiff identified the parallels of ancient shamanism with the forms of modern expressive therapies.[45] In the intervening years, some art therapists have begun to embrace and integrate shamanic principles into their practices, although this remains a radical idea for many in the profession. In part, this may be due to a respectful unease for attempts by some to apply native healing and spiritual practices to contemporary healing technologies rooted in a completely different culture. We view the world with a specific cultural and historic lens that has little relationship to pre-modern life, and it may be a fantasy to think we could know, really and truly, what the shamanic worldview entails. On the other hand, the legacy of shamanism is not a matter of trying literally to imitate an archaic cultural style so much as one of fostering psychic mobility, as our circle demonstrated, applying a range of visionary experience in a mechanical, disenchanted culture with a mindset that has made the very idea of an enchanted landscape unthinkable.[46]

The circle is ancient, an archetypal form that has come to us because it is so desperately needed in the world. It is larger than all of us; it completes the circle between "I and my environment." If disenchantment is viewed having to do with a loss of art which in turn reflects a loss of soul (or a longing for a return of soul, since the soul can not be lost in a literal sense, as it is always with us)[47] then a revival of shamanic principles may be required, since soul-retrieval was once considered the greatest of all illnesses requiring shamanic intervention. In many traditions, the soul is retrieved only by going into the wilderness to perform the initiatory tasks of its revitalization. The longing we so often spoke in our reflective circle came from having glimpsed the possibility of securing this wildish place in ourselves, or our realization that we may have given too little time to the mystic cook fire or to the dreamtime, too little time to our own creative life, or our true loves.[48] Pinkola Estes warns that we may come to feel so bereft and agitated with longing that we leap up when called and search the land over for a sign that our wildish nature will return or has not been lost.[49] Once found, we are determined not to go on without it. As we saw in our circle, this pattern of call and response shapes the journey of re-enchantment, for both the individual and also for the larger, believing human community that supports his or her soul's wildish, creative dreaming.

MAKING OR BREAKING: ART THERAPY IN A VIOLENT WORLD

We can break the world; we can make the world. Peace making can be learned in this relationship of making and breaking, especially in the art therapy setting. Tolstoy said, "art and art only can cause violence to be set aside."[50] Over the course of my professional life as an art therapist, the work of peacemaker has taken many forms as I encounter the pain and alienation in people's lives through art and the therapeutic relationship. I ask myself, what do I offer the fragmented, harried, deeply wounded people I meet on a daily basis? How do I respond? That is a question that accompanies all others. What would happen if we really listened and heard what our lives, our art, is wanting from us? Several years ago, when I first began exploring the relationship between art and violence, between making and breaking, the intense process of indwelling and immersion in these questions produced the exact effect I was studying: over time, the buildup of the imagery of violence surrounded me and its subsequent feeling states shifted me into an experience of pervasive numbness. Despite every intention to do so, I could not make art. I felt myself living in a void, where all color, artistry, and life energy had abandoned me.[51]

Living and working as a compassionate artist in a culture that tends not to see me nor value me, I have found untold opportunity to be challenged continuously by my own violent needs for justice, security, and recognition. I can identify easily with violence as a human tragedy and the deep-seated need to seek retribution for what seems so unjust and coldly indifferent. Yet essentially an artist is a maker. In choosing to make art we choose peace through wholeness. Both artist and art therapist "take the materials of the world, both inner and outer, and work to connect separate entities, bridge over distance, heal splits, and bring unity into the life space."[52] As we explored in our communal studio, when we cannot make a well-connected life space toxic forces will begin to overtake the gestalt building process of life. The ensuing grief and pain will provoke a realignment of the relative weight of the inner life and anti-life forces, either through making the world or breaking it further into fragments. When we make art, we come to know that one cannot separate the self from the world because the individual affects the world and the world affects the individual. Having made the world, we have to transform it. Creative work acts to realign the balance of what feels unjust, out of balance, and threatening one's orienting framework. In art therapy a person's most rejected, violated, and alienated projections can be reconciled. Thus, an art therapist can be a guide or agent in the process of reconciliation, out of which will be born not merely a better adjusted person, but one who has created meaningful and life-affirming forms.

The metaphors and language of violence permeates the larger society in which we work, especially that of making war. There is the war on drugs, the battle of the sexes, the fight for survival; we give each other a fighting chance, and we want to be on the cutting edge. We conquer disease, attack the antibodies, win or lose in the battle with cancer; we bring in the hard data, and hit the books. Death-dealing industries are completely integrated into our economy. Contemporary business practices are described as predatory, and hostile takeovers characterize the business of doing business. Pro-life advocates kill doctors who practice abortion. We sanction the death penalty in order to preserve the sanctity of life. In the workplace, words like "take out," "kill," and "terminate" greatly outnumber nurturing vocabulary. Survivors of layoffs and corporate mergers struggle with gargantuan workloads and shrinking rewards. One art therapist told me how, immediately and violently, her work reality shifted when treatment teams were dismantled, personnel were reshuffled, units were closed and patients moved. People who had contributed years to the making of a cohesive, comprehensive and effective treatment program were suddenly fired. Valued colleagues disappeared. She said, "I felt like I was in a concentration camp where I was a sole survivor; keeping my head down and not saying anything that might jeopardize my job. I told myself that I was one of the lucky ones, but lucky for what? To keep connected to a dead carcass of what had been a living, vital, wonderful treatment team?"

Art therapists working in managed care also have their war stories.[53] They are part of a systematized treatment approach where the authority for treatment decisions is stratified and ranked, with final approval granted by the distant officers of the insurance company. These art therapists lament that the brief stays of their clients mitigate against forming a therapeutic relationship. This may be the real intention, born of an aggressive model of treatment that reflects our society's obsession with violence and war. Building up connections seems irrelevant where breaking down resistance is preferred. We use to lament that we were only "applying band-aids." Now we use the more sophisticated term "triage," a word from improved field medicine in war that differentiates the life-threatening from the merely suffering in one's treatment responses.

We have found a place in this clinical army because art is such a powerful medium against pathology. The technology of violence draws interest to the technical value of our skills. Art therapy is seen as more effective than verbal treatment because it can so quickly get past the patient's resistance. The treatment is effective because it works behind the lines of the patient's defenses, much like a stealth missile. Art is used as a weapon and only secondarily as a tool for self-understanding: Art for breaking, not making. Attack strategies are encouraged in many settings where therapists explain "we don't have time for much art making, we have to get in there quickly and get them to own their feelings." Our need to survive the war may cause us to adapt to the violence, using alien forms of treatment while being impeded in developing our own forms or practices.

Many solutions have been offered to stop the violence and yet it is vital to understand that no system can bring about reconciliation. Systems, as with managed care, are typically concerned with outward changes and adjustments. In general, they strive for outcomes of predictable knowledge and calculation. Concerned primarily with results and not with the means to obtain them, they can offer patterns of action and variations of ideas but not real transformation. What is decisive in bringing about peace is critical awareness of our everyday conduct. As Krishnamurti said,

> Unless you stop yielding to pressure—physical or mental, religious or political—you will continue to be the creator and the victim of this appalling misery. Therefore you, the individual, are the world problem. You are the only problem because all the other problems are created by your unwillingness to tackle yourself first and to understand yourself deeply and fully.[54]

The trauma of the world is a catalyst for our own healing and transformation for, as Macy writes, "the world itself has a role to play in our liberation."[55] In our cauldron of the community studio, toxins were cleansed and the vessel made clear again. We were not alone in the task but were accompanied each night with a sense of timeless presence in the art we created. Reflections evoked the spirits of ancestors who also suffered and passed their legacy of violence and struggle on to us. Thus we addressed with compassion the legacy of our forbears as well as our own woundedness so that the patterns and attitudes that are destroying us all may be transformed. Each art therapist came to the communal studio committed to transforming the toxic patterns of her work life, saw its connection to the legacy of violence, and discovered her unique way to say "This stops with me!"[56] and break the cycle of violence. Each of us holds within us the seeds of making or breaking and will use them to evolve the methods and practices of art therapy.

Dag Hammarskjold, who was an inspired peacemaker and secretary-general of the U.N. in its formative years after World War II, knew well the tension that arises in the compassionate artist's reconciliation of the desire to retreat to the studio with the imperatives of transforming the social order. He fervently believed that caring with dedicated attention for the world is compatible with inwardness, even offers good soil for its cultivation. His professional life was a matter of appointments and aftermaths, reflections and revisions, disappointment and renewed effort; of remembering his purpose in the midst of the recurrent cross-purposes of people and nations in conflict.[57] He welcomed art into his own life that was already crowded with the pressures of mediation of international violence. The experience of art exerted upon him a subtle, welcome pressure toward sustaining the form of his own life in the midst of trauma and the destruction he witnessed firsthand.

"Dreaming of the studio," then, is deeply connected to a compassionate desire for wholeness. In the studio the art therapist practices the life-generating balance of reflection and action, critical for regenerating creative vitality in toxic realities, and a commitment to engagement that reduces toxifying alienation. Having found a sanctuary in a world that is calling out for healing, art therapists can bring the energies of the sanctuary into the communities of the world. But to generate its larger benefits, art therapists may need to commit to the studio differently. Our longing for the studio need not be literalized or set apart from the realities of the clinic and workplace, but it is nonetheless a real and vital place that can be cultivated in our consciousness. For art therapists it is home, a place of belonging or being-in-longing that ameliorates the "no place" of the toxic landscape. After all, what is this deep longing but an archetypal expression of love or *eros* and a counterbalance to the forces of death or *thanatos?*

The way of peace and reconciliation, then, starts with the individual who is nurtured by a believing, committed community of witness. Where the individual accepts responsibility for the violence, peace finds a foothold. To go far, one must begin near; the first actions are within each of us. Art therapists as peacemakers offer unique value and skills as agents of reconciliation since this potential exists in each art therapy encounter. We help make the world and offer others tools to help turn the tide of violence. Yet I wonder that more art therapists have not expanded their role from clinician to activist or peacemaker.[58] As stewards of people's art that are expressions of their culture, art therapists could contribute more deliberately to advocacy for transforming our violent culture into one that is compatible with life. When we notice the pervasive degree in which we are containers of violence, making art ourselves becomes an imperative for the survival and regeneration of our life force. A tremendous challenge of art therapy in the future will be engaging the diabolical within ourselves, the places where we reconcile our own violence, hate and deadness, in order to use creatively its energy for transformation.[59] Diligently, we must try to be open to learning and to understand one another deeply, to address the task of our own self-transformation, and, through our acts, work to transform our violent culture into one that is compatible with life.

NOTES

1. Frost, R. (1969). The secret sits. In *The poetry of Robert Frost*. (E.C. Lathem, Ed.). New York: Holt, Rhinehart, and Winston.

2. Campbell, J. (1988). *The power of myth.* New York: Doubleday. p. 3.
3. Reinhold, B.R. (1996). *Toxic work: How to overcome stress, overload, and burnout and revitalize your career.* New York: Dutton/Penguin. p. 3.
4. Ibid., p. 15.
5. Palmer, P. (1990). *The active life.* New York: HarperCollins. p. 59.
6. Ibid, p. 15.
7. Wheatley, M. J. & Kellner-Rogers, M. (1996). *A simpler way.* San Francisco: Berrett-Koehler.
8. Fromm, E. (1973). *The anatomy of human destructiveness.* New York: Fawcett Crest.
9. Wheatley & Kellner-Rogers, p. 85.
10. Palmer, p. 60.
11. Ibid., p. 31.
12. Ibid., p. 156.
13. Campbell, J. (1949). *The hero with a thousand faces.* Princeton, NJ: Princeton University Press, p. 387.
14. Ulanov, A. & Ulanov, B. (1987). *The witch and the clown: Two archetypes of human sexuality.* Wilmette, IL: Chiron. p. 1.
15. Pinkola Estes, C. (1992). *Women who run with the wolves.* New York: Ballantine. p. 459–460, who writes "If you are on the verge of breaking away, taking a risk–daring to act in proscribed ways, then dig up the deepest bones possible, fructifying the wild and natural aspects of women, of life, of men, of children, of earth. Use your love and good instincts to know when to growl, to pounce, when to take a swipe, when to kill, when to retreat, when to bay till dawn. To live as closely as possible to the numinous wild, a woman must do more head tossing, more brimming, have more sniffing intuition, more creative life, more get-down-and-dirty, more solitude, more women's company, more nocturnal life, more fire, more cooking of words and ideas. She must do more recognition of sorority, more seeding, more root stock, more kindness to men, more neighborhood revolution, more poetry, more painting of fables and facts of the wild feminine. *More terrorist sewing circles* and more howling. Much more *canto hondo,* much more deep song" [italics added].
16. I thank and acknowledge the seven art therapists who formed the Reflective Circle of Peers as co-researchers in an art-based inquiry into the imagery of disenchantment and the transformative power of community in restoring creative vitality. They gave permission to have their artworks and written reflections included in this chapter so that their experiences might serve as a resource for other art therapists. Leah is a pseudonym for an art therapist who wished to remain anonymous in the study; the other art therapists are Sonnie Albinson, Melody Todd Ashby, Michele Burnie, Min Kennedy, and Debra Mickelson. My sincere appreciation is extended to all.
17. Gablik, S. (1991). *The reenchantment of art.* New York: Thames and Hudson, p. 27.
18. For practices and guidelines for conducting the circle form of council among a group of people, see Baldwin, C.(1998). *Calling the circle: The first and future culture.* New York: Bantam Books.

19. Baldwin, pp. 71–73. See also W. Isaacs (1999). *Dialogue and the art of thinking together* (New York: Currency) which describes in detail additional skills of listening, respecting, suspending, and voicing, as well as other excellent practices of creating dialogue and building capacity for transformational behavior in organizations.
20. Schaverien, J. (1992). *The revealing image: Analytic art psychotherapy in theory and practice.* New York: Routledge. p. 142.
21. Ibid., p. 144.
22. McNiff has discussed this principle throughout his body of work; see especially *Art as medicine* (1992) for a discussion of using aesthetic means such as poetry, sound, movement, and performance art as further interpretations of imagery. See also Allen (1992).
23. Schaverien, p. 144.
24. Ibid., p. 63.
25. Meade, M. (1993). *Men and the water of life.* New York: HarperCollins, p. 405.
26. Gablik, p. 11.
27. Cockburn, B. (1984). Lovers in a dangerous time. On *Stealing fire* [sound recording]. New York: Columbia Records.
28. Ulanov, p. 35.
29. Wesselow, E. (1993). Making or breaking: Art as education. *Fellowship [the magazine of the Fellowship of Reconciliation], 59*(1–2), 8.
30. Krishnamurti, J. (1993). The way of peace. *The Sun* (206), 12–13. (Original work published in 1948), p. 14.
31. Williams, T. T. (1995). Excerpts from *An unspoken hunger–Stories from the field.* New York: Random House.
32. Ibid.
33. Ibid.
34. Ibid.
35. Krishnamurti, p. 14. For a detailed discussion of the theories of violence and its impact on contemporary society, also see Gilligan, J. (1996). *Violence: Our deadly epidemic and its causes.* New York: G.P. Putnam's Sons.
36. Ibid.
37. McLaughlin, M. (1997). Bring us the peace. On *Daughter of Lir* [sound recording]. Felton, CA: Gourd Records.
38. Krishnamurti, p. 15.
39. Ibid.
40. Travis, J. W. & Callander, M. (1990). *Wellness for helping professionals: Creating compassionate cultures.* Mill Valley, CA: Wellness Associates.
41. Wagoner, D. (1994). Lost. In Whyte, D. (1994). *The heart aroused.* New York: Doubleday. pp. 259–260.
42. See Whyte, D. (1994). *The heart aroused.* New York: Currency. He writes, "We cannot neglect this interior fire without damaging ourselves in the process. A certain vitality smolders inside us irrespective of whether it has an outlet or not. When it remains unlit, the body fills with dense smoke. I think we all live with the hope

that we can put off our creative imperatives until a later time and not be any the worse of it. By refusing to give room to the fire, our bodies fill with acrid smoke, as it we had converted the flame and starved it of oxygen. The interior of the body becomes numbed and choked with particulate matter. The toxic components of the smoke are resentment, blame, complaint, self-justification, and martyrdom," p. 92.
43. Zukav, G. (1989). *The seat of the soul.* New York: Simon & Schuster. pp. 40–41.
44. Ibid.
45. McNiff, S. (1981). *The arts and psychotherapy.* Springfield, IL: Charles C Thomas.
46. Gablik, p. 47.
47. McNiff, S. (1992). *Art as medicine.* Boston: Shambhala. He writes "the soul cannot be lost in a literal sense because it is always present with us. However, we do lose contact with its movement within our daily lives, and this loss of relationship results in bodily and mental illness, rigidification, the absence of passion, and the estrangement from nature. It is the nature of soul to be lost to that aspect of mind that strives to control it. Mind has to dissolve, to let go of its control, in order to experience what is not itself. The loss of soul is a necessary element of our work, a prerequisite, because it absence stimulates a longing for its return. The experience of soul is a fleeting sensation of consciousness, and never a permanent or fixed condition," p. 22.
48. Pinkola Estes, pp. 7–8.
49. Ibid., pp. 7–8.
50. Tolstoy, quoted in Wesselow, p. 8.
51. Kapitan, L. (1997b). Making or breaking: Art therapy in the shifting tides of a violent culture. *Art Therapy: Journal of the American Art Therapy Association, 14,* 4, 255–260. Excerpts that appear in the conclusion to this chapter are reprinted with permission from AATA, Inc.
52. Deri, S. K. (1984). *Symbolization and creativity.* New York: International Universities. pp. 16–17.
53. Kapitan, L. (1994, November). Sleeping with the enemy. In L. Kapitan, K. McCormick, & L. Vance. Weaving new visions: Art therapy in collaboration with allied professionals. Paper presented at the Annual Conference of the American Art Therapy Association, San Diego, CA.
54. Krishnamurti, p. 16.
55. Macy, J. (1991). *World as lover, world as self.* Berkeley, CA: Parallex Press.
56. Louise Dunlap, quoted in Cane, P.M. (2000). *Trauma healing and transformation: Awakening a new heart with body-mind-spirit practices.* Watsonville, CA: Capacitar. p. 262. Patricia Mathes Cane's handbook is an exceptional resource for grassroots leaders, professionals, and individuals who desire to heal and transform the experiences of traumatic stress. The manual is based on research and workshops in Central America with people affected by widespread trauma and political violence. See www.capacitar@igc.org.
57. Lipsey, R. (1996). For the other Mahatma. *Parabola, 21*(3), 12–17.
58. Lori Vance is an art therapist who is working to heal communities through collaborations with creative arts therapists and community activists. See Vance, L. &

Clark, C. (1994, November). The myth of collaboration: The peace bridge project. Paper presented at the Annual Conference of the American Art Therapy Association, San Diego, CA.
59. Robbins, A. (1996, November). (Moderator). The soul and art therapy: A meeting place for cross-cultural currents. Panel presented at the Annual Conference of the Art Therapy Association, Philadelphia, PA.

Chapter 5

PLAYING ON THE THRESHOLD OF THE OPEN CLOSING DOOR

*When we are so far from our own country...we are seized by a vague fear
and an instinctive desire to go back to the protection of old habits.
At that moment, we are feverish but also porous, so that the lightest touch
makes us quiver at the depths of our being.
We come across a cascade of light, and there is eternity.*
—Albert Camus.[1]

PLAYING WITH WOLVES

The bitter wind drove the temperature down to ten degrees above zero on the high desert plateau where we huddled on that mid October day. Feeling deprived of the recent comforts of coffee and the warm cabin interior we'd left, I brought my stiff fingers to my face and blew a warming breath on them. A light dusting of early winter snow painted the barren, arid landscape a grayish white. It cast a dusty pallor that rendered the place unfamiliar, like the surface of the moon. Warily, I eyed the dark canine shapes moving in the near distance against the scrubby mesquite and creosote bushes. I stiffened, my body recoiling slightly, warning me of danger. Like a shadow, my fear and self-doubt go everywhere I go, stopping me in my tracks and signaling when to build up the defenses, the delay tactics, the control strategies. Or to bludgeon that prickly sensation into submission with some form of distraction or denial.

Caught on the edge between continuing on and turning back, I feel suspended. What was I thinking? I came here with the question of how to keep working in places that murder the spirit, to do what is needed without getting killed in the process. Though my mind in the present tells me I am safe enough, the breath on my hands is the only sensation in my now frozen state. The taunting voice returns from a childhood memory: *"Come on, you stupid girl! What are you, chicken?"* Trampled and made raw with new fear, the memory is blown into the barren desert and left dangling from a barbed wire fence, pummeled by ever-shifting winds. I look into the stark empty space toward some unknown encounter or in reverie of something lost to me. The real question is not about getting killed but rather, how boldly do I live? "Greet this fear and allow it to take you farther along, despite your certain belief that you will suffer and this long night will be lived forever," I whisper to myself. "Life is lived along the dark edges and in the overlapping spaces. Your creative spirit calls you here; surrender to your vulnerability."

Something moves and I see a wolf pacing back and forth. My companion Fred says, "Let's go." Until committed, there is always hesitancy. I take a deep breath. What was dispersed in the wind we now gather into pools and spirals of generating energy. In the opening space beyond my instinctual fear there is a small point of contact being offered me. I can't help it; I am being drawn to the threshold between worlds, between what is known and therefore certain, and what is as-yet unexperienced and open to strange wonder. "Whatever you can do or dream, you can begin it," I remember. "The secret is to drop it—whatever *it* is."[2] I make a leap of faith across the threshold and step forward. I am falling through, falling apart, falling into a waiting world. The world as a loving partner comes alive with shapes, colors, and textures that draw me into it, demanding that I play with them.

Two large wolves charge at me, stopping within an inch of my face as I hunker down to give them a soft-eyed greeting that says "I am here in play; I will not harm you."[3] Making my body contours rounded, I hold out my arms to them like a gesture of an open bowl. I have no agenda, no goal nor objective. I have only one clear intention that I hold firmly in my mind: to touch them with my heart in the play of giving and receiving love. An invisible playground encircles us. From the outside, I appear to be a middle-aged woman stroking some lively wolves and getting her face vigorously washed by enormous tongues from their very toothy snouts. Wolf play. But inside the enchanted circle, poof! I have disappeared! All categories of *wolf, woman, self,* and *other* are gone. I see no *wolf.* There is no wolf; that is only a category of thinking, not the actual being in the space with me. And you can't play with a category. If I were thinking *wolf,* the wolf would likely be thinking in a category of his own: *food.*

"Leading with my belly," I discover a visceral gateway to a half-forgotten meeting place deep within my spirit. This hidden place of sanctuary resonates outward in my gestures of primal, loving touch through play. I feel a complete satisfaction that recalls me to my ancestors who routinely lived in rhythm with the natural world that was how they created. I have no aim other than to scamper and play until we feel like stopping to rest. Nothing else is in the space with me. There is no other reason to be here. I gently let go of fixed notions or rules, accepting the stricter, deeper rules–rules of the dreamtime, rules of the mythos, the rules of rhythm.[4] There cannot be any thought of what I am going to *get* from this encounter, for if there were, we would no longer be playing. The enchanted landscape would congeal back into something deadly and the very real danger of an encounter with wolves would return.

I do not will this act of play; "I" am not "doing something."[5] We share a mutual gesture of joy-filled allowing, opening our body spaces to each other's touch.[6] This joy sweeps the space clear of fears, worries, and preoccupations. "What if's?" are held off indefinitely, for now. They no longer seem to exist at all. It is exhilarating. The wolves and I are in the spacious clearing of *this,* a unitary field beyond the polarities of ordinary reality, yet still real, embodied and directly experienced. Fear, my constant companion, is gone. It had never entered this place.

The high desert wind freezes my fingers past the point of forgetting, forcing me to notice the pain that comes back into my awareness. Just then a gentle illusion drifts across my mind, a subtle separation in my presence: "Why, these actions of mine," I impulsively think, stroking the furry wolves, "they feel so familiar to me. I know I've done this before. Oh yes, of course–I am really just petting them and they are really just like dogs." This is not true. They are wolves. As if they know I've forgotten, fleetingly diverting my attention to other times and places, the wolves suddenly swing around and–in an instant!–attack. I had not noticed the other wolf that sneaked past and grabbed my wolf's bone while we were playing. Now the two rush violently at each other, snarling and snapping. They lock their teeth into each other's throats and do not let go. They go for the kill.

I am surrounded as all the wolves spring to tense alertness. I expect to recoil in terror and fear but strangely I feel none, even as I witness the escalating fight just a few feet away. Though the space has shifted violently, I feel complete calm. Our playing has altered my thoughts, centering my focus to a still point of connection that is alive with feeling and pulsing through me. Everything has a crystal-like clarity and beauty. My first thought is a revelation: *This is not my fight*. To join the struggle I would be claiming a place in the wolf pack where clearly I did not belong. I would be acting out of an illusion that I shared some special place because of our play, or that they had accepted me on their own terms and I was no longer a stranger. Such arrogance would have made the situation very dangerous indeed. Especially for the wolves, since I would become another element in the attack. It was so clear: in a flash I simply knew it without thinking. Then came my second thought: *I should leave now*.

"You discovered that you can't be their playmate and have a cultural role at the same time," Fred said later. "Certainly, in the culture of your work you can step in do what others want and need you to do—just do them with the compassion and clarity of play. Playing says 'I trust'. Period. There are no conditions, no obligations."[7] "I trust," I reflected. How can I transfer this receptivity, compassion, and free flow of play to everyone and everything I touch?[8] Simply to give and receive love, and expect nothing in return? Soon I would be playing with the wolves again, calming their agitation with compassion. I would get another hug and face washing from the very wolf that had tried to rip the face off of a rival two hours earlier. Play would awaken deep patterning or instincts of my own, spontaneously signaling what to do, when to stay and when to leave. It would not matter that I had just witnessed the realities of the wolves' predatory, killing instincts. I would release that violent image and sure knowledge of their destructive power; I would open my body space once again and slip into realness with them.

"Ah, to not be cut off, to live without the slightest partition between your soul and the distant stars,"[9] mused my companion, as if hearing my unspoken wonder of loving, fearless play amid danger, among and between the spaces of life and death. "Away from your star," after all, is what is meant by the word "desire" in its original sense.[10] The gifts of love awaken a powerful, magnetic pull to get back to the source, to be near again, not solely in closeness but in the tension of intimate contact and intimate risk.[11] As I stepped away from the wolves and our playspace, and left for the evening's meal, I could feel a stretching, like an archer pulling a bow in awareness that the target and arrow desire to be one. In the deep, dreaming night, a chorus of wolves serenaded me to sleep.

But when we return to the desert the next morning, we learn that the wolf pack has had another "wreck." Strange tensions have caused them to gang up on each other and attempt to eliminate their weakest member. The alpha male has inflicted a serious leg wound on him, possibly a fracture, while the alpha female looks on placidly. He is driven off and kept on the fringes of the gang's territory, bloodied and wounded. His lonely corner identifies to the others his lowest status in the pack. When I move near him, he turns toward me slightly on his injured leg, and lets out a quiet whimper of pain. At the sound, the rest of the pack becomes quickly alert and starts to circle him ominously. I hear a scream: The researcher who invited me to play with the wolf pack rushes to separate the wolves and impending disaster.

There will be no playing today. With cool detachment, I recognize how the "wreck" serves to rebalance a stressed-out family system. Juveniles will do a similar thing: offer themselves as a focus for their family's attention to create the connection and relationship everyone needs, often to prevent exposure of the deeper pain of a tragic marriage or partnership. The controlling parental unit, human or alpha wolves, will use its power to protect or to scapegoat members in ways that keep them in line with cultural roles, rules, and expectations. My mind, when it functions like this as a trained therapist, knows how these things usually work. I consider the way of the wolf researcher, who has devoted years of study to learn their intimate social dynamics. She has enlightened me with her theories, garnered from their signals, various moods, and the pack's rules of behavior. But play is more of a dream state, not a defined activity with rules and playing field and designated participants. Play can occur only in the absence of knowing so much. Your mind cannot be occupied with what you know, for then you are just playing with a category in your mind: what you know about the wolf and not the actual wolf itself standing before you. And with wolves, there is so much you would have to know so as not to misunderstand the cues and put yourself in danger. "I keep telling you," my play companion Fred reminded me, "play is a gift of creation, not an artifact of culture. Playing is when we don't know we are different from each other. You must let go of knowing. Let go of everything so you can be there completely. In this way you pass beyond competence to presence."[12]

It is difficult to allow this presence. I believe I offer it unconditionally from my years of experience as a therapist, but the reality is that I am not completely there yet. I get attached to the forms and conditions that once satisfied me and that I expect, if they reoccur, will satisfy me again. I am eager to play with the wolves again and feel impatient that they will not join me now. I hold onto the joyful memory of the frisky black wolf, my new friend, and want it back. In this way I acquire and categorize my experience, separate and divide it, and weigh its relative worth to me. Thus my life spaces will become fossilized and constricting as they move me farther from the core rhythms of my life. "What keeps us feeling so disconnected from the world, from ourselves, from one another, and from the sources of our creative power?" I ask my companion now. He quietly answers, "Fear and yearning. You yearn for community with the other because you know that with it you would feel more at home in your life, no longer a stranger."

"Yes," I told him. "We feel 'at home' in our own circles, but it is more than satisfying a need to connect with our own familiar thoughts and those who think like us. We also need the rich materials of otherness and diversity. Otherwise our inner landscapes would be flat and lifeless. We would wither and die, cut off and isolated in our aloneness. But if we found meaning only in communion with others, we would wither and die also, for we were meant to connect inward in solitude as well as outward in healthy communion with others.[13] We need spaciousness in our at-home-ness, as open and vast as the desert sky, in order to be able to hold the paradoxes of our natures without fear, like breathing in and out. Creativity demands that we play with paradox." The wolves carried me to the play space, as though poised on the threshold of the open closing door. The threshold is a meeting place; there I awaken and come home to an old, old memory stirred and brought back to life. This is the memory of my undeniable and irrevocable human kinship with the elemental energies of the wild, encounters with alien "otherness" in which the other is free to be itself and to speak its own truth, whether that other is a wolf, a human companion, or a self-dissenting voice within.[14]

INTERLUDE

My hand moves across the paper in circles as I explore the matter further in the solitude of my studio. Making my body contours soft, my entire attention is directed at connecting with my heart through play. I stroke gray paper, sensing the grainy feel of charcoal between my fingers and the sensuous mark it leaves on the surface. I hesitate, waiting to receive and not knowing if something will, in fact, emerge from the formlessness that begins my creative engagement. From the outside, I look like a middle-aged woman at her drawing board, beginning a pastel painting. But inside the enchanted circle between the paper and me, all categories of *artist, image, self,* and *other* disappear as I am drawn in, my senses alive and alert. I am gone; I have taken myself away. For art to appear, I have to disappear.[15] Time is suspended; nothing is with me here but a hovering presence. I slip into that place of realness with my art, in a direct, eye-level relationship. I play with pigment and paper for no other purpose than to keep the play going and to see what comes next.

I have drawn overlapping circles; I am circling. I place them near the center of the paper, becoming centered. Only when at the center, then I am drawn to the spaces between these circled forms, which I color in deep, inky shadows. I follow the shadowing shapes and get lost in their mystery for a time. Now their forms become rounded, emerging from the gray paper, colored in blues and lavenders, or left gray (Figure 39).

I look at the image I have created. What is central? I ask myself. A huddle of stones. When at the center of it all, a huddle appears, of overlapping, piled-upon stone. They huddle together in a close space where edges touch and merge in shadow. A pool of blue forms at the bottom of the pile, between a single white rock and its smallest counterpart. Pooling at the base, the stony huddle rests. As I stroke them with color and shadow, their surfaces appear smoothly polished, like the stones I used to find every summer on the beach at grandmother's cottage. They emerge in the pooling waters, polished impossibly smooth from the timeless, everlasting turbulence of the sea that carried them to this place.

Now an enclosing, circling boundary appears in the painting, gathering up the huddle of stones at the center of the paper. Inside, a deep

Playing on the Threshold of the Open Closing Door 223

Figure 39. Playing with wolves.

realm of rock, shadow, and water, playing over smooth surfaces or slipping into the hollows between them. Beyond the boundary, I have covered the gray paper in milky white. Like a covering of milk, it seeps to the edges of papered grayness. It is as though what is outside doesn't truly exist; it flows off the edges into milky space. Suddenly, at the threshold between huddled stone and milky space, four dark figures arrive. While a sinuous, black snake comes to encircle the huddled stone, a crow appears on its right, and a pair of wolves on the left.

The snaky boundary touches the crow, whose spreading wings and jutting toes are poised for landing. Perhaps the crow has fluttered down from a higher place, gathering itself into the huddle of stones. The snake has slithered into a central place, now that the guardian crow is here at the threshold. What is left, but two wolves?

I remember such crows and snakes coming into my art many times before, but in this painting the two wolves are new to me. Their rounded body contours and frisky energy tell me they are here in play. Meet us at the boundary, my strange companions say. We are neither here nor there, but *this*. When you step into our circle, when you huddle or pool together for warmth and grounding, polished from the relentless turbulence of life's waters, we will guide you. We will lick your face until its surface is polished clean, until your many masks have fallen away and there is no *you* anymore. Melting surfaces away, and displaying the infinite that was hid,[16] it will be as one face of god greeting another.

But tread carefully in places of power, they say, lest you fail to stay present, thinking of the danger you know exists at the threshold place. It does no good to crow your achievement, your success for having stepped into the circle this time. You could just as easily step on a snake, slithering out unexpectedly. *This,* the hub of all things, the intersection where you cross over, will change you and you must be ready for that. Without the stability that is born of respect for the threshold, change overruns its bounds. You must not think to go there alone; that is why guardians always appear at such doorways as guides or intermediaries for those who cross them.

For a space to be a space, I reflected further, it must be open as well as bounded. The art therapist's studio—whether in community or in solitude—seems to have this configuration, like the open closing door or the begging bowl offered to the world for one's own transformation. The studio is felt to be a safe but contained space, held apart from the distractions of the world. It is a *temenos,* a magic circle: a delimited, sacred space within which special rules apply and in which extraordinary events are free to occur.[17] A space that, when clearly bounded, opens to make a clearing for a meeting to take place and a relationship to form. The sanctuary stills my restless movement and with stillness I begin to grasp what is moving within or without that is calling for my living presence. With presence, my perceptions change and I can open to new, unforeseen possibilities.

Now I look to the center of the painting and see that it is not quite clear. Something central appears to be out of focus, hazy and melting back into grayness. The lonely "I" ecstatically dissolving into the "we" of hoped-for, blissful merger? This enchantment, the common denominator of every form of bliss—what if it is sought only to escape some fear-filled danger?[18] From the encounter on paper I consider the encounter in the other studio spaces of my life. My eye is arrested by that murky place and impatient for it to become clear to me. I remember what my companion said about being utterly clear, getting clearer and clearer at my center. I need such clarity. I do. It is not enough to have a vision that can change who we are, but it must be embodied in a sensual, visceral practice of realness to activate the transformation.[19] I must seek out the masters, those who have not lost how to be real. In *lila,* or divine play, innocence and experience fuse.[20] "I shall find a child," I decide, "to practice playing."

IN THE CROSSROADS

A cage went in search of a bird.
—Kafka[21]

"I couldn't get into the world," a man once simply told me, to explain his frozen state. He could not express it fully in words because what he was saying concerned a deep level of his spirit. I had some inkling of what he meant, that sense of moving through a place without being able to touch or be touched by it. Always stuck on the outside surfaces of things, wanting to reach through whatever it is that is keeping you apart. I thought of him now, as I reflected on the separations that fed my disenchantment. Fear cuts me off and dwindles my perception. Fear is everywhere—in our culture, in our workplaces, in ourselves—it invades the space of sanctuary and dissipates the life-giving energy that brings creative action; it can create tremendous doubt about the value of our life, our work and art. When fear takes hold on either side of the paradoxes I am living, in trying to choose I become divided and embattled.

I know that in creative surrender a new element can appear that can change the composition of my world. But it feels so awkward whenever I pause in my relentless movement forward, like I am expected to be doing something to make it happen. In my workplace, everyone is always rushing by, frenetically going from one activity to another as though checking things off the mental to-do list for that day in the ever-expanding vista of work before them. It all seemed to be a matter of slowing down to see where the little openings or taproots were, so that a ripple of change in my awareness could take hold. So I decided to stand in one place, disrupting the flow. People streamed by, quickly scanning me to see what I was selling. I discovered that if you just stand still, looking at something—anything—people will follow your gaze, pausing momentarily to wonder what the hell it is you are looking at.

"What are you doing?" someone asked me.

"I'm meditating," I answered, looking for a still space to make my studio.

"You picked a place like *this* to meditate in?" she asked, incredulously.

Yes, I thought, this is where I need to be. Finding a "playground" or *temenos* is a mutual choosing; it chooses you and you choose it.[22] How strange that I had stopped in the middle of the trafficked way, like a stubborn bump in the road people had to walk around or over. Yet my desire for a living studio called me to find the most active, peopled spaces in my work environment. I was certain there I would find some unfolding play taking place to be sculpted by my consciousness into art. I stopped at the *crossroads,* as alive a place as I could find in the modern, numbing efficiency that encircled me.

Above ground, the campus was serene. A picture perfect place of sweeping lawn, bell tower, red roofed halls, and statues of Mary, the divine feminine honored. People often told me it was a pleasant shock to arrive here from the teeming city that surrounded it, a timeless, cloistered place of sanctuary. This was but a comforting illusion. The roiling, untidy, energetic comings and goings of people actually take place below, in the underground passageways that link the various buildings, a pragmatic feature in a snowy northern climate. Really, you could spend weeks on campus without ever going outside, above ground, to get some fresh air. There is a lesson in this configuration, I think, of what is the veil and what is real, for art therapists dreaming of a perfect place in which to practice.

As I stood still in meditation where the main passageways crossed, a little child darted out of the nearby lunchroom and ran gleefully down the hall. His mother appeared immediately after and called him to return to put his backpack on, which he ignored. She glanced at me sitting there–a watchful bystander–and I heard her say, "What does that tell you? He runs from authority."

I smiled in response but my mind catches on this small event made vivid by my attentive presence. *Lila* arrives as a small god with a message, I think reflectively, the most potent of muses. Standing in the underground crossroads, I feel the rigid forms of the enduring architecture and the hierarchy of the new administration press down on me from above. Massive structures have been built to contain and direct this free flow of energy rushing past me, channeled into ever-expanding tasks and goals. This hard exterior wraps around me; it is the protective armor with which the institution attempts to operate in safety and enduring self-preservation. But beneath these rigid forms a shaping, molten destiny lives on in the real life forces of the place. In my still alertness I can hear the breathing of the fissuring, heaving earth that always moves beneath my feet. Bubbling up from below, there is an earthquake always in the offering. Cracks that appear in the armor are simply opportunities created so that we can come to terms with the inner place of spirit, the life force. In the depths is a luminous child demanding that we come out and play.

I have no business standing here, doing nothing. I am outside, looking for yet another passage that would take me in. For the past few years it had been especially hard; the winds of change blew cold and barren. Actually, I had come to miss the old days of the nuns who ran the place and all we did to appease them, which was never enough. At least you always knew where you stood, even if that was at the foot of the table. Casting a dusty pallor over that once familiar past was a new layer of the corporate mind-set where we spoke an alien language of initiatives and task forces, strategic planning structures, and the reallocation of resources. Nothing was clear, nothing was direct and true. It all felt gray and milky white; a thing imposed upon us out of fear of encroaching change rather than coaxed patiently from what was already present deep within the soul of the place. The cultural change felt engineered, with doublespeak and contrived motivational strategies, and fear was an ever-present partner. A doctor would notice the toxic effects of introducing inorganic structures on the organism; a craftsperson would warn that no material can be shaped against its true nature.

With the waning influence of the aging nuns, a new pair of alpha leaders had appeared at the top of the hierarchy of our group life. I recalled the day they sat across the table from me at a council meeting. Our leader was energetic, charismatic. She spoke passionately of the changing needs of the community and asked us to search deeply and reflect upon what we could help bring forth that would offer new life to the institution. Her co-leader then spoke. With a fixed, toothy grin, she arranged her words around certain numbers she'd read somewhere that had impressed her greatly and encouraged us to replicate those numbers here. What was wanted was a sure thing, an a priori product whose value had been ratified by the authorities.[23] The contrast was chilling; I returned to my office and pulled out paper and paint to capture what I had just experienced. I drew a tunneling series of boxes within boxes, black and sickly green, rigid borders, ending in two red squares at the center. Squinting, they looked like the red eyes of a dragon peering at me through rigid, tunnel vision. Ah, the green scales of the dragon's power–I had seen this specter many times and in many places. "Wait! I've been here before, I've met you before and I'm not doing this again!" I told it, stiffening in fear, alert to danger. I peered into the stark emptiness toward some unknown encounter and in grief for lost illusion. "How boldly will you live?" the image whispered, as my fear of her killing energies crept closer.

I could tell right away that she came from a different place, a sterile land where I did not want to return. I heard her say that her favorite activity was making policies and I pictured the flow of creative vitality put into very small boxes. I could feel my breathing constrict with the shrinking space. The word got out that if you stopped by her office just to say hello, you'd end up on yet another committee or task force or some part of the efficient flow chart that was becoming our work life. Yet every interaction missed in a peculiar way; somehow making contact yet never really touching. She seemed to have no center line around which to organize a focus and from which to orient toward the world.[24] Everything was changing quickly and all at once through an ever-expanding web of initiatives she drew us into and controlled, creating a deadening, inertial mass that filled up space and blocked interaction. Our alpha leader, preoccupied with other matters, watched from afar as the wreck began to take place within our family system.

"I hate what has been placed in my bowl to transform me!" I howled. I remembered what it felt like to be betrayed the first time, the second time, the third time–it hurts! The free play of imagination creates illusions and illusions bump into reality and get disillusioned.[25] Yes, I know it's called growing up–again and again. I don't care. I try to avoid it. My main strategy was to not go down that hall and bypass her office lair. It felt silly and childish, but actually it was her eye contact I was trying to avoid. These eyes seemed to look right through me but never seemed to see. I put her into a category of my own making: *Wolf.* I retreated to a small, safe corner I found where I hid out, seeking other people I could work through, whom I placed between me and the dangerous other. In doing so, I moved to the edges, the fringes of group life, becoming vulnerable. I squelched any noise that might attract attention. Without consciously realizing it, I was preparing for her dark circling and attack.

Why was I afraid of her? Why did I cower so that I stayed out of her line of sight and avoided her at every opportunity? That day in the desert with Fred, I discovered my instinctual reaction when I am caught off guard, when someone comes up suddenly and tries to grab me. Not one to fight, each time he bounded toward me in playful attack I politely smiled and unconsciously pulled him toward me while moving to get out of his grasp. Fred called this *collapsing* into the aggression, just like any victim will do. He noticed my head dropping and my shoulder curving inward toward self-protection. This is fear expressed in my body as an unspoken desire to flee the world of form, wanting to dissolve into formlessness.[26]

Victim. How I hated the word. I had heard it so many times in stories of disenchantment that it seemed a faithful, shadowy companion trotting along behind me. It conjured up for me the old phantoms of bullies who could appear out of nowhere, disrupting my trance-like play space with their taunts and jeers. This inhibiting specter haunts the lives of many artists as an invisible, bullying force that seems to stand in our way.[27] As the chilly winds whipped around me and cactus spines of the desert floor warned me to keep upright and balanced, I swallowed hard and closed my eyes against the hated memory. I breathed deeply and gathered up energy through a taproot of power from the molten, energetic earth below. Now I visualized a completely steadfast and powerful energy extending out of my arms and legs, rooting to me the earth, connecting with and locking into everything these points of contact touched, like strong, fluid cables of light or color. I would not go away and avoid the troubling thing but rather confront it in a new framework, taking back all the specters and reaching for a clear, unobstructed transmission of creative energy. Extended and steady in the space of *this,* the rest of my body moved fluidly and now I found that with only the slightest bit of energy, I could pull Fred off balance simply by noticing where his body/energy wanted to go.

I didn't get this, at first. I couldn't connect, couldn't get into this fluid world where Fred waited for me. My fear of and attachment to the hungry ghosts had taught me to vigilantly scan the visual environment. I learned it was easier to respond and move with Fred when my eyes were closed, physically reminding myself, in this gesture, to let go. But still I failed to open my heart or live from within my whole body. As he taught me to open and feel this abundant energy extending out of me, suddenly it became easy. In that moment of inner spaciousness and generosity, I went from a disconnect I didn't even know I had to connecting with total, embodied presence.

There was a fleeting realization that all my niceness and smiling self came from a fearful need for the other to be nice in kind. Even with the wolves, in those odd moments when I forgot playing, I remembered my smiling niceness was an illusion of wanting, ultimately, to control their aggression and make me safe. It was not, as Fred said, building my courage to be with wolves, which would merely be another form of behavior designed to conquer something. That would put me back in the realm of trying to control either my fear or a wolf. I recognized this pattern in me and in many of my peers. I did not want to believe it but it was honest truth. How often we smile at others and invite them to our dance, while fear and control lurk behind our civilized masks. This us-against-them attitude merely invites the obstacles back in another form. But they can be absorbed and harmonized in play, where there is no contest, no control.[28]

"I am a middle child, Fred. I believe there is a place between the poles, a middle ground between fight and flight. This middle way is the critical path I walk."

"No," he replied. "It isn't a decision to step down from the contest. It is a decision to step out of the contest entirely. It takes place in a whole different space, not in the middle. Somewhere 'other' than this being nice and smiling, or being snarly and bad. Either way, it is not real. It is still the defense of the self, engaged in some sort of contest behavior. Come; be real with me. Play is not a road."

Getting "grabbed" by wolf or human or life circumstance can take place at any time, physically or verbally. "But here is the secret," my companion said. "You can always choose whether it is an attack or a play opportunity. When you choose that it is not an attack, then the attack stops and that's an incredibly powerful way to be in the universe. Open your arms, totally present. Not weak or mushy, but with a fierce, steady heart that is clear. To really touch, with no intention of selling or getting something in return. This touch is not a cultural signal, like a handshake, but a real and complete connection. In the play touch is at-home-ness and belonging. Not self-defense, but self-disappearance."

I understood, then, that I don't always get to that place of self-disappearance, and that's where I get grabbed by so many things. Like a knock in the side of the head, or trampled by frisky energy barreling down upon me, over and over Fred taught me the price I pay for my contest-created self which is the need to self-defend endlessly from all assaults, real or imagined, in order to keep from being undervalued, pushed to the fringe, or put in my place. "This is an extremely dangerous attitude," he gently reminded me. "You are pinning your well-being to the arbitrariness of the contest order, in whose every action you see something to gain or something to lose."[29]

"Why do we keep playing this game?" I asked him, thinking of how, when we are disempowered, we choose what Quinn calls "peace and pay,"[30] a strategy that maintains the status quo in work environments that offer the trade-off of security for the soul's integrity.

"Because the rewards are great," he said. "First, we get membership in the group which annuls the fear of being alone in a dangerous world. Second, we get an enemy on whom to redirect our anger and aggression. Finally, we get a false, comforting sense of justification for our actions. Out of fear, we still choose to pay the price of endemic violence to maintain our allegiance to the game. Rather than choosing love and dissolving the game itself."[31]

Unlike play, games have their rules, goals, and objectives. Unlike play, which strengthens vitality, contest behavior in the work environment drains us of life while it reinforces strong cultural codes of behavior for dealing with power. At the highest risk for stress-related illness are people whose work makes high demands on them to perform but gives them few opportunities to act freely and make choices.[32] When the game at work takes away personal power and teaches helplessness, the body's vital reactions actually slow down or eventually collapse. Under chronic stress, hormones no longer ebb and flow but stay abnormally high, repressing the immune system's ability to ward off toxins. It is no wonder that work can kill.

In any system, play is a measure of its health and vitality. A common element in the life histories of mass murderers and drunk drivers who kill themselves in accidents is a chronic lack of play.[33] So, too, fundamentalist and totalitarian regimes make it their first order of business to restrict or eliminate the flow of free speech, art, film, and other avenues of creation, expression, and communication.[34] People who are severely play deprived are toxic to themselves, to their bodies, to their families and to others. Often, they are workplace bullies. They are commonly found in the helping professions where there are many opportunities to abuse power over vulnerable others disguised by a public show of how caring they are or want to be perceived. Play-deprived institutions unconsciously promote this and other "horizontal workplace violence"–the harmful behavior between colleagues that seeks to control, humiliate, denigrate or injure the dignity of another.[35]

For consummate players, in contrast, work is play and play is work. They gravitate toward those environments where they are given a clear sense of direction and then are empowered to design and carry out what is needed. They know how to find little openings for play in the flow of work and then stretch those magical moments until they blend with the energies around them. Even in the worst situations, players have a way of "taking all the crassness and stupidity of the world and making it the occasion for play."[36] They understand that the issue is not control, which is the legacy of games, but dynamic connection. High performers play at a high level of risk, express their awe and wonder, and live life along the creative edge needed for re-generating vitality.

In the crossroads–the crosscurrents of swirling, life energies–I was seeking this very connectedness in a way I had not felt for some time. I knew art therapy could be practiced freely as play but over time, culture-bound expectations had turned it into more of a game. I knew that when left to myself, depleted, tired and disempowered, I would not be able to create or attract mutually enhancing relationships.[37] Nor could I create an art that is communal and participatory without opening my hand in a gesture of generosity, without embracing the physical act of fierce-hearted play in the spirit of doing and being for no purpose other than its own pure joy. Gablik inspired this art I was looking to create, saying,

> . . . Gestures of reciprocal touching, gestures that bring together, receive and welcome . . . the possibilities are so profound as to imply a whole new social and cultural order . . . a belief in the restorative action of care. Given our characteristic modern forms of defiance, protest and attack, and our postmodern forms of parody and ironic indifference, the notion of art embodying the good act really does change the nature of the game."[38]

But taking my studio into the crossroads was not a simple matter of parking myself there as some force to be reckoned with. I struggled and had many doubts. I could not get into the space, preoccupied as I was for a long time with trying to intervene in some way and slow down the busy energies of the harried people walking through. Without realizing it, I was clinging to a hoped-for outcome. My intention was to act as a change agent but the paradox of play is that I had to let go of any and all such intentions. *No conditions, no obligations. Play is not a road to some goal. Let it go.* The challenge was to tune in and flow with what was already there, to establish a dialogue with the place and cooperate with its subtle web of interrelated processes.[39] Eventually I understood that all I really needed to do was make an offering and leave it to others to decide whether they wanted to participate or not. I would play, even if it meant playing alone. Perhaps playmates would appear, perhaps not. I set up my paints, brushes, and a four-foot-long canvas propped across two small cafe tables in front of the vending machines. Twice weekly, during the busy lunch hour, I painted in the crossroads.

Now that is the funny thing. When I was no longer banging on the door but simply poised, alert in the threshold, the door opened. In whooshed clarity, power, and freedom; thus, the muse appears and can speak. Immediately, a woman strolled up to me as I painted, curious. Spontaneously, she slipped into a reverie of how her family had discouraged her from a career in art. Twenty years later she is here, finally studying her heart's desire. She was surprised to learn that I had been afraid of the blank canvas for many weeks. She suggested purple for the sky and walked away.

My community play practice got easier as it expanded my field of action. I practiced "soft eyes"—open enough to not get so focused on the work of painting that a wall of energy would be drawn around me, keeping people out, yet focused enough to not impinge on or "capture" people going by. As attention and intention fused, I could see things just as they are and respond in the flow with any number of aesthetic, multi-leveled conversations. Slowly it dawned on me that painting in the crossroads was simply a gift to my work community, with no strings attached. I had known for years as an art therapist that you cannot change people but only invite them to the dance. But I had been "grabbed" by the fear-driven drama going on in the new culture surrounding me. I was here at the crossroads to let that go and remember my gifts. I do have a choice, always, I realized with utter clarity: *this is not my dance alone.*

The child appeared. I knew he would come. I spied him running down the hall and coming by to eat lunch with his mother. I stopped, gave him the play look; soon he was showing me the bottom of his shoe that had an impression of a little truck. Week to week, our friendship grew, gradually drawing in his mother, her friends, and other students and children. Little rituals appeared to guide my practice, to mark otherwise ordinary activity, rendering it intensified, even sacred.[40] A young mother came in, quickly scanned the environment, and placed her little child at a distant table "because of the painting." So it is we domesticate and keep the child apart, breeding predictable environments to serve our purposes. I invited her back, assuring her that there was nothing to fear. Meanwhile, the little guy was back, popping his goldfish crackers and raisins into my mouth with his tiny fingers, raptly studying my dental work.

Painting and playing with the little child and all those in his circle, I realized I had found the playground, *temenos,* studio—*in me.* It is a place and also a no-place; that is another secret. I slipped into the flow of the paint and its pleasures while keeping soft eyes and open heart-centered energy that connected me to everything. Fools and coyote tricksters, the child and the sacred clown, the many archetypes and intermediaries that inhabit the magic circle were drawn out and made visible to me in the spirit of our play. A security guard came by every week to check on how the painting was coming along and to tell me stories about his long-lost love of art from childhood. A nun came to ask me why I didn't post a sign that announced what I was doing, this artist-in-residency, to others in the place. I didn't need to, I considered. This play was a gift, a holy gesture. Free of obligation and expectation. Play is without why.

Then one day, near the end of the painting, a remarkable thing happened. I think it had been waiting on the edges of my consciousness from the very beginning. My painting time was unusually quiet, as the early spring weather had drawn the regulars outside. I brought my focus in a little, to concentrate on painting small details. I decided to lighten the sky with blue, as the purple now looked too gloomy and depressing. After a long winter, I could see that my mood was lifting. The room was silent, expectant. In this moment, the *wolf* came into the painting space.

"It is not good vision alone that allows one to see a wolf in the wild," a native man once told Fred. "One must take a second look. And this is done with the heart. The real wolf is two looks away."[41] As though picking her up on my radar screen, I sensed the wolf's approach, catching her movement with my soft eyes. I lifted and cocked my head to one side, flashing her a play look—and invited her near me. She smiled and came close, and asked what I was doing in the lunchroom. I told her, with a steadfast heart, that painting was my play, my nourishment. I told her what it was like to paint in the crossroads and its therapeutic effects on the community. She cocked her head and listened, placidly gazing down at my painting. She seemed to think this was interesting.

How strange that she who did not often venture beyond the administrative halls came to the crossroads that day, paused in her movement, and had drawn near. It felt as though the universe had put me in her path, or that I had become a "strange attractor."[42] But remarkable still was the fact that, wolf or not, it did not matter to me. I did not clench in fear, did not startle or smile in self-defensive posturing. I felt clarity; nothing grabbed or clung to me. I was rooted in that still, centered moment. I opened my heart, I connected with her, and spoke my truth. I stood in my circle, grounded and embodied from the painting play process; nothing could throw off my balance there. I felt at home, relaxed in the wild artistic nature that had gifts to give and would not be walled off, penned up or channeled into games or policy. To be pure, to not have an agenda, the clarity of being a playmate does indeed transcend the categories, the dualities that keep us apart.

But once you co-create in the play space, you can never be the same way or the same person you were before. Play changes you irrevocably. You have shown a sort of vulnerability that you both share. We experience love but then are called to commit to love's labors and the hard lessons that come when illusions are stripped away. It took so little energy to throw her off, but that was a consequence, not my intention. I do not know what thing shifted in her after our encounter in the crossroads, but things did get worse for me in the group life, not better, after that. I was exposed, no longer hidden from view. I had shown myself free of arbitrary restrictions and able to move flexibly, with creative power, in unforeseen ways. Thus I felt her circling nearer, reasserting her control by vaguely threatening dire consequences if I failed to perform a specific task she assigned to me. As danger approached, I performed the task, but already my play-spirit had loosened her hold on me and I became unattached, rooted elsewhere and finding other places of contact where I was free to play. The power of creative play blew me away from her, tangled no more in old scripts and rigid expectations.

One day, I stood before the group assembly and reported the results of the various tasks and duties she had assigned. I had to ask my colleagues to endorse the recommended action. I faced a stony wall of silence, followed by a passive refusal to act or move. I could feel hostility boiling below the polite surface of our assembly, and sensed tense alertness in a narrowing circle of stonewalling resistance, anger, and worse. The alpha wolves entered the fray and resorted to shaming; everyone was baying for the blood sacrifice. I expect to recoil in terror and fear but strangely I felt none, even as I witnessed the wreck breaking out all around me. With a crystal-like clarity and beauty, I understood: *This is not my fight* and *I should leave now*. It was right to depart this stressed, joyless environment. I was already somewhere else.

In the end, though, I stayed. Because that same afternoon, as though a larger purpose fulfilled, the wolf announced her resignation and disappeared.

* * *

"I see," said the troubadour, when I told him the story, "that you have been practicing your therapeutic artistry, beyond the categorizing that binds up so much energy in your profession and results in conditioned, domesticated confidence. Wherever you go, you can create the *temenos*, the studio, because it exists in this free and flexible attitude, a spirit, or way of doing things. You discovered the secret is all in how you perceive things. All these choices are possible when you embrace the place of the threshold. By going through the experience faithfully, you came through on the other side of the crossing point and found that your faithfulness had borne a new quality into the world."[43]

Yes, I considered. You don't have to choose the one or the other place where the divided self lives. The energy you seek is in the third place, always there to use for transforming your perception and the perceptions of others. Once you do that, the kind of energy you give out to the world has fundamentally changed, which changes the quality of your artistry. You begin to experience the free play of creativity as one with ordinary, daily activity now invested with luminosity, depth, and the simplicity-within-complexity we associate with inspired moments.[44] People will understand and receive your gifts and start to interact with them.

But the place of the threshold is hard, for it contains beauty and horror, joy and the terror, when being faithful to whatever presents itself there. Invited in, the opportunity is unsettling. Do you really want the encounter? It might change you—you may not have anything of value to give in return for such hospitality. You feel your otherness. Maybe you see frightening beauty inside the doorway and want it, but settle instead for a temporary refuge. This feeling of being pulled between opposites, after all, can be taken as a sign that it is time to listen more deeply to other voices. The active awakening to these voices, described in my final story, results in "unconditional confidence"[45]–a source of the art therapist's capacity to discard assumptions and gain creative presence in the midst of on-going transformation in the threshold space.

THE THRESHOLD

Across the doorsill the breeze at dawn
has secrets to tell you.
Don't go back to sleep!
You must ask for what you really want.
Don't go back to sleep!
People are going back and forth across the
doorsill where the two worlds touch.
The door is round and open.
Don't go back to sleep!
—Rumi[46]

The threshold is *between;* it is not the place of life and not the place of death.[47] In the doorway, you might find intuition, imagination, anxiety, threat, and safety. The hungry ghosts of your past, shadows flitting through. One moment I was walking through leafy woods and the next moment—whoosh! I have stepped through an opening in the earth and fallen into a tunnel of orange leaves, landing on the other side in a vivid memory from my childhood home on a crisp, fall day. The place of play, a timeless, magical "fairy circle" I called it; a ring of stones, a child's Stonehenge.

Someone, long ago, had built a semicircle of large, flat stones in a grove of trees in a park across the street from the house of my childhood. I thought I had "discovered" this haven; it was my playground. Here was the birthplace of my dreams where I returned home, to overcome for a time the alienation of being an adult. The ring of stones cast a spell to protect me, returned me to belonging in a way I knew intimately but had forgotten. The four trees that surrounded the circle were its guardians. I saw in them my four sturdy grandparents from the old country and far-off times. They towered over me, even though I had grown and now lived away from home. They renewed my belief in magic.

Magic, in this case, is power. Not power of control over others but power beyond over others. On the play threshold I have enough power, exertion, and energy to view things as they are, properly and directly. I experience the brightness and the haziness of life, the fantastically sharp-edged quality of living in the world in direct and realistic relationship to it.[48] My play spirit has a rich heritage, recalling the tumult of clannish families moving across continents and cultural divides. It can't be tied down, separated, and categorized because play, like art, is the movement of the spirit back and forth across the threshold. Even when magic disappears, I know that I have the inner memory patterns to bring it back into my body and living. This renews my practice with hope, inspiration, and love.

But I remember when I began this journey. It was in the dark days of winter; I was helplessly caught up in the speed of the world around me that swept me up and pulled me in. Work, marriage, and family were negotiated in brief spaces lived between the seventy-mile an hour commute that hurtled me through space morning and night. The hard, exoskeleton body of my car enveloped my increasingly soft, inactive body. I consumed great quantities of fatty foods, as if to lubricate my brain being culturally hot-wired for excessive stimulation and frenzy. The fax, cell phone, palm pilot, answering machine, voice mail, e-mail, and computer all pulsed with accumulating expectations to respond with full and immediate attention to every demand placed there.

I knew I wasn't meant to live this way. The speed of light is not the speed of life. My ancestors roamed the Eurasian steppes at a pace in keeping with the movement of animals and the cycles of weather. I learned this lesson through pain and humiliation, having attempted to please the most demanding of masters and failing utterly. Then, the dark days of winter moved into my soul and body. I surrendered to its bitter root, and there saw that life was out of balance. In the spring, the freeway I traveled came under construction. Deprived of immediate access to that ribbon of unimpeded movement, I was forced to seek alternative routes and detours, and had dreams of catastrophic accidents where soft bodies were pinioned inside piles of twisted metal.

Having slowed to a crawl, it occurred to me that I could walk. What started as a gesture of seeking balance became many long, thoughtful walks in the company of crows. When I came home my pockets were full of their feathers. I remembered who I am and so returned to my studio. In the heat of summer I sorted through piles and piles of stuff, shedding and casting out, creating space in which to work. It happened that my studio was located in the basement, next to the laundry. I thought it was a terrible place to paint, like some dirty corner where we toss the clothes to be washed. But as I connected more intimately with it, I came to see it as a place to cleanse my soul and to wash off the residue of daily, scruffy living.

One day, I read in the news a story about a white swan that lived in a pond of a small New England town, and how two homeless men attacked the swan and knifed her forty times. The people in that town were so outraged that they called for the death penalty to be served upon the two men convicted of stabbing the swan. What could be behind such a virulent outpouring of violence? I tried to imagine the image of purity being stabbed forty times, thinking of what it meant to have destroyed the illusion that the swan represented. It must have been important in that town that everything remain ok, unchanged, undisturbed.

The image of the murdered swan that provokes murderous rage and retaliation grabbed at my mind and soul, like an old, old memory stirred and come back to life. She was a shadow that signaled me to pay attention to my discomfort. She pulled me to the threshold, demanding that I come out and play with *her*. But I do not want to; I know she will pull my heart open. She is part of a timeless pattern, her appearance a mythic invitation to reexamine the killing of creative spirit and what is required to reverse the conditions of the wasteland. Beauty, terror, and death are all calling from the other side of the door and the only way to heal the conditions of the soul is to cross the threshold.[49] On the threshold, the New England pond rematerializes as a symbolic landscape and the mythic swan is the old dragon queen, the keeper of the waters of life and death. Whatever is lost eventually reaches her castle.[50] The homeless men are timeless exiles who must descend to the queen's underworld where spells are broken and innocence traded for a price.

Beauty is imprisoned and all who try to release it with a force of will are slain.

As an art therapist, I knew that illusion well. I have heard the seductive force of the swan's disembodied purity in the voices of many suffering people I knew, as well as within myself. "Whoever has the power to project the vision of the good life make it prevail has the most decisive power of all,"[51] she whispers in a cold, prickly breath upon the back of my neck. "I am that illusion, promising beauty, eternal life, and perfection, reflected in the smooth marble floors and mirrored hallways of my castle, and in the gleam of money. White on white, I am clean and pure and I promise to marry you and bring you utter happiness. Enter my detached and floating world, and I promise you will be transformed, liberated from bodily existence, a paradise free of pain and suffering. But you mistake me—I am a lie."

The white swan wants to be forever at our side; we fear the void, so she fills us with distractions, consumptions, obsessions, and compulsions, envy and powerlessness. She is the shadow we create by our inattention to the living pain of the world. She fills all life space with excessive, compulsive attachments that consume energy and lead us to the slavery of addiction. She imprisons aesthetic joy and offers the opposite: anesthetic numbness to keep us asleep, our pain blunted. "I stimulate you with constant images of perfection you must have all the while draining you of your own images," she laughs menacingly, "the destiny you could have created for yourself. I will flatten you out, making it no longer possible to feel what it means to reflect deeply or to aspire to great heights. I will never let you go," she threatens. To pause and reflect allows a space, an emptying. A wonderful, empty space is generated when we notice and surrender, but we think of it as terrible.

She is the dragon Vritra, the Dark Queen of the Underworld, La Llorona, the Ice Queen whose frozen palace is a house of mirrors, a hologram, where there is no connection to anything, nothing truly shared, no living memory. "Fool! You think you can administer to these souls through your art, your creative process? Do you forget that they are asleep and walking wounded and dead? I killed them, remember?" she screams at me now on the threshold. "The only way you can reach them is to encounter your own dark void, your own deadness inside of you. To look past illusion and free your shadow—it needs your creative compassion to release its power. I don't believe you know how to do that," she accuses me. "I have seen to that, because I walk with you, too."

Finding her voice in my bowl—the dream voice echoing the voices of many with whom I have walked in the misery of their woundedness—I feel raw and antagonized by the specter of nothingness and death. Her purpose is to pull us into the reversal of life energies, into the void of all life can offer. Such illusions always block and obliterate our human capacity for symbol formation and for the enlarging transformation of our imaginations. With the loss of inner space, outer space constricts. There are only surfaces, nothing exists inside of things, and worst of all we are not even sure anything is awake and alive in us. The possessor becomes the possessed. We drift in and out, lost and seeking home for our exiled souls.

Like a foreign agent, scrubbing along my nerve pathways and taking me to a new place of consciousness, I feel the strain and ache of paying attention to what presents itself on the threshold, of trying to see correctly without my own blinders. Absent my play companions, it is wrenching to let go of hubris and to accept other perceptions. But when in play, I am able to tolerate ambiguity, paradox, and mystery, and I no longer need so desperately to find all the answers, or be compelled to attack everything with tooth and nail. I can choose step outside the pull of competing polarities, and when our Divine Partner speaks, I will be listening and I will hear. When called, I will come, and when requirements are set upon me, I will fulfill them with whole heart.[52]

The threshold invites me to enter the sacred wound, in order to gain regenerative energies. It is a wordless place within and beyond each of us that holds "the bitter, unwanted passion of your sure defeat," or "the place of the fierce embrace."[53] "To arrive where you are, to get from where you are not, you must go by a way wherein there is no ecstasy... in order to possess what you do not possess you must go by the way of dispossession."[54] I close my eyes and see the reds and browns of blood and flesh; they give form to the memory of my own wounding. The threshold now becomes, in my mind's eye, the passageway of my own bloody throat. I hear my mother asking me "Why are you taking so long to eat your food?" and "you'll have to sit here and keep eating until you finish everything on your plate." As a child, my throat had only a tiny opening for air and food to pass through. On the day of my surgery, four nurses to hold me down and give me too much ether, causing a violent reaction. I retch on the blood for hours. I think I am dying. Yes, this is a little girl's vision of death.

On the threshold that is neither life nor death, I open my heart to compassion for the child and tell myself now, "I survived this death. As my mother had survived her death when her first child was born. As I survived my birth; as my child survived her birth." The bloody channel that was constricted then is the birth channel now: my own, my mother's, and my child's. The constriction of the birth canal and the pain of labor nonetheless bring me to the wide-open space I desire to be born into and have labored to bring to others. I remember the circle of my peers celebrating birthing in their work as art therapists, tied to rhythms of constriction and expansion, where a passage opens by its own accord connected to a right and natural timing to which one must surrender. We move through the labor of birth much as the budding plant must have the constriction of the earth to yield to it and to push up and through. Sacred space expands inner, constricted space; I would not learn this had I not known life-threatening, constricted space. On the threshold, my wounded, bloody throat is a birth canal and the sacred channel of creativity is moving through me.

I paint the memory (Figure 40) and it becomes a nautilus shape that spirals inward and outward, oscillating with the rhythms of inner and outer experience simultaneously. This is a potent image, for as the animal grows, the nautilus must continuously create new and ever expanding space. Each chamber is a chapter in the animal's journey as the life force spirals outward. I imagine the chambered thresholds as chambers of the heart. I see layer after layer, as though looking into heart muscle. Deep in the center of the endless spirals of the paradoxes, I see a tiny, fetal shape. Some tiny being is nestled safely into the sheltering large, blue form; something is being born here, from my travels inside the black wound and the crossing of the limen.

I like the solidity and vibrancy of my painting; I enjoy the pleasing rhythms of the small shapes juxtaposed with the large blue form and glowing background. The opened, blue form yields to an inner core of interconnected, spiraling shapes. They shelter an inner doubled, blue form that in turn shelters a tiny orange, fetal or bud-like shape. Alive and growing, it has both the ephemeral quality of the spirit as it also has the deep vibrancy and forms of the material world. Many shapes, many voices and persons, held in community by the one large shape or purpose. As each of us nestles inside the larger purpose, we, in turn,

Figure 40. Nautilus.

hold a deeper purpose that is the blue, sacred space out of which our spirits are sheltered and something is born. The sensuous, open, broken heart is a practice, a living relationship committed to freshness and vitality. Here is the place of healer, *curandera*,[55] the intermediary of the threshold, between heaven and earth, sky and water. To answer her calling, she must negotiate between this temporal, material world and that one, infinite, impossible, and full of grace.

My familiar, the crow, comes at last to teach me on the threshold. Hers is a lesson about perceptual shifts that alter consciousness and consciousness that alters behavior.[56] She has the voice of a trickster, forever mocking me, pointing out the contradictions and values of the paradoxes I study. "Caw! Caw! Pay aw-ttention!" she calls. "You thought you could escape me? All those days of walking in my territory? Under my trees? I saw you down there. I've been watching you. You see my friends and me all lined up, perched on a fence, like an audience of critics ready to steal your food. Haw! You think you are so important. You don't like me mocking you. Too bad. Somebody's got to do it. Nobody else is paying attention—I have to caw it like it is.

"I am Crow. I fly between the worlds. I perceive what's up there and what's down there and where you are heading. And the worst place of all is that place where there are no big trees, no hills, and no chasms. Life as a flat screen of things passing you by and you just watching it, where everything is the same, in time and space, leveled flat. I live in trees, you know, and I learned from them that you can't grow up without also growing downward, deepening life through the roots.[57] And the tree doesn't hang onto everything, oh no, it sheds its leaves from time to time. And sometimes it gets cut down, to make room for the little ones to come up in its place. In the spaces between the trees, there are new patterns that emerge and grow out of nothingness. Why fear nothingness?

"I live in the void; I see simultaneously the three fates—past, present, and future.[58] When you know me, you will have my power to address what is out of harmony, out of balance, out of whack, or unjust. I am a messenger calling you to honor harmony that comes from a peaceful mind, an open heart, a true tongue, a light step, and forgiving nature, and a love for all the creatures, in right relationship, without denial of your body and soul. Honor the past as your teacher, honor the present as your creation, and honor the future as your inspiration. Then, I will fly away and find another tree, for no other reason than to be."

I tell the guardian crow that my question is whether we can embrace life's ambiguous interplay of light and shadow, life and death, and learn to live in the creative center of this paradox so that through us our work might be born.[59] All is holy ground, the ordinary as much as the extraordinary, the common as well as the uncommon. The work of the *animadora* is to stretch out those momentary flashes, extend them until they infuse the activity of daily life. Then we can say we have no art because everything we do is artistic practice. At the threshold, we seek a sacred experience that is mitigated, to live its power without it destroying us. We seek to live, not as fully as possible within the sacred, but *between* the sacred and the profane.[60] We hold the polarities, and these take us to the place beyond the polarities in the unifying field of *this*. "Haw!" the crow cries, carrying me across the threshold into the wide-open space. I look down and see our shadow flying over the living currents of the world's soul.

BEYOND THRESHOLDS

"What is *this*?" guided my creative contemplation and actions as I explored the phenomenon of the art therapist's disenchantment on the threshold of the "open closing door." This doorway is both open, as a route to freedom, and closing: stepping into a magical circle marked off from ordinary rules of time, space, and culture. If fear and habit disconnect me from the beauty and terror of life's energies, then playing at the crossroads of the self and the other, with fear and the absence of fear, helps bring me back to enchantment. This place is located neither here nor there, this place nor that, not divided nor categorized but fully present to what is alive right before us and however we are called to practice.

In truth, I have faced many wolves, not only the real ones described in the beginning of this chapter, but the ones that keep appearing and reappearing in my work and life. They bite at my confidence with their snarling accusations that I couldn't possibly know what I am talking about, correcting my "mistakes" with new and improved categories for what and how to practice my therapeutic artistry. I frequently mistake them for real threats and withdraw for protection or in anticipation of attack. But what we pay attention to always attracts energy; truly I always have the power to choose that it is not an attack but merely another play opportunity and then the attack ceases. Or maybe the attacker tries again, but there is nothing to catch on and grab me for I am standing in another place with a fierce, steady heart that is clear and ready for a real and complete encounter. Not in self-defense, but in self-disappearance, which is the essence of play.

I imagine enchantment will return to art therapy when practiced as an extraordinary gift of creation guided by the deeper rules of instinctual, dynamic interconnectedness with and loving compassion for the world. Art therapy, then, becomes an attitude, a playful spirit, or flexible way of being and responding; it is not form-defined. This takes commitment to deeper integrity and a willingness to face the queasy feeling of emptiness that arrives when the world doesn't love us back, doesn't appreciate the loving gestures of our art therapy practices. The world's great indifference pulls at the heart, cracks appear in our professional armor and get patched over again by cornering the wild flow of creative vitality into neat little boxes of who we are and what we do that, of course, builds up the armor again.

The inner spaciousness of the open closing door is populated by a staggering variety of living and non-living things and energies. We don't have to do battle with them, just invite the interplay, the collaborations with "other-ness" that inspires new vitality. Called to the threshold, we commit with a fierce heart and loving embrace to whatever arrives to transform us, especially those shadows that erupt from the mythic substrate and take human form. Letting go of that which no longer fits, I find a potential space that is bigger than I ever knew it could be. The "much bigger" is sacred space, playing us into and out of existence, awakening and restoring us, breathing new life into and out of form. The legacy we leave to our children is this very alive, sacred space in which to live and work.

NOTES

1. Camus, A. in Palmer, P. (1998). *The courage to teach*. San Francisco: Jossey-Bass, p. 39.
2. Nachmanovitch, S. (1990). *Free play: Improvisation in life and art*. New York: Jeremy Tarcher, p. 194.
3. "Playing with wolves" is a true story about events that took place as part of a mentorship with Dr. O. Fred Donaldson at the Raised By Wolves research station in Grants, New Mexico run by Dr. C.J. Rogers. I extend my gratitude to C.J. for her permission and access to the wolves for my research. With regards to the "play look" described, a clear signal that "this is play" is needed to activate the suspension of ordinary boundaries, a glance that can pass so swiftly as to be unnoticed by others. Soft body contours, a slightly cocked head, and a twinkle in the eye that invites the encounter is about the best way I can described this subtle yet all important communication taught to me by Fred Donaldson.
4. Nachmanovitch, p. 81. He describes the beauty of playing together in the context of improvisational music as follows: "I play with my partner; we listen to each other; we mirror each other; we connect with what we hear. He doesn't know where I am going, I don't know where he's going, yet we anticipate, sense, lead, and follow each other. There is no agreed-on structure or measure, but once we have played for five seconds there is a structure, because we've started something. . . . the work comes from neither one artist nor the other, even though our own idiosyncracies and styles, the symptoms of our original natures, still exert their natural pull. Nor does the work come from a compromise or halfway point, but from a third place that isn't necessarily like what either one of us would do individually. There is a third, totally new style that pulls on us. It is as though

we have become a group organism that has its own nature and its own way of being...", pp. 94–95. This passage also describes, I believe, a model for an art therapist's experience of treatment in the co-created therapeutic, aesthetic relationship with a client.
5. Ibid., p. 4.
6. Maitland, J. (1995). *Spacious body: Exploration in somatic ontology.* Berkeley, CA: North Atlantic Books. p. 118.
7. Donaldson, O. F. (1993). *Playing by heart.* Nevada City, CA: Touch the Future. p. 150.
8. Nachmanovitch, p. 69.
9. Rilke, R. M. in Mitchell, S. (Ed). (1995). "Ah, not be cut off," in *The selected poetry and prose of Rainer Maria Rilke.* New York: Modern Library. p. 191.
10. Nachmanovitch, p. 165.
11. Ibid., p. 166.
12. Ibid., p. 21.
13. Palmer, p. 65.
14. Ibid., p. 57.
15. Nachmanovitch says "For art to appear, we have to disappear.... Mind and sense are arrested for a moment, fully in the experience. Nothing else exists. When we 'disappear' in this way, everything around us becomes a surprise, new and fresh. Self and environment unite. Attention and intention fuse. We see things just as we and they are.... This lively and vigorous state of mind is the most favorable to the germination of original work of any kind. It has its roots in child's play," p. 51.
16. Blake, W., in "The Pickering Manuscript," (1803) as cited in Nachmanovitch, p. 4.
17. Nachmanovitch, p. 175.
18. Yalom, I. (1989). *Love's executioner.* New York: HarperPerennial. p. 39.
19. Donaldson defines his practice as "original play," referring to a primal encounter that is "simultaneously inside all life and beyond all separations. Original play is transformative because it is more than a vision that can change our view of who we are individually and collectively; it is an accompanying practice that activates this transformation in all our relationships with each other and all of nature," p. 21.
20. Nachmanovitch, p. 197.
21. Kafka, F., in Donaldson, p. 37.
22. Donaldson, p. 127.
23. Nachmanovitch, p. 121.
24. Maitland writes "having no core means having no sense of one's own identity and having no place from which to orient and relate . . . [and] often misperceives the movements of his own energies and feelings as something external that is attacking or influencing him. The no-core person, having no centerline around which to organize his perceptions and from which to orient toward the world, frequently has problems and difficulties with being present. Their manner and mode of occupying space is always somewhat uncanny and inappropriate. Their psychospatial orientation says, "I don't know where *here* is," p. 62.

25. Nachmanovitch, p. 125.
26. Maitland writes, "Not wanting to be present is the way I define fear psychospatially. [It is an] unspoken desire to flee the world of form. She accomplishes this flight by spatializing her body as a form that wants to be formless. Her manner of being present displays the desire not to be present in the present," pp. 44–45.
27. Nachmanovitch, p. 133.
28. Donaldson, p. 122.
29. Ibid., p. 69.
30. Quinn, R.F. (1996). *Deep change: Discovering the leader within.* San Francisco: Jossey-Bass. He says that the peace-and-pay strategy is a form of mental illness and that individuals who choose this strategy are also contributing to the slow death of the organization. "Actively choosing peace and pay means deliberately joining the legions of the walking dead. Making deep change is not something we do for the organization; we do it for ourselves. It is a choice to be alive," pp. 22–23.
31. Donaldson, p. 69.
32. Reinhold, B. B. (1996). *Toxic work: How to overcome stress, overload, and burnout and revitalize your career.* New York: Dutton/Penguin, p. 22.
33. Brown, S. L. (1995). Through the lens of play. *Revision, 17* (4), pp. 4–12. Stuart Brown is a psychiatrist who served on a research team in 1966 assigned to understand the motives and life of the notorious Texas Tower mass-murderer Charles Whitman. Brown interviewed and collected the "play histories" of hundreds of people who committed mass murder, of young murderers, and from studying the lives of fatally injured drunk drivers. His research repeatedly showed the one common element was not childhood abuse, as commonly suspected, but rather that all shared a life history almost entirely devoid of play. Brown has determined that people who are severely play deprived are toxic to themselves, to their bodies, and to their families and others. There is a neurological continuum between play states, dream states, and REM states. All serve important regulatory functions. People who are sleep deprived risk physical breakdown and death; REM deprivation leads to psychosis and hallucinations. Play deprivation, it can be theorized, leads to a form of psychological pain and an antisocial orientation toward death. It is alarming to consider how sleep and play deprived modern cultures are and where this phenomena may be leading the human species.
34. Nachmanovitch, p. 182.
35. Nurse Advocate: Nurses and workplace violence. (n.d.) A horizontal violence position statement. Available from World Wide Web: http://www.nurseadvocate.org/hvstate.html.
36. Aaron Copland, cited in Nachmanovitch, p. 123, made an interesting remark when discussing what is was like to be a composer in 1920, a period of great indifference or hostility toward non-European, non-classical music. Instead of complaining, Copland said, "The fun of the fight against the musical Philistines, the sorties and strategies, the converts won, and the hot arguments with dull-witted critics partly explain the particular excitement of that period."
37. Quinn, p. 42.

38. Gablik, S. (1991). *The reenchantment of art.* New York: Thames and Hudson, p. 71, describes forms and methods of socially active art making. A notable example of this "artist-in-residency" within a social action context is Mierle Laderman Ukeles, who worked as an unsalaried artist with the New York City Department of Sanitation, culminating in an eight-hour-day performance work where she'd come in at roll call, walk the routes with the sanitation workers, made tapes and videos of them and completed a ritual in which she faced each person, shook their hand, and said "Thank you for keeping New York City alive." Gablik writes, "By offering her hand in a gesture of openness and generosity, a space of enchantment is opened up, if only for a moment. The archetypal reach of her open hand . . . extends way beyond the horizons of our immediate social world; it responds to needs so deep they are not even recognized until the gesture has touched them with kindness." Quoting a sanitation worker who participated: "If that's what art is, it's fine with me," pp. 70–71.
39. Ibid., p. 91, describing the environmental artwork of Andy Goldsworthy, who inspired this insight.
40. Nachmanovitch, p. 74.
41. Donaldson, p. 10. He also states that the "first look" kind of consciousness organizes life into a succession of rigid categories and structures. To survive we perceive the world rationally, order it according to fixed values, and attempt to master it systematically.
42. Wheatley, M. J. (1992). *Leadership and the new science.* San Francisco: Berrett-Koehler. The chaotic movements of an open-ended system have a shape known as a "strange attractor," which is a basin of attraction, an area displayed in computer-generated phase space that the system is magnetically drawn into, pulling the system into a visible shape of order inherent in chaos, p. 122.
43. Richards, M.C. (1973). *The crossing point.* Middletown, CN: Wesleyan University Press. p. 63.
44. Nachmanovitch, p. 19.
45. Quinn, p. 77.
46. Rumi, quoted in Singer, J. (1990). *Seeing through the visible world.* San Francisco: HarperSan Francisco. p. 22.
47. Thomas Moore (2000), in "Neither here nor there" (*Parabola, 25,* 1), describes the threshold as the means by which the deep soul prospers—neither in life nor entirely out of life, saying "This is a good place from which to make a decision and get a hunch. It is the true home of creativity. It is also the claustrophobic place of greatest fear. Anything of moment takes place in these interstices—in the tunnels and passages and waiting periods. They are indispensable and yet must be kept tangential. It takes considerable courage to stay as long as needed in a place of between, and it requires a degree of holy foolishness to seek one out," p. 37.
48. Trungpa, C. (1996). *Dharma art.* Boston: Shambhala. p. 94.
49. Meade, M. (1993). *Men and the water of life.* New York: HarperCollins, pp. 400–405.
50. Ibid., p. 348.
51. Leach, W. (1993). *Land of desire.* New York: Pantheon Books. p. xiii.

52. Singer, p. 220.
53. Whyte, D. (1995). *Fire in the earth*. Langley, WA: Many Rivers Press.
54. Elliot, T. S.
55. Sewall, L. in Roszak, T., Gomes, M. E., and Kanner, A. D. (1995). *Ecopsychology*. San Francisco: Sierra Club Books. p. 203.
56. Bly, R. (1996). *The sibling society*. Reading, MA: Addison-Wesley.
57. Hillman, J. (1995). *Kinds of power*. New York: Currency Doubleday. pp. 50–52.
58. Sams, J. and Carson, D. (1988). *Medicine cards: The discovery of power through the ways of animals*. Santa Fe, NM: Bear and Company. pp. 133–135.
59. Palmer, P. (1990). *The active life*. San Francisco: Harper. p. 6.
60. Miller, A.L. (1992, Winter). Living with sacred power: Promise and threat. *Parabola, 17,* 4, pp. 4–9.

CONCLUSION

You do not have to be good.
You do not have to walk on your knees
for a hundred miles through the desert, repenting.
You only have to let the soft animal of your body
love what it loves.
Tell me about despair, yours, and I will tell you mine...
Whoever you are, no matter how lonely,
the world offers itself to your imagination,
calls to you like the wild geese,
harsh and exciting—
over and over announcing your place
in the family of things.
—Mary Oliver[1]

I fall in and out of love; my heart breaks over and over again. This is what happens when saying yes, yes, yes! I have more joy but also more agony. Possibilities grow visibly, tangibly larger and more spacious in just a few moments. Say no, no, no! and the world gets smaller and heavier.[2] Over a long period of time, no-saying turns into a hardened lump in the middle of your chest, and your dreams of the deep, underground river become a distant, desperate longing. This is certainly one possibility when the practice of art therapy loses its creative vitality.

Sometimes, I must say no. I need to take myself away and find a place to nurture myself again. I will say no, defiantly! But other times, I simply whisper *later*. Later, when I have more time, when the children are out of the house, after I clean the studio or when I finish organizing the paper work. I will say yes, I will help bring change to the world, but first I need to learn more, know more, become a better person, become more enlightened, or be much more evolved as an artist or a more skilled, self-aware therapist. I get caught in the thrall of my own stinginess and illusory belief in what could be, should be, if only might be.

I placed disenchantment in my begging bowl and carried it with me, holding it out to others who also sought to see it clearly, name it, and dissolve its roots. Thus we might become reconciled to the nature of our therapeutic, artistic practices and free the transformational energy bound there. I witnessed the question in my own life as well as in my interactions with others. One night, when I was nearing the end of my inquiry, I dreamed again of the "open closing door."[3] It seemed so long ago that I had dreamed of the solid black door which I could open only a crack before the fierce, glaring woman marched up and pushed me away, slamming it shut. A guardian of the threshold, she had appeared and reappeared over many months in many guises–the cruel white swan, trickster wolves, security guards and priestesses of purity, fiery dragons, managers of care, "bad company," the hungry ghosts of ancestors, and my own unnamed fears. I remember the night I stepped through the threshold and was lifted up by the big, black crow. I flew over the wild river below me, following its course to the headwaters, believing I would never come home again. I loved the spaciousness of the freedom I found in the place of the inward sky, where the constellations shift and form anew.

The next morning, I went early to the studio, opening windows to the early spring air to prepare the space for the others arriving soon to make art together in our space of sanctuary. In the quiet energetic embrace of my fellows, I moved my arm in an arc of flight over the surface of my paper, vaguely recalling the dream from the night before. My hand responded with small strokes; I allowed whatever needed my attention to come to me. Gradually, the image formed, grew larger, and expanded outward in cascades and threads of blues, whites, and smoky blacks. It was different from the one I painted of the dream, so many months ago; I see that, as a result of my inquiry, it and I have transformed (Figure 41).

I feel myself move through threshold upon threshold as I paint this new image of the open closing door. I thread my way through narrow places, reminiscent of the obstacles I witnessed in all the art therapy stories. These narrow places open to exquisite expanses. The dark shadows now are luscious mysteries; the white glows with new worlds spinning and threading their way into form. Layers of bone, pearly shell, water, stars, and the remnants of hearth fire, I can picture them

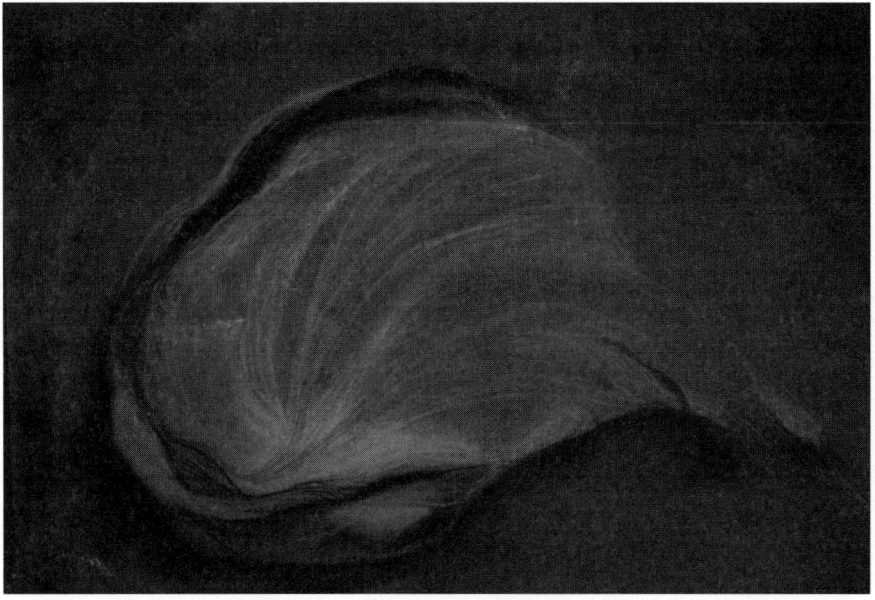

Figure 41. Open closing door.

mingled in the cauldron, made into a rich stew. I look into the river of vitality that is, this time, a quiet pool, so still I see through its depths with bright clarity. Other times, it is a torrent that sweeps me up, threatens to drown me, and carries me downstream with all the mess of its mud, silt, and waste. In the cross-currents are life's playgrounds wanting to play me into and out of existence. Everything is in movement; there is no immunity, no permanence.

I thought I could hold out a bowl and find there all I needed for transformation. But when I opened my hands and let go of what I was carrying, I found myself inside the bowl of the ensouled world that Grandmother holds; she holds me so I don't have to. I run past the edge, past the threshold space; I run into sky and fall with a shock into her cool waters, and come swimming up to the surface for a gulp of air.

But oh, how we do fear this river and its creative, unleashed power! We want those encounters with living art and soul on our terms. We want somehow to control their outcomes so they will not threaten our view of the world and the self.[4] Throughout my inquiry, in art and story, art therapists told me of the myriad ways we use to protect ourselves from being so alive, from the threat of a live encounter with the dragon of our creative power—or with the living river that pulls us along, incessantly, into truth, integrity, authenticity. We bind the power with carefully built structures to channel and control it at the very same time we wail and thrash at their constraints. It is a paradox that we see the walls around us but don't recognize the many that are created from our own conditioned perceptions. Taking the opportunity to embrace the walls and obstacles, as did the individual art therapists I witnessed and the "radical women's sewing circle," we discover the power contained in them that is ours to make living art with, like the story of the delicate vine that pushes through the cracks in the walls of health care agencies, or the art therapist whose withdrawal deep inside the cave brought her to the jewels embedded within its walls.

Sometimes we take pride in our separateness, dedicating ourselves to purity in the methods we once learned and continue to practice, as though investing enchanted, talismanic power in them to protect us from the roiling mixtures and messes of a healing creativity. We collaborate with the structures of separation because they promise to protect us from "the encounter with the other who is free to be itself, to speak its own truth, . . . to tell us what we might not wish to hear"[5] or to look at what we don't want to see. Thus, we split off and cast out what is "other" to protect ourselves from contagion or a disenchanting reality, at the same time that we walk through the world feeling alienated, exiled, and further disenchanted, toxic to ourselves and others. But art ushers in the relationship, whether we embrace it or not. It is an interaction that challenges us, always, to reorder ourselves. As Gilkey writes:

> When [the transcendent in art] is there, it is of vast creative power: this is the role of art in making us see in new and different ways, below the surface and beyond the obvious. Art opens up the truth, hidden behind and within the ordinary; it provides a new entrance into reality and pushes us through that entrance. It leads us to what is really there and really going on. Far from subjective, it pierces opaque subjectivity, the not seeing of conventional life, of conventional viewing, and discloses reality.[6]

This is the utterly essential role of art and the artistic: to re-create ordinary experience into enhanced, meaningful experience.[7] Art therapists who embrace their work and their clients with deep compassion open themselves to the ever-present possibility—even if only infrequent or momentary—that the transcendent function will appear when an event we name "art" stops the heedless flow of time in an enhanced moment, a moment of new awareness or understanding, and a moment of intense seeing and of participation in what is seen.[8] To knowingly approach and bear witness directly through artistic practice can be liberating and exhilarating, but also devastating and terrifying. This direct, eye-level relationship with "that which is other and also myself" pierces opaque illusion created for protection born of fear–fear of discomfort or pain, of suffering anew, or of deeper, unsettling voices that threaten to awaken us from our illusions of emotional equilibrium or the costly peace we have negotiated within a divided self.

THE COSTS OF DISENCHANTMENT AND LOST CREATIVITY

I began my inquiry assuming that art therapists did not value or had forgotten how important it was to stay connected to their primary sources of creative power found in the practice of making art. But my witness to their experiences showed me otherwise, as all had been called to practice art therapy because they so greatly valued art in their lives and understood its healing influence in the lives of their clients. So, too, I wondered about the effects of working in the toxic waste of the terrible suffering told and shown to them pictorially by their clients who had been raped, abused, ravaged, abandoned, betrayed, tortured, ignored, discarded, and destroyed. Perhaps that is why they no longer made art, no longer cared to work in dispirited places but dreamed instead of enchanting, peaceful weekend retreat centers in the mountains, away from the depressing tedium and madness of it all, tending to the healing of already healthy, privileged people. It is true that some work environments can kill or crush our spirits, where it is seemingly impossible to serve the creative function in the face of overwhelming odds. Yet it is not the survivors who drain us; their resilience and capacity to bring themselves back to life can be energizing. As one observer has written, "Rape is hell, trauma is pain; but the power we have to change the world is always a source of joy."[9]

I have walked with wounded and empty souls, and have despaired that a safe place, a place of sanctuary for healing, either did not exist or was desperately needed. I believe now that this was my own desperate need. I witnessed in my inquiry art therapists who felt orphaned by health care organizations where there is no special place for them at the table. The longing for the studio, a clear and free space of their own making, runs deep. But truly and ultimately, there is no safety, no protection from life's difficulties, no immutable barrier from the realities of certain or potentially toxic work. People who are not privileged with an abundance of material wealth and safety already know that life will not grant them immunity as neither will the protection of the studio. When, in the discourse of the art therapy profession, we reify making art as a singularly defined activity that promises longed-for bliss, or separate it from its living context of human and other relationships, we weave another enchanting illusion that art will save us from the messy difficulties of suffering and pain. The full embrace requires "dirt time"—getting messy with people and their messy problems, and having the courage to go with them wherever they need to go and however they need to go there, whether or not that includes our preferred tools and favored environments.

In disenchantment, I found that many are profoundly ambivalent or estranged from the love and fearlessness of creative power that art therapists readily access in the play of their artistic creations and therapeutic artistry. We are aware, in our work-lives as art therapists, that the powerful gifts we offer others carry with them terrific freedom. But in the stories and art I witnessed, I saw that we often are deeply afraid or resentful of the responsibility asked of us in return. When the dragon of power rises up we are like the art therapist who told her dragon "Wait a minute! What will this get me? You can keep your lands, I will go back to where I came from." To avoid conflict with a difficult, possibly transformational situation, many resign themselves to the strategy of "peace and pay": don't rock the boat, keep your head down, accept and tolerate the deadening environment while assuming that you are not also dying, and go along with the status quo. The promise of a ready-made pattern in which to fit one's aspirations requires, over time, a costly trade-off. Especially for art therapists with stable homes and families, established or becoming established in their careers, the practice of their arts may put them at some level of risk of destabilizing all they have worked for. This is all the more threatening when the practice of art entails commitment to continual openness that might rearrange their capacities and their very identity, to be used in unforeseen ways.

The fast-paced, technology-driven and fear-driven work culture in which we labor isn't likely to change for the better in the near future. Neither will we be able to do our work productively where it is most needed if we fear contagion and attacks on our creativity, or deny the transformational promise that various creative, psychological, and symbolic deaths may bring. When we embrace both the divine and the diabolical within ourselves, when we pay as much heed to shadowy voices that threaten or challenge us as we do ecstatic moments of bliss, we will begin to retrieve ourselves from the middle of a trafficked way where the creativity killers do their best work on us. When we dare to move through the fear, we give up the illusion of control and enter a partnership with the world, accountable to and contextually rooted in a living relationship with it. This relationship is the artist's canvas upon which we do our soul work. As co-creators in the play of life, the risk we feel, I believe, is that we know we must trust the relationship to go in any way, unencumbered by our desires and passions. Often instead, it seems, we prefer a relationship with our own known and closely held passions, and this itself is a form of spell or enchantment that keeps us out of life's flow. As my companion told me,

> Fearlessness is living this realization in everyday life . . . we are no longer special, yet we are committed to a practice that is a lifelong training of spirit . . . we experience an unconditional state, if only momentarily, in which all winning and losing is impossible, for we have nothing to prove, hide, or lose. We feel the great relief of letting down our guard to become a conduit for an empowering, inexhaustible source greater than we can imagine. Drawn from our inner depths, from a realm beyond culture, this wisdom is available to all humans.[10]

But perhaps the hardest thing of all is to demand a return to art making and restored creativity from the fearful person who feels unlovable.[11] Indeed, if I have never felt love I wouldn't know how to let go and trust that I could be held in the arms of the world. I might tell you that my life is too filled with demands to give attention to the rhythm of my creativity; or that I have had to give up my artistic identity in favor of a clinical one. I might tell you that I don't have enough: enough time, space, freedom, money, or power. I might accept the dictatorial judgment that as an art therapist who does not freely make art at every turn, I am not artist enough or really art therapist enough. But what is "enoughness" if not my own fear that it is *I* who am "not enough?" I believe the deeper truth is that when I go to face my canvas, without my professional role to grant me protection or immunity,

I risk encountering what I am as "not enough." I risk suffering and rejection. The muse that guides me may not be kind; I might hear the angry voices on the threshold, of brutal introjects telling me how stupid I am to think I can paint, how clumsy, how inept. If I believe I am not beautiful myself, how could I ever produce a thing of beauty?

RE-ENCHANTMENT AS A PRACTICE OF GENEROSITY

In the various contexts of my inquiry, I practiced building generative, co-created relationships as a path for witness and reconciliation of whatever energies were calling my attentions. Whether with one's muse or creative power or with the practice of art therapy, the creative relationship can have all the elements of a stormy love affair or a committed marriage. The discomforting problem is that when this space is truly alive, ordinary fears are felt more intensely, evoking "the failure of efforts, the loneliness of isolation, the awareness that the process is necessary, the shock of rejection, the endurance of beginning again and again, the pain of letting go."[12] But when we don't offer ourselves generously to that encounter, neither do we let the other reciprocate. For protection, we put our energies into keeping things small, contained, private, and even special. If, out of fear, we don't ask for more, as the "radical women's sewing circle" articulated so passionately, we won't receive the gifts others bring that would connect us to the whole cloth of our creative work where re-enchantment is made possible.

In my own experimentations with and practice of generosity, I experienced it as the cultivation of an inner spaciousness out of which creative power arises. In some traditions, this space is called heaven. The space of heaven is the primordial mind that is free from conditions. It is empty but not vacant; it is a charged, potential space pregnant with possibilities that have not yet arisen. There is room to stretch out, to rest, to kick, dance, and play. Art therapists, consciously or not, aspire for this pre-condition of generativity in their practice. This kind of unconflicted space is integral to the process of creation and was the essence of my method of inquiry in its various contexts. Before we produce anything at all, we have to have at the very least a felt sense of free and open space with no obstacles. When there's enough space and no struggle, we can afford to relax; "we can begin to discover what is known as sacred world, in which any artistic endeavor is regarded as sacred."[13] This, I believe, is the archetypal promise of the studio–in relation to my art, in witness to others, and in communal and particular forms–which can be brought to whatever space and people who need it.

On the other hand, to live in the world is to live with limitations. As the old joke goes: "Gravity: It's not just a good idea. It's the law." The perception of obstacles in our lives is a manifestation of real limitation. Everything in nature "arises from the power of free play sloshing against the power of limits."[14] The essence of my method for restoring creative vitality was an understanding that if our actions are grounded in truly allowing the living encounter with the self and the world, we may surrender to the limitations that appear and use them for transformation. Obstacles confront us with the demand for transformation and only limit us when we recoil from that demand. As Maitland says, "when you embrace limitation completely through allowing, you take the most important first step toward creative transformation. Limitations that were once limiting begin to suggest new ways of living as new possibilities arise."[15] This is not to say that we must accept unjust conditions arising from limitation, but rather allow full awareness of the pain or injustice and move into relationship with it. As one art therapist so clearly stated, such awareness "helps kick you out of the unhealthy place."

When opened to the sources of their disenchantment, art therapists revealed that in losing their connection to a reciprocating, participative creativity in the world, they lose a vital part of themselves. They are no longer entirely alive and present to themselves or to the world, and they feel this loss of presence as a loss of love. The dream voices of their art spoke of intense yearning for what had been lost. Our relationship to the world, nurtured in the potential space of transformation, grew naturally from our first relationship to those who loved us as a child, from whom we learned to trust that the world would hold us and love us back.[16] When we lose that dimension of our relationship to the world, we lose our lover as well as our place or home in a loving world. We are not seen nor heard; we are invisible, an orphan. A lack of presence or loving connection to the world manifested in feelings of homelessness and the deeply felt longing for at-home-ness in the disenchanted and isolated art therapists I witnessed.

What allows the transition to generativity? We need to have faith in the constancy of who we are when the edges of the world meet and collide, and demand our reciprocating, loving attention. Constancy, a psychodynamic term, refers to having established a wholeness of self despite the ongoing stressors that threaten to disrupt continuity. Paradoxically, with wholeness of self, one can let go of self and allow a larger process to move through one. Constancy enables us to bend with the shifting winds and still remain rooted to that which nourishes us. We can trust the ebb and flow of creative power, and not despair when it leaves us from time to time. The resiliency of those art therapists I witnessed who could sense this creative flow in their lives seemed to have such constancy and deep trust that the beloved would return, and this allowed them to move in and out of enchantment without feeling disconnected. Alternately, constancy that is reclaimed through the loving presence of others, such as that found in the circle of peers or collaborative witness, offers the opportunity to reconnect and regain presence.

When we are grounded on the earth, lifted toward the heavens, centered in the core of being, and moving with unencumbered ease in the fullness of time, a generous space of clearing arises from which we can realize our creative powers.[17] Even when temporarily cast adrift, the constancy of our loving sense of worth holds us and helps us find our place in the ecosystem of reality where we might more clearly discern life-giving actions from those that are not, and participate more fully in our own destinies.[18] This relational way of knowing can help us reclaim the capacity for generativity upon which good art therapy depends.

Wholeness survives only in the contexts of partnership and community, when individuals decide to live "divided no more" and seek a new center for their lives, a new place to stand. This is the generative space art therapists can create in their role of *animadora*—one whose practice is committed to restoring and remaking the life-giving world at every moment. It is, the poets say, where "your deep gladness and the world's deep hunger meet."[19] Convergence of intention occurs when others answering the same call to wholeness join together, from which community becomes possible. A true community, Peck says,[20] will be inclusive, simply because it is always extending itself through a willingness for differences to coexist. It will respond more realistically, out of appreciation for the whole of the situation, than is possible for anyone operating alone or in isolation. A community is contemplative; it examines itself and knows itself well. Most importantly, it is recognized as a place where one is not cut off, hence, it is a safe place. Its members look at one another with "soft eyes" of respect and caring through which one learns to take in more of the world.

The art therapists who came together in the reflective circle of peers demonstrated these principles in their embodied commitment to live divided no more, to risk and to re-discover the connections that would transform their therapeutic artistic practice. The studio they created was not a literal space as much as it was a heart place, in living community. Although they met as a "radical sewing circle" of women from which they celebrated their mothers' and grandmothers' heritage of transformational rehabilitation, the obligation they felt to address these concerns was not itself feminine, but was instead, urgently human. They brought their pain and frustrations with the walls and doors that seem forever locked or guarded by fierce stinginess and sacrifice. But they transformed these walls into the sacred cave walls their ancestors used for their canvas in communion with their instinctual creative natures. They did so by accepting the paradoxes their work lives presented them, since paradox is the same as creative tension: holding the polarity creates an energetic charge that keeps us alive.

One image all wrestled with, often at the core of their disenchantment, was *victim*. It has significance in any community where people feel disempowered and made invisible by the dominant, contest-oriented, power structures that order and control their daily work lives. But art therapists throughout my inquiry did more than share their wounds and stories of how they'd been hurt and discounted. When victimhood consolidates into an identity, mirrored and made special by others who share that identity, we only strengthen the workplace culture of violence by collapsing into its toxic, contest-oriented value system. Instead, we asked each other "what can be done about this?" We could live a divided life, protecting ourselves by just doing our jobs, delivering professional caring but undergoing a personal detachment from the violence of our experiences that called us to respond. We could defend ourselves by insisting on our specialness, thus making the "rest of the world" into the *evilizer*–the unseeing enemy who is unappreciative of our gifts as art therapists. Or we could take a third way and stand in a different place entirely. We could "make the great leap of heart and stretch of imagination, seeing the hellfire clearly and yet admiring the strength of the survivors . . . but that would require thinking highly of ourselves," unapologetically encouraging one another to claim and exert our power more effectively.[21]

Knowing the difficult realities of our work, one purpose for practicing generosity, creating and re-creating with our arts, is to detoxify and regain clarity, aliveness, and wholeness. This practice is akin to drawing up water from the underground river of creativity, making us as supple, flexible, and adaptable as a willow tree. Our rootedness allows us to embrace and pass through shifting states of fear, pain, grief, and desire, as well as ecstasy, love, and innocence. Exile is just the other side of belonging; dryness is a signal for where one is in relation to the river. Thus, when on the ascendant, light-filled side of the cycle of enchantment, we will recognize its occasional passage into disenchantment and the spaces that open in us need not fill with fear of the void or creative death. The dragon of power may threaten to tear us apart and cast us out, our energy dispersed and formless. But this is simply one side of a larger wholeness that brings us the needed tension of opposites that gives birth to re-enchantment. With this knowledge we can trust in the elemental generativity of the universe and allow its full embrace in our practices.

Generativity, which is the transformation of creative power into action, arose throughout my inquiry as a commitment to come together and witness one another's creative risk taking, found at the thresholds between the self and the other—whether the other is a wolf, the blank canvas calling my response, the shunned image, the wounds of the heart, another art therapist, or an unknown possibility cooked in a communal cauldron. Bearing witness to each other, we are granted the possibility of standing in a different place between and beyond the poles of fight or flight, self or other, fear or bliss. This third possibility creates in us constantly renewable capacity and this is where re-enchantment lies. As therapists, we cultivate bounded relationships that are neither objective nor subjective but intersubjective. As art therapists, we risk a deeper relationship with our creative power that might be ecstatic or terrifying, knowing that after a while terror always turns to deeper faith.[22] As socially responsive artists, we hold in our active visions the capacity for becoming master change agents by practicing transformation in ourselves, our relationships, and the constantly changing world.

The centered heart opens only through risk. In order to live fully, we must not be afraid of life. In the collective dreaming of art therapists, I saw visions of a fire burning within us that can light and sustain our communities; there are waters within us that can cool these passions and quench our deep thirst. If we deny the waters, the world we live in becomes a wasteland and our raging fires will consume everything we touch. When in a state of self-violation, we create the internal conditions for violating those with whom we work. To thrive as a community, the fires of change need to be acknowledged, the waters need to flow, and the risks need to be accepted so that the powers of creation are freed to do their work of transformation. We will respond to the cries of the world as artists, not through our intentions alone, but by committing differently to our work and to each other. We will accept the myriad potentially transformative invitations that come to us, asking for our loving attention.

NOTES

1. Oliver, M. (1986). Wild geese. *Dream work*. New York: The Atlantic Monthly Press. p. 14.
2. Nachmanovitch, S. (1990). *Free play: Improvisation in life and art*. New York: Jeremy Tarcher. p. 55.
3. The "open closing door" is an image used by Chris Squire of The Impossible Theater as the title of a theater project with criminal offenders in Great Britain. See Squire, C. (1996). The open closing door: Impossible theatre's video art work with offenders, victims and observers of crime. In M. Liebmann. (Ed). *Arts approaches to conflict*. (347–368). Philadelphia and London: Jessica Kingsley.
4. Palmer, P. (1998). *The courage to teach*. San Francisco: Jossey-Bass. p. 37.
5. Ibid., p. 37.
6. Gilkey, L. B. (1996). Can art fill the vacuum? In D. Apostolos-Cappadona (Ed.). *Art, creativity, and the sacred*. New York: Continuum. pp. 189–190.
7. Ibid., pp. 189–190.
8. Donaldson, F. (1993). *Playing by heart*. Nevada City, CA: Touch the Future. p. 57.
9. Wolf, N. (1993). *Fire with fire*. New York: Fawcett Columbine. p. 157.
10. Donaldson, p. 149.
11. Ibid., p. 57.
12. Ibid., p. 57.
13. Trungpa, C. (1996). *Dharma art*. Boston: Shambhala. pp. 111–112.
14. Nachmanovitch, p. 33.
15. Maitland, p. 121.
16. The mother's practice of care and the infant's experience of being cared for is one of the first, if not the earliest, human aesthetic. It is a profound occasion when the nature of the self is formed and transformed by the loving other who is

experienced as the environment. The aesthetic experience is an existential recollection of the time when communicating took place primarily through this illusion of deep rapport between subject and object. See C. Bollas. (1987). *The shadow of the object: Psychoanalysis of the unthought known* (London: Free Association Books) for an intriguing discussion of the uncanny experience from the theoretical perspective of object relations psychology.
17. Nachmanovitch, p. 174.
18. Palmer, p. 56.
19. Buechner, F., quoted in Palmer, p. 30.
20. Peck, S. (1987). *A different drum: Community-making and peace.* New York: Simon and Schuster.
21. Wolf, p. 156.
22. Quinn, R. E. (1996). *Deep change.* San Francisco: Jossey-Bass. p. 12.

BIBLIOGRAPHY

Allen, P. B. (1992). Artist-in-residence: An alternative to 'clinification' for art therapists. *Art Therapy: Journal of the American Art Therapy Association, 9* (19), 22–28.
— . (1995a). *Art is a way of knowing.* Boston: Shambhala.
— . (1995b). Coyote comes in from the cold: The evolution of the open studio concept. *Art Therapy: Journal of the American Art Therapy Association, 12* (3), 161–166.
American Psychological Association. (1994). *Diagnostic and statistical manual of mental disorders, fourth edition.* Washington, DC: Author.
Bachelard, G. (1969). (M. Jolas, Trans.). *The poetics of space.* Boston: Beacon Press.
Baldwin, C. (1994). *Calling the circle: The first and future culture.* New York: Bantam.
Bender, S. (1995). *Everyday sacred: A woman's journey home.* New York: HarperCollins.
Berman, M. (1981). *The reenchantment of the world.* New York: Bantam.
— . (1989). *Coming to our senses.* New York: Bantam.
Bly, R. (1996). *The sibling society.* Reading, MA: Addison-Wesley.
Bollas, C. (1987). *The shadow of the object: Psychoanalysis of the unthought known.* London: Free Association Books.
Burns, R. C. (1972). *Actions, styles and symbols in kinetic family drawings: An interpretive manual.* New York: Brunner/Mazel.
Braud, W. & Anderson, R. (1998). *Transpersonal research methods for the social sciences.* Thousand Oaks, CA: Sage.
Brown, S. L. (1995). Through the lens of play. *Revision, 17* (4), 4–12.
Byrne, P. (1995). From the depths to the surface: Art therapy as a discursive practice in the postmodern era. *The Arts in Psychotherapy, 22,* 235–239.
Campbell, J. (1949). *The hero with a thousand faces.* Princeton, NJ: Princeton University Press.
— . (1988). *The power of myth.* New York: Doubleday.
Cane, P. M. (2000). *Trauma healing and transformation: Awakening a new heart with body-mind-spirit practices.* Watsonville, CA: Capacitar. Available at www.capacitar@igc.org.
Capronigro, P. (1991). Writing with light. *Parabola, 16* (3), 54.
Casteneda, C. (1991). *Journey to Ixtlan.* New York: Simon & Schuster.
Chapman, L., Appleton, V., Kapitan, L., Gussak, D., & Anderson, C. (1997). Violence and vulnerability: A developmental perspective. Panel presented at the Annual Conference of the American Art Therapy Association, Milwaukee, WI.

Clements, J., Ettling, D., Jenett, D., & Shields, L. (1998). Organic research: Feminine spirituality meets transpersonal research. In W. Braud & R. Anderson. (Eds.). *Transpersonal research methods for the social sciences* (pp. 114–127). Thousand Oaks, CA: Sage.

Deri, S. K. (1984). *Symbolization and creativity.* New York: International Universities Press.

Dissanayake, E. (1992a). Art for life's sake. *Art Therapy: Journal of the American Art Therapy Association, 9* (4), 169–175.

— . (1992b). *Homo aestheticus: Where art comes from.* New York: Basic Books.

Donaldson, O. F. (1993). *Playing by heart.* Nevada City, CA: Touch the Future.

Dooling, D. M. (1986). The alchemy of craft. *A way of working.* New York: Parabola Books.

Eliade, M. (1958). *Rites and symbols of initiation.* New York: Harper.

Fromm, E. (1973). *The anatomy of human destructiveness.* New York: Fawcett Crest.

Frost, R. (1969). The secret sits. In E.C. Lantham (Ed.). *The poetry of Robert Frost* (p. 362). New York: Holt, Rhinehart, and Winston.

Gablik, S. (1991). *The reenchantment of art.* New York: Thames & Hudson.

— . (1995). *Conversations before the end of time: Dialogues on art, life, and spiritual renewal.* New York: Thames and Hudson.

Gergen, K. J. (1991). *The saturated self.* New York: Basic Books.

Gilkey, L. B. (1996). Can art fill the vacuum? In D. Apostolos-Cappadona (Ed.). *Art, creativity, and the sacred* (pp. 187–192). New York: Continuum.

Glassman, B. (1998). *Bearing witness.* New York: Bell Tower.

Glendinning, C. (1995) Technology, taming and the wild. In T. Roszak, M. Gomes, & A. D. Kanner. (Eds.). *Ecopsychology* (pp. 41–54). San Francisco: Sierra Club.

Grentz, S. (1996). *A primer on postmodernism.* Grand Rapids, MI: William B. Eerdmans.

Gustafson, J. P. (1992). *Self-delight in a harsh world: The main stories of individual, marital and family psychotherapy.* New York: W.W. Norton.

Guntrip, H. (1971). *Psychoanalytic theory, therapy, and the self.* New York: Basic Books.

Hammerschlag, C. A. (1993). *The theft of the spirit.* New York: Simon and Schuster.

Hillman, J. (1989). (T. Moore, Ed.). *A blue fire: Selected writings by James Hillman.* New York: Harper Perennial.

— . (1995). *Kinds of power.* New York: Currency Doubleday.

Isaacs, W. (1999). *Dialogue and the art of thinking together.* New York: Currency.

Johnson, D. (1994). Shame dynamics among creative arts therapists. *The Arts in Psychotherapy, 21* (3), 173–175.

Josephson, S. G. (1996). *From idolatry to advertising: Visual art and contemporary culture.* New York: A.M. Sharpe.

Kapitan, L. (1994). Sleeping with the enemy. In L. Kapitan, K. McCormick, & L. Vance. Weaving new visions: Art therapy in collaboration with allied professionals. Opening plenary of the Annual Conference of the American Art Therapy Association, San Diego, CA.

—. (1996). Making or breaking: Art therapy in the shifting tides of a violent culture. Paper presented at the Annual Conference of the American Art Therapy Association, Philadelphia.

—. (1997a). Consuming art therapy: Paradoxes and perils in a market-driven society. Paper and performance presented at the Annual Conference of the American Art Therapy Association, Milwaukee, WI.

—. (1997b). Making or breaking: Art therapy in the shifting tides of a violent culture. *Art Therapy: Journal of the American Art Therapy Association, 14* (4), 255-260.

—. (1998a). In pursuit of the irresistible: Art therapy research in the hunting tradition. *Art Therapy: Journal of the American Art Therapy Association, 15* (1), 22-28.

—. (1998b). (Coordinator). Gathering the village, stirring the sleeping dragon. Opening plenary of the 29th Annual Conference of the American Art Therapy Association, Portland, OR. Denver: National Audio Video, Audio tape 121-1.

—. (1999). In H. Wadeson, M. Junge, R. Vick, & L. Kapitan. Why do you make art? Panel presentation at the Annual Conference of the American Art Therapy Association, Orlando, FL. Denver, CO: National Audio Video, Audio tape, 156-5.

—. (2001). Dying river, depleted wells: Loss and restoration of art therapists' creative vitality. Paper presented at the Annual Conference of the American Art Therapy Association, Albuquerque, NM. Denver, CO: National Audio Video, Audio tape 108-1036.

Kapitan, L. & Newhouse, M. (2000). Playing chaos into coherence: Educating the postmodern art therapist. *Art Therapy: Journal of the American Art Therapy Association, 17* (2), 111-117.

Kapitan, L. & Vance, L. (1991). Being in creation: Re-visioning the artist in the art therapist identity. Paper and performance presented at the Annual Conference of the American Art Therapy Association, San Francisco, CA.

Kramer, E. (1971). *Art as therapy with children.* New York: Schocken Books.

Krishnamurti, J. (1993). The way of peace. *The Sun* (206), 12-13. (Original work published in 1948).

Kwiatkowska, H. (1978). *Family therapy and evaluation through art.* Springfield, IL: Charles C Thomas.

Landgarten, H. (1987). *Clinical art therapy: A comprehensive guide.* New York: Brunner/Mazel.

Lawlor, A. (1994). *The temple in the house.* New York: G.P. Putnam's Sons.

Leach, W. (1993). *Land of desire.* New York: Pantheon Books.

Lippard, L. (1995). *The pink swan: Selected feminist essays on art.* New York: New Press.

Lipsey, R. (1997). *An art of our own: The spiritual in twentieth century art.* Boston: Shambhala.

—. (1996). For the other Mahatma. *Parabola, 21* (3), 12-17.

Lorca, F. Garcia. (1940). Poema doble del lago Eden. *Poeta en Nueva York, 1929-1930.* (B. Bellitt, trans.). New York: Grove Press.

Macy, J. (1991). *World as lover, world as self.* Berkeley, CA: Parallex Press.

Maitland, J. (1995). *Spacious body: Explorations in somatic ontology.* Berkeley, CA: North Atlantic Books.

Malchiodi, C. (Ed.). (1995). Studio approaches to art therapy. *Art Therapy: Journal of the American Art Therapy Association, 12,* (3, Special Issue).

Malchiodi, C. & Good, D. (1998). Secondary traumatic stress: Self-care, self-empowerment and authenticity. Paper presented at the Annual Conference of the American Art Therapy Association, Portland, OR.

Margulies, A. (1989). *The empathic imagination.* New York: W.W. Norton.

McNiff, S. (1981). *The arts in psychotherapy.* Springfield, IL: Charles C Thomas.

—. (1988). *Fundamentals of art therapy.* Springfield, IL: Charles C Thomas.

—. (1989). *Depth psychology of art.* Springfield, IL: Charles C Thomas.

—. (1992). *Art as medicine: Creating a therapy of the imagination.* Boston: Shambhala.

—. (1995). Keeping the studio. *Art Therapy: Journal of the American Art Therapy Association, 12* (3), 179–183.

—. (1998). *Art-based research.* Philadelphia: Jessica Kingsley.

Meade, M. (1993). *Men and the water of life.* New York: HarperCollins.

Miller, A.L. (1992). Living with sacred power: Promise and threat. *Parabola, 17* (4), 4–9.

Moore, T. (2000). Neither here nor there. *Parabola, 25* (1), 35–37.

Morales, R. L. (1990). The importance of being artist. In M. O'Brien & C. Little. (Eds.). *Reimaging America: The arts of social change* (pp.16–24). Philadelphia: New Society.

Nachmanovitch, S. (1990). *Free play: Improvisation in life and art.* New York: Jeremy Tarcher.

Natterson, J. (1991). *Beyond countertransference.* New York: Jason Aronson.

Naumburg, M. (1973). *An introduction to art therapy.* New York: Teachers College.

Newhouse, M. (1999). Personal, professional, and creative holding environments: An existential and postmodern approach to art therapy. Unpublished master's thesis. Milwaukee, WI: Mount Mary College.

Oliver, M. (1986). Wild geese. *Dream work* (p. 14). New York: The Atlantic Monthly Press.

Palmer, M., Ramsay, J. & Xiaomin, Z. (Trans.). (1995). *I Ching: The shamanic orcle of change.* San Francisco: Harper Collins.

Palmer, P. (1990). *The active life.* San Francisco: Harper.

—. (1998). *The courage to teach.* San Francisco: Jossey-Bass.

Peck, M. S. (1987). *The different drum: Community-making and peace.* New York: Simon and Schuster.

Pinkola Estes, C. (1992). *Women who run with the wolves.* New York: Ballantine.

Quinn, R.F. (1996). *Deep change: Discovering the leader within.* San Francisco: Jossey Bass.

Reinhold, B. R. (1996). *Toxic work: How to overcome stress, overload, and burnout and revitalize your career.* New York: Dutton/Penguin.

Remde, G. (1991). Close to the earth. *Parabola, 16* (3), 49.

Richards, M.C. (1973). *The crossing point.* Middletown, CT: Wesleyan University Press.

Riley, S. (1997). Conflicts in treatment issues of liberation, connection, and culture: Art therapy for women and their families. *Art Therapy: Journal of the American Art Therapy Association, 14* (2), 102–108.

Rilke, R. M. (1995). *The selected poetry of Rainer Maria Rilke*. (Stephen Mitchell, trans.). New York: Modern Library.

Robbins, A. (1973). The art therapist's imagery as a response to a therapeutic dialogue. *Art Psychotherapy, 1* (3/4), 181–184.

—. (1987). *The artist as therapist*. New York: Human Sciences.

—. (1996). (Moderator). The soul and art therapy: A meeting place for cross-cultural currents. Panel presented at the Annual Conference of the American Art Therapy Association, Philadelphia, PA.

—. (1998). *Therapeutic presence: Bridging expression and form*. Philadelphia: Jessica Kingsley.

—. (1999). Chaos and form. *Art Therapy: Journal of the American Art Therapy Association, 16* (3), 121–125.

Rossiter, C. (1985). Sudden thunder. *Modern Haiku, 16* (1), 55.

Sams, J. & Carson, D. (1988). *Medicine cards: The discovery of power through the ways of animals*. Santa Fe, NM: Bear and Company.

Schaverien, J. (1992). *The revealing image*. London: Tavistock Routledge.

Sewall, L. (1995). The skill of ecological perception. In T. Roszak, M. E. Gomes, & A. D. Kanner. (Eds.). *Ecopsychology* (pp. 201–215). San Francisco: Sierra Club.

Singer, J. (1990). *Seeing through the visible world*. San Francisco: HarperSan Francisco.

Smithers, S. (1992). The sleeping dragon and the waters. *Parabola, 17* (4), 29.

Spaniol, S. (2000). The withering of the expert: Recovery through art. *Art Therapy: Journal of the American Art Therapy Association, 17* (1), 78–79.

Squire, C. (1996). The open closing door: Impossible theatre's video art work with offenders, victims and observers of crime. In M. Liebmann. (Ed). *Arts approaches to conflict* (347–368). Philadelphia and London: Jessica Kingsley.

Stolorow, R. D., Atwood, G. F., & Brandchaft, B. (Eds.). (1994). *The intersubjective perspective*. Northvale, NJ: Jason Aronson.

Sweig, T., O'Rourke, R. C., Sarnoff, J., & Urspring, W. (1998). Vicarious traumatization and the creative therapist: Personal perspectives on the clinical underworld. Panel presented at the Annual Conference of the American Art Therapy Association, Portland, OR.

Thompson, W. I. (1991). *The American replacement of nature: The everyday acts of outrageous evolution of economic life*. New York: Bantam Doubleday Dell.

Tracol, H. (1991). Birth of a sculpture. *Parabola, 16* (3), 66.

Travis, J. W. & Callendar, M. (1990). *Wellness for helping professionals: Creating compassionate culture*. Mill Valley, CA: Wellness Associates.

Trungpa, C. (1996). *Dharma art*. Boston: Shambhala.

Ulanov, A. & Ulanov, B. (1987). *The witch and the clown: Two archetypes of human sexuality*. Wilmette, IL: Chiron.

Valle, R. & Mohs, M. (1998). Transpersonal awareness in phenomenological inquiry: Philosophy, reflections, and recent research. In W. Braud & R. Anderson. (Eds.). *Transpersonal research methods in the social sciences* (pp. 95–113). Thousand Oaks, CA: Sage.

Vance, L. & Clark, C. (1994). The myth of collaboration: The peace bridge project. Paper presented at the Annual Conference of the American Art Therapy Association, San Diego, CA.

Wadeson, H. (1998). Burning out burn-out. Workshop presented at the Annual Conference of the American Art Therapy Association, Portland, OR.

—. (1999). Commentary: Where are the wetlands? *Arts in Psychotherapy, 26* (5), 345–348.

Wagoner, D. (1994). Lost. In Whyte, D. *The heart aroused* (pp. 259–260). New York: Doubleday.

Walter, E. W. (1988). *Placeways: A theory of the human environment.* Chapel Hill, NC: University of North Carolina Press.

Wesselow, E. (1993). Making or breaking: Art as education. *Fellowship (The Magazine of the Fellowship of Reconciliation), 59* (1–2), 8.

Wheatley, M. (1992). *Leadership and the new science: Learning about organizations from an orderly universe.* San Francisco: Berrett-Koehler.

Wheatley, M. & Kellner-Rogers, M. (1996). *A simpler way.* San Francisco: Berrett-Koehler.

Whyte, D. (1994). *The heart aroused.* New York: Doubleday.

—. (1995). *Fire in the earth.* Langley, WA: Many Rivers Press.

Williams, T. Tempest. (1995). *An unspoken hunger–Stories from the field.* New York: Random House.

Wolf, N. (1994). *Fire with fire: The new female power and how to use it.* New York: Fawcett Columbine.

Wright, W. A. (1936). (Ed.). *The complete works of William Shakespeare.* Garden City, NY: Doubleday.

Yalom, I. (1989). *Love's executioner.* New York: HarperPerennial.

Young, J. (1995). The reenchantment of art therapy. *Art Therapy: Journal of the American Art Therapy Association, 12* (3), 193–196.

Zimmer, H. (1946). *Myths and symbols in Indian art and civilization.* Princeton, NJ: Princeton University Press.

Zukav, G. (1989). *The seat of the soul.* New York: Simon and Schuster.

INDEX

A

Abbenante, 57; dragon story, 44–48
Abyss, image of, 44, 48, 90, 163; *see also* Void
Acceptance
    in art and stories of communal witness, 180, 188–194, 203
    and belonging, 97, 141, 149
    struggle to accept disenchanting reality, 91, 13, 144, 160
Alchemy, 55, 71–72, 74, 100, 103–104, 109
Aliveness
    allowing the encounter with aliveness, 253, 259
    annihilation of, 178
    of art and the creative process, 48, 97, 104–105, 242
    keeping art therapy alive, 47
    "making alive" as an art therapeutic practice, 13, 21, 65, 75, 260–262
    of matter, 67, 72, 86, 94, 104
    in the play state, 219
    and re-enchantment of the world, 19, 86
    staying alive, 154, 248
    and the toxic work environment, 165–168, 175, 262
Allen, 9–12, 75, 100, 157–158, 164, 265
Allowing, 72, 221, 259
    and the unwilling will, 143
Ambivalence, 17, 20, 32, 179, 256
Ancestors, 85–86, 154, 161, 218, 252, 261
    in art and stories of communal witness, 183, 193, 194, 210
Anesthesia or numbness, 8, 9, 93, 166, 167, 178, 240
    cultural anesthesia, 18–19
Anger
    in art and stories of communal witness, 190–192
    in art and stories of disenchantment, 131–133, 139, 145, 163
    as a transformational force, 50–53, 65, 68, 165, 231, 236
Animadora, vii, 20, 65, 76, 108–109, 244, 260
Appleton, 58; dragon story, 44–48
Archetype, 89, 160, 234, 249
    archetypal psychology, 100, 249
    of the circle, 206
    of the studio, 14, 259
Art
    communal, 168–173, 232–234
    compared to craft, 70–71
    feminist models of, 98
    function of, 71, 96–99, 208, 254–255
    inhibition of artists, 229
    intelligence of, 73
    place in art therapy, 12, 41, 96, 175–176, 201–202, 255
    reifying art, 256
    socially responsive, 93–99, 169, 249
    and transcendence, 89, 254–255
    to transform violence or toxins, 49–50, 62, 104–108, 180, 188, 207–211
    as witness, 89, 254–255
Art making
    of art therapists, vi, 9, 37, 97, 111–113, 59, 174, 201, 257
    of artist books, 66–71
    as an artistic love affair, 60, 66–71
    in collaborative witness, 104
    in the crossroads, 233–235

meditative or reflective, 18, 75–85, 222–225, 252–257
with clients, 33–34, 175–176
Art therapy
as a career, 35, 72–73, 88–89, 92
and peacemaking, 207–211
place in the work and art worlds, 34–35, 95–96, 144, 174–177
as play, 232–235, 241, 246–247
post-modernist view of, 25–30, 232
practice of, 7, 13, 40, 95, 150–151, 169, 188, 205, 208–211, 226, 232–235, 243, 245, 255, 258, 261
professional association, 40–41, 149–150
as psychotherapy, 12
as salvation, 19, 256
and shamanic practice, 206
as socially responsive art, vi, 16, 21, 95–99, 169, 178–179, 232, 262–263
survival of, 175–177
Artistic journal, 171
Artistic practice
in art and stories of communal witness, 173–211
place in art therapy, 12, 66, 88, 93, 95, 96, 98, 257
practice of craft informing art therapy, 68–70, 72
in re-enchantment, 65, 93, 244, 252, 255, 261
as a way of knowing and discovery, 15–16, 105
Artistry, *see* Therapeutic Artistry
Ashby, 57; dragon story, 33–35
Attachment
to forms of practice, 95, 221
to a goal or outcome, 69, 233
to identity or ownership of ideas, 30, 54, 105
unattached, 235, 241
Attack
choosing attack or play, 229–231, 245
as a control strategy, 131, 209, 218–220, 235–236, 241
fear of, 229, 231, 245, 257
Attention
attracts transformational energy, 29, 55, 172–173, 241, 245, 252, 260, 263
in council meeting, 170
to discomfort and living pain of the world, 239, 240–241
fused with intention, 233, 247
to images, 75–85
to what is already there, 66–70, 202, 241, 243
with "soft eyes," 233–234
Attraction, 232
strange attractor, 235, 249
Attunement, 37, 120–122, 152, 233
Ault, 33, 57; dragon story, 33–35
Authenticity, 14, 73, 109, 254
Authority, in art and stories of communal witness, 175–177
Awakening
as "animadora," 65, 75, 98
to creative power or chaos, 38, 45–47, 54–56, 115–116, 255
to consciousness, 35–37, 39, 47, 91–92, 237
to restored life, 32, 54, 74, 206, 221, 246
through play, 219, 221

B

Bachelard, 47, 101, 265
Balance
in art and stories of communal witness, 183–184, 188, 201–202;
between common sense and imagination, 87
of energies and dynamic connection, 199, 201–202, 229, 235
eros and thanatos, 178, 208, 211
of a family system, 220
illusion of, 80, 255
of polarities, 92, 108
role of creative tension, 34
see also Polarities; Holding
shifting or renewing balance, 80, 239, 244
Baldwin, 64, 99, 170, 212, 213, 265
Banality, 49
Bear, image of, 180–188
Belly
in art and stories of communal witness, 181, 183, 185–186, 201
of the dragon or darkness, 32, 44, 50, 63
leading with, 218

Index

Belonging or fitting in, 20, 86, 95, 97, 160, 219, 230–231, 238, 262
   in art and stories of communal witness, 190, 211
   in art and stories of disenchantment, 125, 129, 133, 138, 145–149, 160
Bender, 105, 161, 265
Berman, viii, 18, 86, 87, 100, 101, 265
Betrayal, 44–45, 228
   in art and stories of communal witness,190–191, 194
Birth
   in art and stories of communal witness, 176–179, 187–188, 242
   in art and stories of disenchantment, 113, 124, 151–157
   birth canal, 158, 242–243
   "dar la luz," 62, 20, 63, 65, 99
   and death, 48, 71–72, 242
   labor of, 179, 187–188, 242
Blake, 224, 247
Blindness or not seeing, 35–38, 38–39, 69, 123, 128, 139, 162, 175, 176, 241, 254
Bliss, vii, 12, 19–20, 32, 120, 224, 241, 256–257, 262
Blood
   in art and stories of communal witness, 174–175, 179–181, 183, 187, 190–194
   blood sacrifice, 155, 181, 190–194, 236
   of wounding, 220, 241–242
Bly, 243, 251, 265
Bollas, 264, 265
Bowl
   begging bowl, 61–62, 66, 71, 86, 159, 224, 252
   as a conception of art therapy practice, 69–70, 74, 76, 98, 104, 106, 172
   as a gesture, 217
   for transformation, 20–21, 60–61, 103–104, 159, 169, 172–173, 179–180, 188, 228–229, 241, 253
   sacrificial vessel, 63–65, 179–180,190–193
Braud and Anderson, 15, 17, 265
Breathing, 46–48, 55–56, 63, 72, 221, 227–228
   breathing life into, 65, 246
   of sacred objects, 95
Bricolage, 27, 94, 98
Brown, 231, 248, 265

Buber, 104, 160
Buechner, 260, 263
Bullies, 229, 232; *see also* Voice
Burns, 58, 265
Byrne, 25, 26, 56, 265

C

Campbell, viii, 31, 32, 33, 54, 57, 59, 65, 70, 87, 90, 91, 93, 93, 96, 99, 101, 105, 109, 114, 144, 158, 161, 162, 163, 164, 165, 167, 212, 265
Camus, 216, 246
Cane, 214, 265
Capronigro, 72, 73, 100, 265
Captivity, 137–138, 163, 233
   in art and stories of communal witness, 197–199
Casteneda, 78, 100, 265
Categories
   categorizing creative flow, 18, 28–29, 49, 238, 245
   fixed or bounded categories, 73, 74, 95, 228, 236, 249
   playing with a category, 218, 220–221
   transcending, 235–236, 245
Cauldron, image of, 168–169, 180, 194–195, 253, 262
Cave, image of, 32, 91, 159, 254, 261
   in art and stories of communal witness, 174, 195, 200
   in art and stories of disenchantment, 110–114, 122, 138, 159, 197–199
Center
   in art and stories of disenchantment, 111, 129, 149–150, 151, 158, 163
   centered heart, 262
   centering, 219, 222, 224
   creating centers of personal power, 29, 187
   lack of, 29, 191, 228, 247
   mythic or generative center, 31, 64, 90–91, 169
   therapist's psychic center, 13, 43, 260
   through connection, 229, 235
Certification, 9, 49; story of, 49–54
Change
   change agent, 149–150, 151, 194, 199, 232–233, 262

changing times, 55, 183
"deep change," 110, 149, 172, 235–236, 248
in the work environment, 165, 227–228
catalysts for change, 13, 194, 224, 225, 264
in health care, v, 7, 41–44, 123, 130–131, 158, 166
Chaos, 20, 40–45, 90, 123, 249
creative, 24–33, 35, 47, 54, 94
vs. order, 31–33, 39, 41, 48, 54–55, 249
waters of, 31–33, 90, 131
Chapel, 91
Chapman, et al., 9, 265
Chasm or gap, 48, 77, 81–82, 85, 131, 161
Child
in art and stories of communal witness, 178, 181, 183, 200, 201
in art and stories of disenchantment, 113, 117, 164, 180
childhood play, 234, 237–238, 247
element in dragon stories of creative power, 35–38, 38–39, 40–41, 51–52
first relationship, 154, 259
in the play space, 225–227, 233–234
protecting the lost, wounded or unsanctioned child, 76–78, 86–87, 164, 178, 241–242
Circle
archetypal form or structure, 69, 92–93, 106, 206
art and stories from the Reflective Circle of Peers, 173–211, 221, 242, 261
circling, 65, 220, 222, 229, 235–236
enchanted or magic, 155, 169, 217–218, 222–224, 234–238, 245
as an intervention, 64–65, 168–173, 188, 206
in stories of disenchantment, 113, 148–149
Clarity
in art and stories of disenchantment, 117, 123, 128, 139–141, 162
clear unwavering contact or insight, 69, 70, 83, 229–230, 233, 236
clearing mind or perceptions, 73–74, 108, 109
detoxifying and becoming clear again, 220, 260, 224, 262
of the play state, 219, 235, 245

Clements, et al., 16, 266
Clinification, 9, 11–12, 111–12,
Cockburn, 174, 213
Collaboration, 98, 105, 152, 157
with images, 171
Community
accountability to, 221
in art and stories of disenchantment, 130–136, 145–149, 152–157, 160
belonging to, 21, 63, 83, 261
communal art-making, 98, 173–211, 225–236
creating, 29, 50, 86, 160, 242–243, 263
elements of, 48–49, 260–261
for restoring creative vitality, 168–173, 188, 193, 206, 263
Companion, *see* Guide
Compassion, 48, 90, 219, 242, 245, 254
to release creative power, 37, 103–104, 240–241
Confidence, 52–53, 245
"conditional" vs. "unconditional," 114–116, 122, 162, 236–237
Conflict, 12–13, 49, 50, 68, 192, 256
Connection
creating connections as a vital practice, 66, 70, 73, 145, 261
lack of, in disenchantment, 209, 221, 240; *see also* Separation
symbol of the stairway, 162
through art making, 178–179, 208, 222–225, 234–235
through play, 219, 222–225, 229–230, 232–235
with sources of strength and vitality, 31, 116, 152, 174, 184, 194, 201, 199, 219–220
with the subjectivity of the world, 86
Consciousness
art awakening consciousness, 47, 65, 98
asleep to, 32–33, 47, 111, 241–243
and co-consciousness, 85, 117, 162
creating a place for, 88, 93, 94, 171
journey of transforming consciousness, 68, 73, 87, 90–92, 120
and perception, 68, 249
Constancy, 14, 73, 260
Contemplation, vi, 9, 88, 94, 245, 260
Container, of practice, 14, 18, 73

Contest, 230–231, 261
Contradiction, 48, 89
Control, 28–30, 70, 228, 253–254, 257
    through being nice, 46, 230
    vs. dynamic connection, 54, 199, 232, 235, 238, 245
Copland, 248
Council, practices of, 170–173, 212
Countertransference, 162
Craftspersons, vii, 97
    lessons of, 66–74, 89, 227
Creation myth, Hindu, 20, 32–34
Creative combustion, 54–55
Creative power, 20, 36, 41, 43, 49, 54–56, 63, 90, 96, 161, 169, 174, 87, 224, 239–241, 244, 253–255, 258, 260
    accepting demands of, 28, 32, 46, 54–56, 71, 244, 259, 261–263
    ambivalence of art therapists with, 5, 17, 20, 30, 32, 109, 179, 183, 221, 253–254, 256
    categorizing the flow of, 28–29, 221, 228, 231, 235–236, 238, 245, 249
    creating centers of, 29–30, 91, 106, 152
    power-to-make-things-happen, 31, 33, 49, 110, 183, 233, 235
    as the source of art therapy, 21, 30, 74, 141, 150, 219, 221, 254–255, 262
    and transcendence in art, 174–175, 254
Creative process, 13, 24–30, 33–34, 70, 75, 111–112, 122, 258
    as a cycle, 27, 29–30, 33–35, 48, 151, 158, 179, 180, 260, 262
    as a practice of bringing back to life, 27, 240–241
    in research, 161
Creative spirit, 6, 13, 94, 217, 255
    in the image of an elfin woman, 137–144
Creative tension, 31, 34, 107, 232, 261
Creative vitality, v, 3, 7, 9, 13, 14, 20, 62, 34, 122, 144, 211, 228, 245
    as an elixir, 137–144
    lack of, 3, 129, 138, 148, 172, 193, 232, 251, 255–260
    regaining or restoring, 17, 115–116, 154–155, 157, 168–173, 193, 210–211, 232, 236, 239, 246, 259; *see also* Transformation
    see also Creative Power; Water

Creativity killer, 7, 20, 24, 46, 257
    in the image of the swan, 239–241
    in the workplace, 226–225, 257
    see also Categorizing creative flow, Toxic Work Environment, Violence
Crossroads, 92, 184, 245
    crosscurrents, 151–152, 232, 253
    crossing over, 120
    story of, 225–236
Crow, or raven, image of, 6, 197, 223–224, 239, 252
    story of crow as an intermediary, 243–244
Culture
    cultures of anesthesia, deadness or rigidity, 18, 28, 136, 159–160, 178, 211
    cultural shifting, 25, 49
    genuinely felt meaning with, 14
    vs. play, 219–220, 230–233, 257
    pushed to the margins of, 163–164, 207
    roles in, 219–220, 245, 257–258
Curandera, 243

D

Dam, image of, 146–147, 158
Dance or dancing, 48, 80–81, 89, 103, 233
    in stories of disenchantment, 111, 152, 157
Darkness, 38, 44–45, 63, 76–77, 90, 109, 217, 222
    in art and stories of communal witness, 174–175
    in art and stories of disenchantment, 118, 144, 162
    on the threshold place, 238, 252
Death or deadness, 3, 37, 44, 48, 71–73, 76, 86–89, 97, 103, 106, 136, 154, 178, 208, 218, 221, 239–242, 244, 256
    in art and stories of disenchantment, 118, 129, 132, 139–140, 154–155
    creative death, vi, 11, 109–110, 256–257, 262
    and play deprivation, 248
    "slow death," 110, 248
Deconstruction, as part of the creative cycle, 27–30, 71–72, 109
Deri, 208, 214, 266

Desert, 61, 63, 65, 160, 216–218, 229, 251
   in art and stories of communal witness, 190, 193–194
   see also Landscape, desert or wasteland
Desire, 22, 55, 61, 141, 145, 219; *see* Longing
Destruction, 20, 33–34, 39, 41–44, 53, 62, 71
   in art and stories of communal witness, 175, 178, 179–180
   in brokenness, 179–180
Devouring, 37, 90
   swallowing up space of creation, 20, 32, 44–46
Diagnosis, 26, 50–51, 53, 58
Disappearance of self, 217–218, 222, 230–231, 245, 247
Disenchantment, v, vi, vii, 3, 11, 14–17, 21, 36, 64, 76, 97, 104, 106, 245, 252–263
   art and stories created from, 76–85, 105–109, 110–160, 190–191
   causes of, 8, 55, 97,157–160, 165–168, 172, 199–200
   costs of, 110, 255–258
   defined, 18–19, 206
   in postmodern art, 25
   sadness in, 133, 188, 193, 199
   transforming through community intervention, 168–173, 193
   of the world, 172, 206
   see also Re-enchantment; Creative Vitality, loss of; Separation
Dissanayake, 71, 99, 266
Divergence, 145, 149, 158
Diversity, 48, 50, 53, 55, 148, 179, 189, 221; *see also* Other or otherness
Divine, partner or source, 51–52, 82, 90–91, 98, 158, 181, 241
Donaldson, F., viii, 217, 219, 225, 226, 230, 231, 234, 246, 247, 248, 249, 255, 257, 258, 263
Dooling, 71, 72, 100, 266
Door, image of, vi, 4, 90–91, 113, 128, 237, 252, 261
   in art and stories of disenchantment, 137–138, 140–141
   as threshold, 90, 224, 233, 237–246
   see also Open closing door; Passageway; Portal; Threshold
Dragon, of creative power, 20, 31–33, 54–55, 90, 175, 228, 240, 252, 262
   in art and stories, 33–54
   of injustice, 35, 52;
Dreams, 75, 106, 203, 251
   of the bear, 180
   of the bowl, 61–65
   of the broken vessel, 179–180
   of the open closing door, 3–7
   of running from the chasing man, 181
Dreaming, 47, 71, 82, 203–204, 217, 248
   art dreaming a story, 106–108
   collective dreaming of art therapists, 203–207, 210, 255, 262–263
   making a space for, vii, 22, 47, 61, 88, 203–207
   and play, 220, 237–238
   suppression of, 66
Drought, 124–130; *see also* Desert
Dunlap, 210, 214

E

Earthquake, 85, 227
Edge or margin, 76–77, 217, 223, 228; *see also* Margin; Narrow Places
Ego, 70, 73, 108, 202
Eliade, 71, 100, 266
Elliot, 241, 250
Emptiness or empty space
   facing emptiness where soul enters, 78, 217, 228, 245
   filled or needing to be filled, 42, 87
   function in art-based research, 108
   generative, as part of a cycle, 92, 158, 240
   in art and stories of communal witness, 183, 187, 190, 197
   in art and stories of disenchantment, 113–114, 131, 133, 158
Enchantment, 19, 49, 67, 72, 75, 92–93, 224, 245, 249, 255, 260, 262
   in art and stories of communal witness, 195, 197, 204
   in art and stories of disenchantment, 113, 137, 150, 154–155
   as a protection from creative chaos, 224, 239–241, 256–257
Energy
   in art therapy practice, 11–12

binding or dispersing, 31, 55, 154, 166, 225–226, 233, 236, 421, 262; *see also* categories
   of empowerment, 229–230, 232, 240, 257
   generative, life-renewing and enhancing, 12, 13, 31, 33, 43, 74, 81–82, 90, 92–93, 103, 158, 172, 175, 178, 180, 217, 229, 232, 245, 255, 26
   of images, 81–82
   moving toward wholeness, 12, 148
   of the studio, 95–96, 172
   see also Creative Vitality; Creative Power; Transformation
"Enough," 53, 96, 131–132, 251–252, 257–258
Evilizer, 42–43, 261
Exhaustion, 47, 61, 78
   in art and stories of disenchantment, 130, 132–133, 159
Exile, 20, 149–150, 160, 239, 262
   of the hermit, 116
   exiled image, 78
   exiled soul, 241
   of the orphan, 125, 255–256
   of the outsider or stranger, 91, 137, 174, 219, 221, 227, 254
Eye or seeing, 38, 69, 82–84, 87, 105, 150
   critical eye of the dragon, 36–38, 228–229
   disembodied eye of art world, 18
   "soft eyes," 217, 233–234, 261
   see also Blindness or not seeing

F

Falling, apart, 27–33, 42, 8, 108, 217, 245
   in art and stories of communal witness, 204–205
   into chaos or void, 44–44, 81, 77
   in love, 67, 251
Fear, 8, 40, 49, 53, 55, 65, 77, 80, 88, 130, 175, 187, 192, 216–217, 219, 221, 225, 227, 229, 231, 233, 237, 245, 248, 249, 252, 255, 258, 262
   absence of, 219, 234–236, 245, 257
   of attack, 229–230
   of creative power or the dragon, 28, 32, 37, 40, 41, 43, 48, 55, 131, 183, 224, 228, 253–256

and scarcity, 148
Fever and illness, in stories of disenchantment, 130–137, 139–140
Fire, 9, 37, 38, 42–47, 53, 55, 91, 103, 261, 263
   in art and stories of communal witness, 181, 193, 195–197, 213–214
   burned out, 47, 132, 193
   consuming or burning out, 47, 131–132, 193, 195–197, 263
   of the hearth, 111, 252
   image of, 168–169
   of life, 61, 65, 114, 117
Flower, in art and stories of communal witness, 201; *see also* Vegetation
Formlessness, 110, 205, 224, 229, 248
   in the creative process, 222, 262
   in fog, 78, 110, 123–125; *see also* Clarity, lack of
Foundation, 92, 152
Fromm, 166, 212, 266
Frost, 165, 211, 266
Frozen state, 77, 80, 217–218, 225

G

Gablik, viii, 18, 19, 25, 26, 28, 56, 101, 169, 172, 206, 212, 213, 214, 232, 233, 249, 266
Games, vs. play, 46, 231
   in the workplace, 231–232; *see also* Contest
Garden, in stories of disenchantment, 123–130, 148, 163
Gate, symbol of, 89–90, 129, 218
Generativity, 64, 81, 87, 93, 122, 161, 240, 258–263
   see also Creative vitality; Re-enchantment
Generosity, 230, 232, 249, 256–263
   "enough," 252, 258
   and stinginess, 252, 258
Gergen, 25, 27, 56, 266
Getting grabbed, 229–231, 233, 235, 245
Gilkey, 254, 263, 266
Glassman, 69, 99, 104, 105, 160, 161, 266
Glendinning, 86, 100, 266
Goldsworthy, 249
Grandmother, image of, 64, 65, 83–85, 148, 193, 238, 253

Gratitude, 61, 69, 133, 148, 188
Grentz, 25, 56, 266
Grief, 45, 80, 132, 137, 205, 228
Ground, moving, 84–85, 92, 184, 187, 227, 229
  grounding or rootedness, 92, 122–123, 124, 133, 141, 167, 223, 235, 244, 260, 262
  lack of, 166
Guardian, 32, 46, 82, 87, 90, 131, 223, 238, 243–244, 252
  in art and stories of communal witness, 175–176, 181, 183, 187, 190, 205
Guide or companion, 87, 159, 188, 219, 224, 241
  fear as companion, 216, 218, 229
  strange companions or helpers, 87, 122, 137–138, 223–224
Guntrip, 86, 101, 266
Gustafson, 146, 163, 266

H

Hammerschlag, 130, 162, 163, 266
Healing, 13, 62, 74, 89, 92, 122, 155, 176, 206, 243, 255
  communal, 172
  healing elixir, image of, 137–141
  healing waters, image of, 130–136, 141
  see also Circle, magic or enchanted
Heart
  in art and stories of communal witness, 181, 196–197, 206
  centered heart as a practice, 70, 73–76, 234
  fierce heart, 181, 229–230, 232, 234–235, 241, 245–246
  listening with or opening the heart, 82, 87, 93, 242, 261–262
  wounded or broken heart, 82, 242; story of, 76–78
Heaven, 200
Hierarchy, 45, 145–146, 163, 226–227
Hillman, 68, 75, 76, 86, 99, 100, 244, 250, 266
Holding, 52, 62, 86–87, 92, 97, 120–122, 221, 244, 253, 257, 259
  in art and stories of communal witness, 173, 188, 190, 195, 198

  in art therapist's consciousness, 221
  holding back, 175
  in stories of disenchantment, 104, 108, 111, 114, 118–120, 137
Home, 42, 51, 70, 160, 197, 221, 230, 249, 252, 259
  in art and stories of disenchantment, 111, 150
  creating homecoming, 168, 199–200
  homelessness, 91, 239–241, 259
  in the studio, 235
Horowitz, 57; dragon story, 38–39
Hospitality, as an image of the therapeutic relationship, 74, 237
House-Tree-Person test, 50, 58
Hunger, 36–37, 55, 260
  in art and stories of communal witness, 180, 187, 190, 194
  hungry ghosts, 229, 237, 252

I

Identity
  artistic identity, 9–10, 27–28, 40, 88, 111, 165, 25
  professional, v, 8, 12, 13, 55, 73, 114, 157, 163–164, 195, 247
  of the self-determined individual, 167
  as a victim, 96, 136, 261
Illusion
  of control, 174–175, 230, 240–241, 257
  of enchantment, 37, 47, 56, 74, 80, 137, 143, 145, 155, 174, 226, 228, 235, 240, 241
  of protection or immunity, 42, 55, 56, 109, 166, 218, 219, 226, 255, 256
  see also Enchantment; Re-Enchantment
Image, 12, 15–16, 58, 68, 75–76, 80, 98, 104, 105, 122, 176, 239–241
  dispirited, 104, 110;
  as a living form, 171–172
  mythic imagery, 107, 167
  postmodern, 26–27, 30
  shunned or discarded, 77–80, 173, 175, 190, 262
Imaginal space, 75, 120–122; see also Imagination; Space; Soul
Imagination, 61, 75, 87, 93, 228, 241, 251, 261
  linked with place, 29, 73, 87, 93

Immunity, 55, 56, 109, 253, 256–258; *see also* Illusion
Initiation, vi, 71, 89, 90–92, 122, 162, 207
Integrity, 35, 47, 231, 245, 254
Intention, 21, 70, 170–171, 217, 233, 247, 260
Interplay, 31, 122, 244, 246
Intersubjective space, 11, 120–122, 162, 246–247, 262; *see also* Co-Consciousness
Invisibility, 174, 207–208, 218, 261; *see also* Margin; Disappearance of Self
Isaacs, 213, 266

J

Jewels, in stories of disenchantment, 110–116, 150, 153, 161, 254
Johnson, D., 11, 266
Jones, 57; dragon story, 40–41
Josephson, 18, 266
Journey or traveler, 73, 76–78, 82–92, 149–150, 161, 238–239, 242
  in art and stories of disenchantment, 116–122, 130, 145, 149–150, 151–152
  in the image of a path, 82, 88–89, 124, 149, 194–195, 206
  as a theorist, 97
  see also Initiation

K

Kafka, 225, 247
Kandinsky, 106, 161
Kapitan, 8, 16, 33, 57, 74, 100, 159, 161, 164, 207, 214, 266, 267
Kapitan and Newhouse, 16, 56, 267
Kapitan and Vance, 95, 101, 267
Killing
  going for the kill, 218–219
  killing creativity, vi, 7, 8, 23, 29, 47, 53, 103, 109, 191, 239, 240, 255, 257
  killing the dragon, 32, 33, 35, 37, 43, 44, 46, 48
  killing energies, 228, 231
  killing images, vii, 181
  killing lovers and children, 178, 179
  killing the swan, 239–241
  killing work, ix, 178, 217, 231, 255
  language and metaphors of killing, 208–209
  see also Violence; Toxic Work Environment
Kirshenblatt-Gimblett, 93, 101
Kramer, E., 12, 267
Krishnamurti, 54, 59, 179, 187, 192, 210, 213, 214, 267
Kwiatkowska, 52–53, 58, 59, 267

L

Landgarten, 12, 267
Landscape
  in art and stories of communal witness, 183–184, 193–194, 197, 200, 206
  and banality, 49
  of a borderland, 123–130, 144–145
  of the dragon, 46–47
  of the desert or wasteland, 55, 86, 160, 183, 193, 216, 228, 239
  enchanted, 85–93, 94, 218
  inner, 56, 76, 108, 221
  of mountains, 200
  of the night, 183, 205
  toxic, 165, 211, 221, 228, 244
Lawlor, 89, 90, 91, 92, 101, 267
Leach, 240, 249, 267
Letting go, 22, 30, 61, 74, 202, 214, 218, 219, 221, 246, 253, 260
  of an ideal, 167–168, 233
  of the image of victim, 173–174
  struggle and the process of letting go, 43, 46, 122, 154, 196, 217, 229, 240–241, 258
  see also Surrender
Liebmann, 263, 269
Limitation, 70, 72–74, 99, 120, 138, 259
Lippard, 96, 97, 98, 101, 102, 267
Lipsey, 88, 101, 105, 161, 210, 214, 267
Longing, 36, 37, 74, 141, 160, 194, 202
  disowned desire, 55, 251
  for home, 200, 221
  for love or the beloved other, 60, 61, 97, 137, 259, 221
  for the studio, 12, 171–172, 256
  see also Desire
Lorca, Garcia, 78, 100, 267

Loss or being lost, 77–80, 116, 160–163, 172, 239, 247, 259
  in art and stories of communal witness, 184–187, 197–198
  poem of, 195
Love
  art created from, 50, 66–72–73, 89, 91, 93, 99, 179
  artistic love affairs, 60–61, 91, 178, 207, 258
  fear and, 175, 231
  function in renewal and re-enchantment, 22, 61, 120, 158, 202, 217–218, 235, 238, 245, 251, 258
  loss of, 77, 257–259
  lovers in dangerous times, 174–179
  loving attention or partner, 60–61, 74, 75, 104
  loving partner, 21, 60–61, 86, 87, 217, 259, 263–264
  primal power of love, 181, 187, 190

M

Macy, 210, 214, 267
Magic, 22, 65, 85, 129, 144, 154–155, 171, 188, 193, 195
  magic circle, 65, 169, 172, 222, 224, 234, 237–238, 245
  magical perception of the world, 171
  transformation by magic, 144, 155, 197
Maitland, 70, 71, 72, 99, 100, 143, 163, 218, 228–229, 247, 248, 259, 263, 267
Malchiodi, 13, 268
Malchiodi and Good, 9, 268
Managed care, 8, 158, 208–209, 252
  in art and stories of disenchantment, 41–44, 123, 130–131, 137, 158
Margin or fringe, 96, 151, 163–164, 220, 23; *see also* Edge
Margulies, 100, 161, 162, 268
Mary, divine feminine, 90–91
Maybeck, 91, 101
McLaughlin, 188, 213
McNiff, viii, 13, 15, 16, 43, 58, 74, 75, 95, 100, 101, 206, 214, 268
Meade, 87, 101, 105, 122, 129, 161, 162, 163, 172, 213, 239, 249, 268

Miller, 30, 56, 244, 250, 268
Mirror, in art and stories of disenchantment, 112–114
Moon, image of, 109, 216
  in art and stories of communal witness, 181–182, 200–201
Moon, C., 57; dragon story, 41–44
Moore, 237, 249, 268
Morales, 96, 101, 268
Mother, image of, 39, 62–63, 85–88, 259
  in art and stories of communal witness, 181, 180–188, 184–187, 197–198, 200–201
  in art and stories of disenchantment, 113–114, 120
  lost or wounded mother, 76–78, 78–80, 120, 184–187, 259
  Mary or Madonna, 90–91, 200–201, 226
  in the play space, 226, 233–234
Mountain, image of, 32, 82–85, 90
  in art and stories of communal witness, 187, 200
Multiplicity, 51, 55, 58, 96, 157
Mundus imaginalis, 86
Myth, 54, 75, 87, 90, 106–107, 109, 122, 124, 167, 218, 239, 246
  mythic story; mystic cook fire, 207
  creation myth, 17, 20, 32–33, 34, 158
  of the magic boon, 143–144

N

Nachmanovitch, 65, 94, 99, 101, 217, 218, 219, 220, 221, 222, 224, 225, 227, 228, 229, 231, 232, 234, 236, 246, 247, 248, 249, 251, 259, 260, 263, 264, 268
Naming
  as an act of power, 47–48
  as making alive, 76
Narrow places, 46, 63, 64, 96, 124, 130, 138, 236, 252; *see also* Margin, Edge
Natterson, 121–122, 162, 268
Naumburg, M., 12, 268
Nautilus, image of, 242–243
Newhouse, 268
Numbness, *see* Anesthesia

O

Obstacles, 69, 109, 159–160, 192, 230, 252
   to creative freedom or power, 4, 23, 32, 33, 38, 109, 226–229, 253–254, 258-25
   to creative process, 229, 251–252
   in the image of a dam, 146–148
   see also Walls
Offering, 61, 64–65, 89, 99, 148, 227, 233
Oliver, viii, 251, 263, 268
Oneness, 37, 48, 122, 154, 219–220, 224, 236
Open closing door, 3–7, 245–246, 252–253, 263
   in the studio space, 172, 180, 224
   in play, 221
Open studio, 11
Opening, vi, 32, 66, 68, 70, 73–75, 78, 90, 103, 174, 217, 241–242, 260
   in art and stories of disenchantment, 43, 105, 122, 125–128, 130, 155
   for play, 218–219, 229–230, 232, 235, 258
   in images, 81–82, 90, 106, 188, 196–197, 237
Order, 23–30, 34, 54, 90, 105
   order into chaos, 31, 48
Organizations, 40–41, 163, 226–227, 231, 248, 256, 261
   and anxiety, 167
   game playing in, 231, 235
   in the image of the kingdom, 144–150
   play-deprived, 231–232
   resistance to creative power in, 28–29, 34–35, 55, 227, 231
   see also Hierarchy; Work environment
Other or otherness, 118, 125, 151, 174, 221, 237, 246, 254–255, 262

P

Palmer, M., et al., 149, 164, 268
Palmer, P., 30, 31, 48, 49, 55, 56, 57, 58, 160, 166, 167, 212, 221, 244, 246, 247, 250, 253, 254, 260, 263, 264, 268
Paradox, 11, 20, 22, 48, 221, 225, 232, 241–244, 254, 261
   in art and stories of communal witness, 180–181, 194, 195
Partnership, 65, 66, 85, 86, 89, 204, 217, 257–260
   in art and stories of disenchantment, 141, 151–152
   in play, 217–218, 241, 246
   see also Love, loving partner
Passageway, 63, 192, 218, 242, 29
   in art and stories of disenchantment, 113, 129, 157
   in the image of an archway, 91–92, 129
   through wounding, 78, 241–242
   underground, 92, 226–227
   see also Door; Journey; Opening; Portal
Passion, 46, 55, 61, 65, 69, 95, 128, 141, 148, 214, 241, 257, 263
   consuming, 195–197
   in art and stories of communal witness, 175, 179, 181, 188, 193, 203, 204
Peacemaking, 188–194, 207–211
   art therapy as, 21, 160, 172
   peace and pay, 231, 248, 255–256
   see also Violence; Wholeness
Peck, 260, 264, 268
Perception, 236, 241, 243–244, 247, 254
Pinkola Estes, viii, 137, 158, 159, 160, 163, 164, 169, 207, 212, 214, 268
Place, 89, 93, 137, 148–149, 227
   dispirited, v, 13, 22, 103, 160, 255
   vs. "no place," 165, 211, 234
   see also Landscape; Space
Plague, as a symbol of toxic work, 131–136
Play, 200, 241, 245–247, 258–259
   adventurous play, 216–225, 229
   lack of, 231–232, 248
   lila or divine play, 225–226
   and playgrounds, 22, 169, 217, 225, 232–238, 253
   play look or touch, 21–218, 235, 246
   play spirit, 235, 238
   playing with wolves, 216–225
   role of will, 218
   vs. game, 231
   vs. control or contest, 226–227, 230, 261
   in the work environment, 225–236
Poison, as a symbol of toxic work, 139, 159
Polarities, 12, 31, 48, 89–91, 108, 148, 164, 181, 262
   in art therapy, 95, 158
   beyond, 218, 230

holding polarities, 13, 19–20, 31, 65, 73, 98, 230, 244, 261
    pulled between opposites, 230, 236, 241, 262
Pollution or contamination, vi, 150, 159–160, 163, 168, 254, 257
    image as cleansing what pollutes, 171, 172
Polyvaritas, 51, 58
Portal, image of, 73, 90, 129–130
    see also Door; Opening; Passageway
Postmodernism, in art and art therapy,11, 18, 20, 25–30
Powerlessness, 33–38, 42–43, 131, 133, 140, 145–146, 166–167, 184, 231, 240, 261
    see also Creative Vitality, lack of
Presence, 143–144, 218, 221, 230, 245, 247, 260
    of the community, 52, 206, 210, 260
    and competence, 221, 237
    loss or lack of, 109, 218, 247–248, 259–260
    therapeutic and creative, 13, 37, 55, 67–70, 92, 118, 210, 222, 224, 230
Process structure, 28–29
Procreation
    in art and stories of communal witness, 183–184, 200–201
    in art and stories of disenchantment,111–114, 150–157
    inner space of, 174, 183–184
    see also Birth; Energy
Prophet, in stories of disenchantment, 145, 149, 152, 155
Prostitution, 163
Protection, 38, 49, 78, 88, 166, 227, 229, 253–258, 261
    in art and stories of disenchantment, 111, 125, 132, 148, 173
    from fear or attack, 216, 229–231, 245
    from pain, 166–167, 192, 220, 254–255
    protective figure in art and stories of communal witness, 87, 183–187
    see also Fear; Immunity; Security
Proust, 75, 100
Purity, 2, 149, 240, 252, 254
    in stories of disenchantment, 137–141, 145, 149, 151, 163

Q

Queen, image of, 145–146, 154–156, 239–240
Quinn, 110, 111, 149, 161, 162, 164, 231, 232, 237, 248, 249, 262, 264, 268

R

Radical sewing circle, 22, 169–170, 203, 212, 254, 258, 261
Reconciliation, 12, 172, 187, 208–210
    see also Peacemaking; Wholeness
Reconstruction, 27–30, 55; see also creative process
Reductionism, 49, 54, 75
Re-enchantment, vii, viii, 17, 18–22, 76, 87, 199, 207, 238–241, 245, 258–263
    art therapist art and reflections on, 173–211
    and artistic practice, 65, 93, 244, 252, 255, 261
    communal practice of, 168–173, 193, 195
    as a cyclic process, 175, 207
    function of love in, 22, 61, 120, 158, 202, 217–218, 235, 238, 245, 251, 258
    as a practice of generativity, 258–263
    as a practice of "making alive," 13, 21, 27, 65, 75, 240–241, 260–262
    of the world, 172, 206
    see also Awakening; Creative Vitality; Connection; Energy; Play; Transformation
Reflective art-making, 168–173
Refuge, 55, 237
Reinhold, 165, 166, 212, 231, 248, 268
Relationship
    art made in the context of, 98, 99, 169, 222, 233, 254–255, 256
    of art therapist to the art image or materials, 16, 50, 72, 75–76, 105
    between action and withdrawal, 22, 210
    between art and violence, 8, 21, 71, 178–179, 187, 207–208
    between self and larger forces of the world, 16–17, 20–22, 28–29, 71, 73, 214

to life-enhancing sources of creativity, vi, 157–160, 243, 255–256, 262
in partnership, 65, 66, 85, 86, 89, 204, 217, 257–260
relational field, 11, 13–14, 18, 82, 85, 92, 95; *see also* Co-Consciousness
rhythms of, 11, 28, 74, 108
therapeutic, 7, 12, 13, 28, 33–35, 35–38, 38–39, 68–69, 96, 116–123, 161, 166, 207, 209, 247
unfolding, 70–76, 95, 224, 232
with what disenchants, 259
see also Holding
Remde, 67, 71, 99, 100, 268
Research
art-based, 14–17, 25–30, 106–108
collaborative witness, 105–108, 157–158
heuristic, 8, 17
phenomenological method, 15, 105, 161
scientific rationalism, 167
transpersonal and feminist, 16, 17–18
Resistance, 209, 236
to creative power, 4, 28–29, 90
to flow of energy, 225, 226–233, 236
Response, creative, 70–71, 75–76, 93
Resting place, 47, 61, 65, 89, 159, 172, 258
in art and stories of communal witness, 179, 180, 183
Resurrection, 8, 34, 71, 89, 103, 167–168
Retreat, 19, 94, 160, 174, 210, 255
Rhythm, 86–87, 91–92, 95, 118, 202, 218, 221
birth rhythm, 179, 242
Richards, 236, 249, 268
Riley, 25, 56, 268
Rilke, viii, 48, 58, 219, 24, 269
Ritual, 69–70, 74, 94, 98–99, 106, 171–172, 234
ritual garment, 49–54
ritual gesture, 89, 249
in the Reflective Circle of Peers, 169–173
River, *see* Water
Robbins, viii, 11, 13–14, 29, 56, 95–96, 101, 211, 215, 269
Rossiter, 30, 56, 269
Rumi, 237, 249

S

Safety, *see* Security
safe harbor, 51–56, 91
Salvation, 19, 88
Sams and Carson, 244, 250, 269
Sanctuary, 74, 88–91, 98, 114, 205, 211, 224–226, 242–243, 255
communal, 166, 169, 172, 179, 252
within, 218, 224
Scarcity, 36; in stories of disenchantment, 125, 139, 164
Schaverien, 105, 161, 171, 213, 269
Security
to heal the split and prevent violence, 86–87
safe space, 73, 174, 205, 224, 217, 228, 244
or safety in the work environment, 42, 44, 56, 109, 166, 226–227, 231, 256
Separation
in art world, 97–98
from presence, 218–219, 221, 235
isolation from other and community, 116, 132–133, 148
and oneness or connection, 85–86, 109, 122, 181, 184, 245, 260
source of disenchantment, 97–98, 109, 122, 132–133, 148, 225, 238, 245
and specialness, 148
split of self and world, 85–87, 91, 225, 236, 255, 260–262
see also Connection; Disenchantment
Serpent, *see* Dragon
Sewall, 243, 250, 269
Shadow, 44, 47, 120, 216, 222–223, 244, 246
created from inattention, 239–241
Shakespeare, 93, 101
Shamanic principles, 201–202, 206
Shame, 133, 163, 236
in art and stories of communal witness, 178–179, 190
Shredding, in re-enchantment, 33–35, 71
Shusterman, 95, 101
Singer, 241, 249, 250, 269

Sky, image of, 4, 60, 63, 84–85, 124, 233–234, 252–253
    in art and stories of communal witness, 133, 183, 184, 186
    sky door, 90
Sleeping, 30, 32, 35–39, 47; *see also* Awakening
Smithers, 32, 57, 269
Smoke, element of, 41–43
Snake, image of, 223–224
Soul, 32, 45, 78, 88, 183, 187, 219, 231, 241, 249
    and art therapists, 157–160, 199–203
    definition of, 200
    familiars, 87, 243
    of the image or aesthetic object, 96, 171
    making or retrieval of, 22, 171–172, 199–203, 206–207, 214, 239–240, 257
    sickness or death of, 21, 129, 137, 154–155, 159–160, 163, 168
    world ensouled, 2, 21, 86, 87, 244, 253
Space
    of between, 22, 78, 80, 110, 158, 162, 178, 202, 217, 219, 230, 237, 243–249
    breathing space, 46–48, 228
    constricted or confined, as a source of disenchantment, 110–112, 221, 228, 240–242, 257
    filled-up spaces, as a source of disenchantment, 42, 44, 110–112, 240
    generative rather than empty, 14, 61, 65, 111–112, 187, 240, 242, 256
    imaginal, images from, 75–85
    inner, 60, 73, 90, 92, 174, 183, 241, 246
    optimal configuration in art therapy practice, 224
    sacred space, 22, 70, 74, 94–95, 179, 202, 224, 242–246, 258–259
    safe space, 73, 174, 205, 224, 228, 244
    spacial transformation, 13, 43, 70, 74, 196, 242
Spaciousness, 32, 48, 61, 74, 105, 133, 192, 206, 128, 221, 230, 242, 246, 251–252
    as a conception of heaven, 258–259
Spaniol, S., 11, 269
Specialness, 71, 97, 98–99, 173, 202, 219, 256–258, 261
    in art and stories of disenchantment, 138, 143, 148–149

Spirals, image of, 80–82, 111, 217, 242–243
Squire, 263, 269
Stairway, symbol of, 118, 162
Steeple, symbol of, 89
Sticking with, practice of, 68–69, 99
Stolorow, et al., 11, 162, 269
Story and story telling, 17, 18, 50–51, 75–76, 106, 175
    attachment to, 30
    dream-story, 106–108
    as narrative, 26–27
Stranger, *see* Exile
Stress, *see* Work Environment, toxic
Structure, 26–29, 46, 55, 65, 105, 123, 226–227, 246–249, 254
    of education, 88–89, 226
Stuck, getting stuck, 47, 113, 154, 164, 167, 175, 198
Studio environment, 13, 31, 92–95, 159, 204, 210, 224, 239, 252, 255–256
    as an archetype, 14, 96, 172, 211, 256, 258
    in art and stories of communal witness, 173–211
    communal studio, 168–173, 179, 195, 210, 232–233, 252
    living studio, 225, 232–234, 236
    as a place of consciousness, 17, 96, 172, 211, 234
    soul-making, 171–172
    temenos, 74, 224, 234, 236
Suffering
    in art therapist disenchantment, 4, 103, 141, 154–155, 174, 206, 255–256
    in art and transformation, 71–72, 171–172, 179, 217, 255–258
    and compassion, 48, 103–104
    suffering the process of creation, 27–30, 31, 71–72, 89, 171–172
Surrender, 46, 61, 71, 73, 217, 225, 257, 259
    in art and stories of communal witness, 173–174, 181, 188, 190, 211
    of the image of victim, 173–174
    see also Letting Go
Survival, 41, 43–44, 99, 175, 208, 255, 261
    in art and stories of disenchantment, 128, 133, 139, 148, 154, 209
    of lovers, 174–179
Suspension, 77–78, 80, 217, 222
    in art-based research, 105, 108, 161

see also Space, of between
Swan
  as a guardian of the threshold, 252
  story of, 239–241
  as a symbol of enchantment, 239–241
Sweig et al, 9, 269

T

Talisman, 42, 254
Tao te Ching, 93, 101
Target, image in stories of disenchantment, 131, 136, 145
Tears, element of, 64, 65, 159, 193
Temenos, 22, 74, 224, 226, 234, 236
Therapeutic artistry, v, 14, 16, 66–74, 96, 98, 108, 122, 157, 236, 245, 256
  and practice, 69, 75, 160, 236
  and space, 11, 73, 74, 96
Therapeutic relationship, 13, 33–35, 35–38, 38–39, 68–69, 96, 116–123, 161, 166, 207, 209, 247
Thompson, 89, 101, 269
Threshold, 8, 64, 90, 105, 217, 221, 236–246, 249, 252–254, 262
  danger of, 224, 249
  guardian of, 205, 223, 252
  in an image, 223, 252–253
  in the symbol of the gate, 89–90
Thunderbolt or lightning sword, 32, 49, 55, 67, 175, 190
Time
  in art and stories of disenchantment, 113, 159
  dreaming time, 204, 207, 218
  slowing down, vii, 67, 70, 98, 225–226, 232–233, 238, 254–255
Tolstoy, 207, 214
Torbert, 113, 114, 162
Touch
  lack of, 51, 228
  vibrant, of aliveness, 60–63, 106
  to transmit love and attention, 67–70, 217, 230, 232
  play touch, 216–218, 222, 232
Toxins, 104–105, 108–109, 160, 172, 208, 227, 254, 262
  and inner fire, 213–214
  in stories of disenchantment, 122, 129, 136–137, 139–144, 159
  transforming, 103–110, 166–168, 180, 187, 210–211, 231
  see also Work Environment, toxic
Toxic work environment, *see* Work Environment
Tracol, 68, 99, 269
Transformation
  in art and stories of communal witness, 173–211
  art for social transformation, 97, 99, 169, 178–179
  art-making as a practice of, 22, 44, 49–50, 61–62, 99, 104–108, 180, 188, 207–211, 246
  in the lessons of the craftsperson, 66–74
  limitation in, 72–73, 167, 259
  in the metaphor of the bowl, 20–21, 60–61, 103–104, 159, 169, 172–173, 179–180
  rehabilitation, vii, 66, 97, 168, 170, 180, 232, 261
  through play, 235, 247, *see also* Play
  transformational energy, 8, 14, 61, 87–93, 97, 172, 241, 246, 252, 256–257
  transforming disenchantment or violence, 16–17, 22, 48, 52, 54–56, 90, 120, 133, 229, 168–173, 208–09, 237, 241–242, 246, 252, 261, 256–257, 262–264
  see also Creative Power; Creative Vitality; Disenchantment; Re-Enchantment
Traveler, *see* Journey
Travis and Callendar, 12, 192, 213, 269
Trauma, 9, 136–137, 197, 255
  in art and stories of disenchantment, 116–120, 136–137, 154–155
  birth, 154
  collective, 86, 210
Tree, image of, 203, 244, 262
  in art and stories of disenchantment, 124–125, 129, 148, 159
  as a form of school, 88
  as sanctuary, 195
Troubadour, 87–93, 98, 103–106, 109–110, 159–160, 236
Trungpa, 238, 249, 259, 263, 269
Trust, 85, 133, 129, 259–260

Truth, 96–97, 105, 108, 192, 221, 235, 253–254
   therapeutic, 161
   vs. lie, 240–241
Tunnel, 92, 130, 205, 228, 237, 249
Turtle, story of disenchantment, 110–116

U

Ukeles, M. Laderman, 249
Ulanov and Ulanov, 169, 175, 212, 213, 269
Unified or relational field, 11, 13–14, 18, 82, 85, 92, 95, 218, 244
Unknowing, 104, 150, 220–221

V

Valle and Mohs, 16, 17, 269
Vance and Clark, 214–215, 269
Vegetation, in art and stories of disenchantment, 110–111, 114, 123, 124–130, 133, 148
Vessel, 62, 74, 103, 155, 210
   in art and stories of communal witness, 179–180, 190–192, 194
   of birthing, 20, 62–65, 72; *see* Birth
   broken cup or vessel, 179–180
   as a cauldron of creative power, 71, 159, 168–169
   as a conduit of life force, 65, 93, 151
   in the image of the chalice, 190–192, 194
Vicarious traumatization, 9
Victim or victimhood, 20, 22, 43, 96, 136, 229, 261
   in art and stories of communal witness, 173–174, 176–180, 210
   in art and stories of disenchantment, 130–137
   in collapsing into aggression, 136, 229, 261
Violence, 9, 53–54, 71, 86, 166, 168, 181, 187, 219, 263
   of the bullying force, 229, 232
   causes of, 86, 166, 187, 248
   culture of, 178, 208–210, 231, 261
   horizontal workplace violence, 232
   and reconciliation, 172, 187, 208–210
   relationship to art, 8, 21, 71, 178–179
   seed of, 154
   transformed by love, 178–179, 207–211
   and war, 178, 187, 208–209
Vital life sign, 20, 24, 55, 206
Vitality, vi, 7, 28, 42, 66, 89, 114, 157, 166, 179, 192, 195, 231–232, 243, 253, 259
   play as a measure of, 231–232
   see also Creative Vitality
Voice
   in art and stories of disenchantment, 113, 117, 149, 152
   listening to voices within, 118, 237, 255, 257
   critical or taunting, 77, 113, 217, 221, 229, 241, 243, 245, 257–258
Void, 44, 55, 60, 77
   fear of, 240–241, 244, 262
   living in the void, 207, 244
   see also Emptiness; Space
Vritra, *see* Dragon
Vulnerability, 35, 48, 78–79, 107, 217, 228, 235
   in art and stories of communal witness, 181, 185, 187–188, 192

W

Wadeson, 9, 158, 164, 270
Wagoner, 195, 213, 270
Walls, image of, 38, 70, 92, 235, 254, 261
   in art and stories of communal witness, 173–174, 179, 192, 205
   in art and stories of disenchantment, 111–113, 123–130, 133, 140, 145
Walter, 87, 101, 270
Wasteland, 21, 63, 263
   in art and stories of disenchantment, 109, 124, 159–160
   see also Landscape, desert or wasteland
Water, image of transformation, 60–65, 80, 85, 252
   in art and stories of communal witness, 173–174, 183, 190–197, 205
   in art and stories of disenchantment, 111–113, 123–130, 130–136, 137–144, 144–149, 150–160, 164
   cleansing, 39, 62–63, 159, 239, 262
   as a confluence, 146–149
   of creation, 20, 21, 31–33, 55, 62, 84–85, 89, 90, 95, 129, 175, 193, 239, 254, 263

as ice, 195–197, 205
as a pool, 81, 91, 141, 193, 222, 253
as a process structure, 28–29, 149, 174
as a river, 6, 21, 28, 35, 125, 133, 144–145, 150, 157–159, 168, 183, 244, 251–254, 262
as a torrent, 67, 158, 183, 193, 253
Well
  in art and stories of disenchantment, 144–145, 163
  as an image of holding, 106, 173
  see also Walls
Wesselow, 178, 207, 213, 214, 270
Wheatley, 28, 56, 235, 249, 270
Wheatley and Kellner Rogers, 29, 56, 105, 161, 166, 167, 212, 270
Whirlwind, image of, 44–45
Wholeness, 12, 21, 48, 70, 74, 76, 165–166, 210, 258, 260, 262
  and brokenness, 179–180
  as peace or peacemaking, 172, 179, 208
  see also Connection
Whyte, 31, 57, 109, 161, 213, 241, 250, 270
Williams, 180, 181, 213, 270
Witness, 21, 75, 85, 89, 96, 108, 187, 255, 258, 262
  art and stories from collaborative witness, 110–157
  art and stories of communal witness, 173–211
  collaborative, 17, 103–110, 157–158
  community, 205
Wild or wilderness, 169, 221, 235
  in art and stories of communal witness, 180–181, 183, 187, 197, 207
Wolf, N., 96, 101, 136, 163, 164, 255, 262, 263, 264, 270
Wolves
  playing with, 216–225, 230

reflective art image of, 222–225, 252
wolves in the workplace, 227–230, 234–236, 245
Woman, image of, 4, 78, 82–85, 138–141, 252
  in art and stories of communal witness, 175–176, 188–190, 192, 197, 202
  power of, 174, 181–183, 197
Womb, 32, 62, 114, 161
  in art and stories of communal witness, 183, 187
Work environment, toxic
  source of art therapist disenchantment, v, vi, 9, 18–19, 34–35, 41–45, 62, 104, 108–109, 136, 159–160, 165–166, 175, 183, 194, 217, 227, 255–257, 261
  and play, 219, 225–236, 231–232
  chronic stress and, 141–142, 165–166, 231
  game playing in, 231
  play deprivation and, 231–232, 248
  stories and images of disenchantment in, 110–160, 167, 193–194
  workplace bullies, 229, 232
Wound
  cleansing or healing, 74, 91, 159, 172, 261–262
  as an opening, vi, 76–78, 78–80
  as a result of seeking the "right place," 137–138
  sacred wound, 241–242
  wounded spirits, 44, 63, 97, 120, 172, 240–241, 255
Wright, 270

Y

Yalom, 19, 224, 247, 270
Young, 19, 270

616.891656 K17r

Kapitan, Lynn.

Re-enchanting art therapy

DATE DUE

NOV 08 2011		
11/15/14		